AppleWorks™
Tips & Traps

AppleWorks™
Tips & Traps

Dick Andersen
Janet McBeen
and
Janice M. Gessin

Osborne **McGraw-Hill**
Berkeley, California

Osborne **McGraw-Hill**
2600 Tenth Street
Berkeley, California 94710
U.S.A.

For information on translations and book distributors outside of the U.S.A., please write to Osborne **McGraw-Hill** at the above address.

A complete list of trademarks appears on page 285.

AppleWorks™ Tips & Traps

1234567890 DODO 89876

ISBN 0-07-881207-0

Cynthia Hudson, Acquisitions Editor
Kay Nelson, Technical Editor
Michael Fischer, Technical Reviewer
Jean Stein, Senior Editor

Elizabeth Fisher, Editorial Assistant
Fran Haselsteiner, Project Editor
Yashi Okita, Cover Design

To Dr. James S.B. Mackie.

D.A.

To my parents, who have each given me so much, in very different ways.

J.M.

To my family and family of friends.

J.M.G.

Contents

Acknowledgments

Thank you to Jean Stein, Cindy Hudson, Kay Nelson, Michael Fischer, and Liz Fisher.

D.A. and **J.M.**

Thank you to Debra Bogel Rothschild, Charlotte McGovern and Sister Miriam Claire Arnold of St. Patrick's School, Ronna Slavin, Brad Roth, and John Newstrom.

J.M.G.

Introduction

AppleWorks has been around long enough that we have seen numerous books dedicated to the enlightenment of its users. Many are well-written presentations of AppleWorks' features. Some are restatements of material covered in the *Apple-Works Reference Manual,* a guide so well written that it warrants few improvements.

The Tips and Traps method is designed to go beyond the typical how-to presentation provided in the *Reference Manual* and in the far too many books created in its image. A Tip is a pointer on how to accomplish a task more effectively, more quickly, or both. A Trap is a situation that can catch you unawares or an unknown ramification of another operation. This book focuses on solutions distilled from actual problem situations or on specific details that have been omitted from the documentation. Thus the emphasis is not so much on how to carry out procedures — those steps are clearly stated in the manual — but on when certain procedures are advantageous and why.

How to Use This Book

AppleWorks Tips & Traps is a book you should have at hand whenever you begin an AppleWorks session so you can refer to it easily when you get into a sticky situation or want to begin a procedure you do not understand. The Tip and Trap headings allow you to quickly determine the nature of the description that follows. Using the index is most helpful as a way to zero in on the solution you are seeking. Of course, if you prefer to read this book from cover to cover, you will certainly benefit from doing so.

Is This Book for You?

Beginner and expert alike can benefit from the Tips and Traps format. Spared of the need to read through reams of self-evident information to extract relevant points, the expert can use this book for augmenting an already developed talent in the most expedient way. For the beginner, these Tips and Traps can provide important directions that how-to materials choose to ignore. Beginners will find the Traps especially valuable as a way to sidestep problems that can add frustration to the learning process.

Whatever your level of expertise, we predict that the Tips and Traps presented in this book will save you so much time and frustration that you will become a loyal Tips and Traps advocate in no time and even begin developing new ones yourself. We encourage you to share your insights with us by writing to

Dick Andersen
2525A Lucy Lane
Walnut Creek, CA 94596

If we use any of your Tips or Traps in subsequent editions of this book, we will be happy to give you credit.

How This Book Is Organized

The following outline presents a list of *AppleWorks Tips & Traps* chapters and brief descriptions of each.

Chapter 1: The AppleWorks Environment

AppleWorks' integrated environments have many important features in common. Chapter 1 focuses on commands used in all AppleWorks environments and presents Tips and Traps appropriate to common operations, such as startup, disk and file handling, and printing. Desktop pointers that apply to AppleWorks as a whole are also presented in this chapter.

Chapter 2: Word Processing

Chapter 2 covers setting up a word processing document and the most effective ways of getting around in this environment. You will learn valuable entering and editing techniques and the best way to make word processing commands work for you. Tips and Traps on printing with the Word Processor are also included in this chapter.

Chapter 3: The Data Base

In this chapter you will learn the advantages of each type of record layout available to you in the AppleWorks Data Base. Tips on changing your record layout and manipulating the information with Data Base commands are presented in this section.

Chapter 4: Data Base Reporting

Chapter 4 discusses setting up a Data Base report, calculating categories, and producing group totals. Table-style reports and label-style reports are discussed, as well as printing techniques for both.

Chapter 5: The Spreadsheet

You will gain insight into all aspects of the AppleWorks Spreadsheet by becoming familiar with the information in this chapter. It covers entering and editing, using the worksheet to manipulate data and view it, and using formulas and functions.

Chapter 6: Data Transfer

The ability to share data between AppleWorks environments via the Clipboard is a powerful feature that is covered in this chapter. Tips and Traps on creating ASCII and DIF files for data exchange between AppleWorks and other programs make this chapter particularly valuable for users who have much to gain from this time-saving procedure.

Chapter 7: AppleWorks Applications For Home, School, and Office

This chapter focuses on designing effective applications for four specific work environments: home, office, school administration, and the classroom.

1

The AppleWorks
Environment

Most of the chapters in this book represent a specific aspect of AppleWorks, but this first chapter presents Tips and Traps that apply to AppleWorks as a whole. The chapter is divided into five sections. The first, "Startup," provides helpful techniques for beginning your AppleWorks adventure. The "Desktop" section presents valuable techniques for dealing with Desktop problems as well as Tips for enhancing Desktop features.

Tips and Traps related to commands that are common to all three Apple-Works environments (Word Processor, Spreadsheet, and Data Base) are presented in the third section of this chapter; they are followed by a section on suggestions related to disk and file handling. The chapter concludes with printing Tips and Traps that apply to AppleWorks as a whole.

You may find it helpful to read this first chapter from beginning to end, though that is not necessary for the other chapters. This is not a hard and fast rule, as one of the most valuable characteristics of the Tips and Traps books is flexibility of usage. You may find, however, that if you get your grounding in the AppleWorks environment presented in this chapter, you will be secure in skipping around thereafter.

Startup

 1.01 Trap: *Don't try to use the original AppleWorks Startup and AppleWorks Program disks that came with your program.*

Your AppleWorks package includes three floppy disks, two of which have information written on both sides. One of these double-sided "flippy" disks contains AppleWorks Startup on one side and the AppleWorks Program on the other side.

Each time you begin an AppleWorks session, you will need to boot with the AppleWorks Startup disk and then, when instructed to do so, switch to the AppleWorks Program disk. However, the original Startup and Program disks that came with AppleWorks have been write-protected and will not accept the information interchange necessary for AppleWorks' operation.

If you use these original disks, you will meet with apparent success in loading the Startup program, but the following screen message will appear when you try to load the Program disk:

```
File: None                    GETTING STARTED
==================================================================




                Your copy of the AppleWorks PROGRAM disk
                must be in Drive 1.  The write-protect
                notch must be uncovered.




------------------------------------------------------------------
Press Space Bar to continue                          55K Avail.
```

If you make a copy of the original Startup and Program disks, your problem will be solved. You will find detailed instructions for carrying out this copy procedure on page 5 of the *AppleWorks Reference Manual*. This is a good time to become familiar with this process, because it is important that you adopt a habit of backing up all your work with duplicate disk files.

1.02 Trap: *Do not write-protect your copy of the AppleWorks Program disk or you won't be able to use it.*

If you are one of those wise people who takes precautions at every turn, you may have already cultivated the habit of covering the write-enable notch on any program disks that you copy. Although this is an admirable habit to develop in some cases, it will render the AppleWorks program useless if you employ it in this situation.

As stated in the previous Tip, an integral part of AppleWorks' performance depends on your being able to write information onto the Program disk as well as to read from it. If you write-protect your AppleWorks Program copy, this exchange cannot take place.

1.03 Tip: *The Apple Presents AppleWorks disk takes you on a detailed tour of AppleWorks.*

If you learn fastest by doing instead of reading, you will probably find it helpful to take the AppleWorks disk tutorial. This tutorial is presented on both sides of the Apple Presents AppleWorks disk and is self-explanatory.

You can go through it from beginning to end or zoom through it at whatever speed is comfortable for you, pausing for tasks that you want to understand more thoroughly and skipping areas where comprehension comes easily. The AppleWorks Tutorial booklet that came with your AppleWorks program augments the disk tutorial. Use both together or in sequence to help you develop a thorough understanding of AppleWorks.

The AppleWorks tutorial offers many opportunities for interaction, but the responses that you are allowed are predetermined. You will be unable to explore the various tangents that occur to you during your learning session. These restrictions apply only to the tutorial disk and will not be present when you are working with the actual AppleWorks program.

1.04 Tip: *Use your Sample Files disk to practice AppleWorks techniques as you learn them.*

If you are frustrated because the AppleWorks tutorial disk restricts you to a predetermined path, try using the AppleWorks Sample Files disk for more widespread experimentation. After you have booted your system first with the Startup disk and then with the Program disk, load the sample files by choosing "Add files to the Desktop" from the Main Menu.

As you become more familiar with AppleWorks and are ready to develop applications of your own, you may find it helpful to use one or more sample files as a model or template that you can change to match your needs.

*1.05 **Tip:** Begin an AppleWorks session by placing the Startup disk in the internal drive and then turning on the computer.*

Unfortunately, the amount of instructions necessary for AppleWorks operation exceeds the space available on one disk. Consequently, the initial operating instructions are on the Startup disk. Do not try to boot AppleWorks using the Program disk alone. For the program to operate, the Startup disk must be read before the Program disk.

*1.06 **Tip:** AppleWorks uses Drive 1 to access program information.*

If you have a one-drive system, this will be obvious to you. However, with two drives before you, you could conceivably attempt to load AppleWorks from Drive 2. You will soon find this unworkable. Not only do you need to start AppleWorks from Drive 1, but you should also expect to leave the Program disk in that drive while you are working with AppleWorks.

From time to time, proper program operation depends on access to information on the Program disk. If you have a one-drive system, you will be prompted to exchange your data disk for the Program disk at these times. If you have a two-drive system, simply leave your Program disk in Drive 1 at all times, and Apple-Works will access it automatically when necessary.

*1.07 **Tip:** The Main Menu is your doorway to all AppleWorks functions.*

The illustration that follows shows the AppleWorks Main Menu.

The AppleWorks Environment

```
Disk: Drive 2                    MAIN MENU              Escape: "Startup"
_____
 |                         |_____
 |   Main Menu             |                                               |
 |                         |                                               |
 |                                                                         |
 |   1.  Add files to the Desktop                                          |
 |                                                                         |
 |   2.  Work with one of the files on the Desktop                         |
 |                                                                         |
 |   3.  Save Desktop files to disk                                        |
 |                                                                         |
 |   4.  Remove files from the Desktop                                     |
 |                                                                         |
 |   5.  Other Activities                                                  |
 |                                                                         |
 |   6.  Quit                                                              |
 |                                                                         |
 |_____|


_____
Type number, or use arrows, then press Return              ∂-? for Help
```

You should become familiar with the choices available from this menu and the effect of each. The options provide a starting point from which you can carry out all AppleWorks operations. No matter where you are in AppleWorks, you can always reach this menu by pressing the ESCAPE key one or more times.

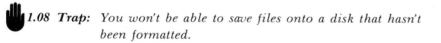

1.08 Trap: *You won't be able to save files onto a disk that hasn't been formatted.*

Once you become familiar with AppleWorks, you will want to begin creating files of your own. To do this, you will need to learn the procedure for saving files onto a disk. Without a permanent record on disk, all your hard work would be lost forever each time you quit AppleWorks.

Before you can accomplish this important saving process, each of your disks must be formatted with the ProDOS format that AppleWorks understands. Formatting a disk is a simple procedure that can be carried out in the middle of an AppleWorks session without danger of losing any of the data that is currently in your computer's memory.

Begin by using the ESCAPE key to get to the Main Menu. If one press of this key doesn't do it, keep pressing it until you see the Main Menu. Then choose option 5, "Other Activities." The procedure you want, "Format a blank disk," will be option number 5 on the Other Activities menu.

When you choose this option, you will be presented with the following screen:

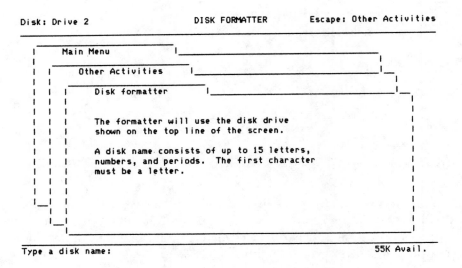

```
Disk: Drive 2                    DISK FORMATTER        Escape: Other Activities
_____
I     Main Menu          I_____
I                        I                                          I
I  I     Other Activities    I_____I__
I  I                         I                                    I
I  I  I     Disk formatter      I_____I__
I  I  I                         I                                   I
I  I  I                                                             I
I  I  I     The formatter will use the disk drive                  I
I  I  I     shown on the top line of the screen.                   I
I  I  I                                                             I
I  I  I     A disk name consists of up to 15 letters,              I
I  I  I     numbers, and periods.  The first character             I
I  I  I     must be a letter.                                      I
I  I  I                                                             I
I  I  I                                                             I
I__I  I                                                             I
I  I                                                                I
I  I__I                                                             I
I  I__I_____I

Type a disk name:                                            55K Avail.
```

Before you can proceed, you will have to enter a name for the disk that you are formatting (notice the prompt at the bottom of the screen). AppleWorks' rules for naming files are shown on the screen. If you don't follow them, your disk name will not be accepted, and you will have to try again. Once you enter an acceptable name and press RETURN, another screen will warn you that you need to make sure that the disk you want to format is in the appropriate drive (the one shown at the top-left corner of the screen).

When you press RETURN or the SPACE BAR, formatting will begin. Don't be alarmed by the sound that this procedure makes — it is completely normal. When your disk has been formatted, you can repeat the process with another disk if you like.

If you want to return to a Desktop file, simply type OPEN APPLE-Q (for quick change), and choose a file from the Desktop Index that will then be superimposed on your screen. If you want to return to the Main Menu, pressing the ESCAPE key a few times will get you there quickly.

Desktop

 1.09 Tip: *The AppleWorks Desktop enables you to keep up to 12 files in RAM at once.*

Using your computer to accomplish tasks that you used to do manually can be quicker, more accurate, and more convenient. The computer facilitates the handling of many tasks. The tasks themselves, however, have changed little. You probably still work much as you did back in B.C. (before computers), when you had a stack of file folders on your desk that contained information to be added to, perused, or manipulated.

With your stack of folders close at hand, you worked on these tasks progressively, from the top of the stack to the bottom, or skipped from one folder to another to refer to related information. Because of the need for quick referral and information exchange, you kept the information you were presently working with close at hand. It wouldn't have made any sense to have had to walk into another room, for instance, each time you needed to refer to information in a different file folder.

Now the information that you work with is in disk files instead of folders, but you still need to be able to get to them easily when you need them. AppleWorks was designed so that you can maintain up to 12 files at once in short-term, accessible memory. Because there are so many similarities between this new setup and maintaining the traditional stack of folders on a desk, AppleWorks has named this convenient RAM holding tank the Desktop.

1.10 Tip: *Switch between Desktop files with* OPEN APPLE-Q.

Having files on the Desktop means that you can switch from one file to another quickly without having to wait for it to load from disk. The second option in the Main Menu, "Work with one of the files on the Desktop," will present you with a list of Desktop files from which to choose.

You can get to this Desktop Index more quickly from any AppleWorks environment or screen by typing OPEN APPLE-Q. This action superimposes a list of Desktop files on your present screen. The following illustration is an example.

```
 File: Desktop                REVIEW/ADD/CHANGE              Escape: Main Menu
========================================================================

  Having files on the desktop means that you can switch from
  one file to another quickly without having to wait for it to
  load from disk. The second option in the main menu, Work
  with one of the files on the Desktop, will present you with
  a list of all desktop files from which you can make your
  current choice.             ._____.
                              |     Desktop Index      |
  You can also access this    |------------------------| m any
  AppleWorks environment or   | 1.  Desktop        WP  |
  Apple - Q. This action su   | 2.  Memory         WP  | files
  on top of your present sc   | 3.  Printing       WP  | on
  shows an example of this.   | 4.  Startup        WP  |
                              |_____|


  Move your cursor to highlight the file of your choice and
  press Return. In no time the specified file will be on the
  screen before you, the whole operation completed in a
  fraction of the time it would have taken to carry it out
  ----------------------------------------------------------------------
  Type number, or use arrows, then press Return              49K Avail.
```

Move your cursor to highlight the file of your choice and press RETURN. The specified file will quickly be on the screen before you, the whole operation completed in a fraction of the time it would have taken to carry it out from the Main Menu.

1.11 Tip: *A message in the upper-left corner of the Review/Add/ Change screen lets you know which Desktop file is currently on the screen.*

AppleWorks makes switching between Desktop files so easy that you may get confused about which file is the current one on your screen. If this happens, just glance at the upper-left corner of your Review/Add/Change screen. The current file name will always be displayed there for easy reference.

1.12 Trap: *There is no shortcut to using the Main Menu when you want to remove files from your Desktop.*

OPEN APPLE-Q provides a way to shortcut access to Desktop files. It would be handy if a similar shortcut were available when you wanted to remove files from the Desktop. But the Main Menu provides the only doorway to this procedure.

Once you have escaped backward to the Main Menu, choose option 4, "Remove files from the Desktop." The following illustration shows the Remove Files screen that is the result of this choice:

```
Disk: Drive 2              REMOVE FILES           Escape: Main Menu
  _____
 |   Main Menu              | _____
 |    _____|_____       |
 |   |   Remove Files        | _____ |      |
 |   |   Name              Status      Document type       Size |      |
 |   |  =========================================================      |
 |   |   Desktop           Changed     Word Processor       4K |       |
 |   |   Memory            Unchanged   Word Processor       1K |       |
 |   |   Printing          Unchanged   Word Processor       1K |       |
 |   |   Startup           Unchanged   Word Processor       1K |       |
 |   |                                                         |       |
 |   |                                                         |       |
 |   |                                                         |       |
 |   |                                                         |       |
 |   |                                                         |       |
 |___|                                                         |       |
     |                                                         |       |
     |_____|

Use Right Arrow to choose files, Left Arrow to undo        49K Avail.
```

If you want to remove only one file from your Desktop at this time, just highlight your choice by using the up and down arrows and press RETURN. You can have AppleWorks get rid of more than one file at a time by pressing the right arrow key each time your highlight is positioned on one of the files you want removed. In the following illustration, the arrows to the left of the file names indicate the files that were marked in this way:

```
Disk: Drive 2              REMOVE FILES           Escape: Main Menu
  _____
 |   Main Menu              | _____
 |    _____|_____ |
 |   |   Remove Files        | _____ |      |
 |   |   Name              Status      Document type       Size |      |
 |   |  =========================================================      |
 |   | --> Desktop         Changed     Word Processor       4K |       |
 |   | --> Memory          Unchanged   Word Processor       1K |       |
 |   |     Printing        Unchanged   Word Processor       1K |       |
 |   | --> Startup         Unchanged   Word Processor       1K |       |
 |   |                                                         |       |
 |   |                                                         |       |
 |   |                                                         |       |
 |   |                                                         |       |
 |___|                                                         |       |
     |                                                         |       |
     |_____|

Use Right Arrow to choose files, Left Arrow to undo        49K Avail.
```

Once these choices are made, pressing the RETURN key begins their removal from the Desktop. If you haven't made any changes to a file specified for removal since it was last saved, removal will be carried out immediately and the Main Menu will then appear on your screen.

If you have made changes to any file that you want to remove, a caution screen will appear for each unsaved file to alert you to this fact and present you with the following options:

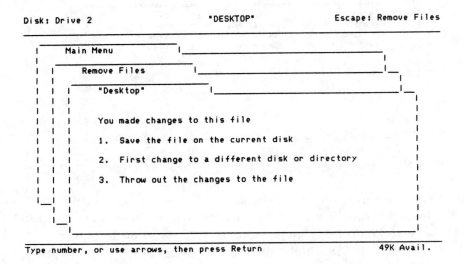

```
Disk: Drive 2                    "DESKTOP"           Escape: Remove Files
_____
I _____Main Menu_____ I_____
I I                             I                                        I
I I   Remove Files_____ I_____ I__
I I I                           I                                         I
I I I   "Desktop"_____ I_____I__
I I I                                                                       I
I I I                                                                       I
I I I   You made changes to this file                                      I
I I I                                                                       I
I I I   1.  Save the file on the current disk                              I
I I I                                                                       I
I I I   2.  First change to a different disk or directory                  I
I I I                                                                       I
I I I   3.  Throw out the changes to the file                              I
I I I                                                                       I
I_I I                                                                      I
  I I                                                                       I
  I_I                                                                       I
    I _____
Type number, or use arrows, then press Return              49K Avail.
```

If you really do not want these files anymore and don't need to save them first, it is quite bothersome to have to go through this procedure for each file you have specified. But AppleWorks has built in these safeguards for you because in the long run they could save you grief.

1.13 Tip: *Selecting Add Files to the Desktop allows you to choose from three sources for your Desktop files.*

Whether you want to load files from a disk, create a new file from scratch, or import information from non-AppleWorks files (ASCII, DIF, VisiCalc, or Quick-File), your first step is to choose "Add Files to the Desktop." Once you have entered the Add Files doorway, your choices have just begun. The following screen illustrates these choices as they are listed on the Add Files menu:

```
Disk: Drive 2                    ADD FILES              Escape: Main Menu

  _____
 |   Main Menu              |_____ |
 | |_____| |
 | | Add Files           |_____| |_
 | |                                                                | |
 | |                                                                | |
 | |     Get files from:                                            | |
 | |                                                                | |
 | |     1.  The current disk: Drive 2                              | |
 | |     2.  A different disk                                       | |
 | |                                                                | |
 | |     Make a new file for the:                                   | |
 | |                                                                | |
 | |     3.  Word Processor                                         | |
 | |     4.  Data Base                                              | |
 | |     5.  Spreadsheet                                            | |
 |_|_|                                                              | |
   |                                                                | |
   |_____| |

  Type number, or use arrows, then press Return            48K Avail.
```

The choices displayed in the Add Files menu involve loading files from disk or creating them. But the choice of importing data from other sources is hidden in a lower menu level. To access this menu, you must choose "Make a new file for the:"

3. Word Processor

4. Data Base

5. Spreadsheet

Each choice calls up a menu that lists the imports allowable within that particular environment. More information about where to go from here is presented in Chapter 6, "Data Transfer."

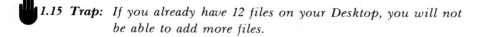 *1.14 Tip: Removing a file from your Desktop does not affect any copy of that file you had on disk.*

Don't be afraid that you might adversely affect your disk copy of a file that is removed from your Desktop. Throwing out a Desktop file does nothing to the copy of that file on a disk.

1.15 Trap: If you already have 12 files on your Desktop, you will not be able to add more files.

Don't expect to be able to continue adding files to your Desktop indefinitely. Even if your Desktop memory limit has not been reached, AppleWorks limits your Desktop files to 12.

If you don't have room for a file that you need on your Desktop, you must first remove one of the current Desktop files to create an available slot (option 4 from the Main Menu). Remember to save the file before you remove it if you haven't already done so since you last made changes to it. If you do this, you can always retrieve it just as it was if you need to refer to it in the future.

 1.16 Trap: You can't always get 12 files on the Desktop.

As stated in the previous Trap, the maximum number of files AppleWorks allows you to have on the Desktop at one time is 12. However, this maximum is further controlled because the limit on Desktop space is 55K of RAM if you have a 128K system; 10K of RAM with a 64K system. (Of course, your available Desktop space will be increased if you have added RAM cards to increase your computer's memory capacity.)

Obviously, you will not be able to add files whose combined size exceeds your Desktop limit. You could reach this limit with one very large file or with five moderately large files.

When you attempt to add a file that there is not room for, a screen such as the following one informs you that the Desktop is full:

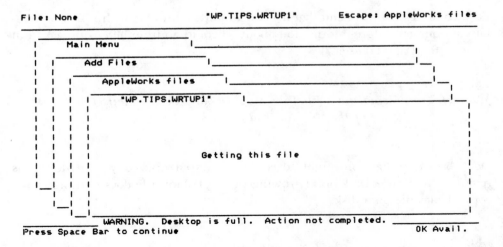

The only thing you can do in this case is remove one or more Desktop files to make room for the file you want to add. Make sure that the file(s) you remove free up enough memory to accommodate the one you are adding, plus a little more to work with.

1.17 Trap: *If you are switching between Desktop files and making many changes, be sure to save all the changes when you are ready to quit your session.*

AppleWorks' Desktop feature allows you to keep up to 12 files easily available. When you are composing a letter, for example, you can quickly refer to related data in a spreadsheet or look up the proper address from a data base file.

If you are working in one Desktop file and are accessing others only for reference purposes, you are not likely to run into problems. But if you are adding, deleting, or moving information in various files as you switch among them, it is easy to forget to save these changes before you end your work session—a serious mistake if it means time lost in having to redo the changes.

If you can trust yourself to perform a quick save (OPEN APPLE-S) each time after working on a file but before switching to another, this is probably the fastest technique to use. Even if you remember to do this most of the time, it is likely that sooner or later you will forget.

To be absolutely safe, it is best to carry out your file saves by choosing option 3 ("Save Desktop files to disk") from the Main Menu just before you are ready to quit your work session. This option calls up a list of all your Desktop files and lets you know which ones have undergone changes since they were last saved. With this information, you can use the right arrow key to mark each file that needs to be saved. The following illustration shows such a file list marked for saving:

```
Disk: Drive 2              SAVE FILES              Escape: Main Menu
_____
 I      Main Menu        I_____
 I                                                              I__
 I  I     Save Files     I_____  I
 I  I     Name           Status      Document type       Size   I  I
 I  I     ===================================================   I  I
 I  I --> Printing        Changed     Word Processor       1K    I
 I  I --> Desktop         Changed     Word Processor      11K    I
 I  I     Memory          Saved       Word Processor       1K    I
 I  I     Startup         Unchanged   Word Processor       1K    I
 I  I                                                            I
 I  I                                                            I
 I  I                                                            I
 I  I                                                            I
 I  I                                                            I
 I  I_I                                                          I
 I   I                                                           I
 I                                                               I
 I_____I

Use Right Arrow to choose files, Left Arrow to undo        42K Avail.
```

1.18 Tip: *Don't worry about losing the files on your Desktop when you take time out to format a new disk or perform any other menu tasks unrelated to your current file.*

Any time you are working with a Desktop file, you can press ESCAPE to get to the Main Menu with the knowledge that the information in your current file will be kept intact for you to return to whenever you wish. In fact, the safety of your Desktop files is not threatened even if you choose to perform several tasks from the Main Menu or any of the submenus that lead from it.

You can take time out from working in a Desktop file to format a disk that you wish to use for saving Desktop information, add more files to your Desktop, or any other side task that seems necessary. Once you are finished with your side trip and want to return to a Desktop file, type OPEN APPLE-Q and choose the appropriate file from the Desktop Index that appears on your screen.

1.19 Trap: *As the size of your file approaches your computer's memory limit, it takes longer to complete simple commands.*

This trap is especially prevalent in AppleWorks' word processing environment. As your file gets closer to the 55K Desktop limit (or whatever your limit is), you will notice that procedures such as Copy, Move, and Delete take a long time. You may notice other strange effects, such as having to press the SPACE BAR over and over just to get it to insert a space within a line. (See the next Tip for how to avoid this.)

1.20 Tip: *You can solve your memory problems by dividing large Desktop files in two.*

If sluggishness begins to bother you when you are working with a large file, it is time to break the file in two. First make sure that you have a copy of the entire file on disk. Then delete everything from the Desktop (OPEN APPLE-D), except the portion of the file that you want to put into a second file. When the second file data is all that is left, give it a new file name (OPEN APPLE-N) and save it to disk.

All that's left now is to load the original file from disk, delete the portion that you have already transferred to your new file, and resave it in its new form. Keep in mind that you will not be able to perform this last step until you have created enough Desktop space to make room for the original file to be loaded. Don't worry about removing your file from the Desktop to create this space. The file you are loading contains the same information as the file you are removing, so you won't really be losing anything.

1.21 Tip: *The Help command tells you how much Desktop space is available.*

You will probably want to know how much Desktop space you have left if you are planning to add a file to your Desktop and want to make sure you have room for it. And if you are adding information to a file that is already large, you may want to check your Desktop space periodically to make sure that you will have room to enter the necessary information before you exceed the Desktop's limit.

It is easy to ascertain how much Desktop space is currently available by accessing the help screen with OPEN APPLE-?. As shown in the following illustration, the bottom-right corner of this screen always displays the currently available Desktop space.

```
File: Desktop                        HELP            Escape: Review/Add/Change
===================|=========================================================

              ∂-C   Copy text (includes cut and paste)

              ∂-D   Delete text

              ∂-F   Find occurrences of....

              ∂-K   Calculate page numbers

              ∂-M   Move text (includes cut and paste)

              ∂-N   Change name of file

              ∂-O   Options for print formatting

              ∂-P   Print

              ∂-R   Replace occurrences of.....

              ∂-T   Set and clear tab stops

-----------------------------------------------------------------------------
Use arrows to see remainder of Help                          25K Avail.
```

This helpful message also appears in the same location each time you choose options 1 through 5 from the Main Menu. It saves you the trouble of determining available Desktop space before you begin one of these procedures.

Common Commands and Features

1.22 Tip: *The* CLOSED APPLE *key works just as well as the* OPEN APPLE *key in AppleWorks commands.*

Throughout the AppleWorks program, various keys are used in conjunction with an APPLE key to initiate certain commands and perform specific functions. The AppleWorks manual refers to these keys in combination with the OPEN APPLE key. For simplicity's sake, we have followed their lead in this book, referring to command combinations as OPEN APPLE-key.

The OPEN APPLE and CLOSED APPLE keys are equally effective partners for all command or function keys. At times you will find it more convenient to use the CLOSED APPLE because of its position on the keyboard. Get used to making this switch if it is convenient; don't be tied to the OPEN APPLE just because it is the one referred to in print.

1.23 Tip: *The* ESCAPE *key always gets you back to the Main Menu eventually.*

The ESCAPE key enables you to backstep through whatever operations you have performed. Pressing ESCAPE generally moves you backward one step at a time with each press. It takes as many ESCAPE presses to get you back to the Review/Add/Change screen as it took to proceed through the current operation.

You can use the ESCAPE key to undo one or more operations whenever you realize that changes are called for before a procedure is completed. You can also press ESCAPE as often as necessary to get out of a procedure completely.

If you press ESCAPE from Review/Add/Change, you will be presented with the Main Menu. From there you can choose any Main Menu option or return to your file in Review/Add/Change by pressing ESCAPE again. A handy prompt similar to the one in the following illustration will always be displayed in the upper-right corner of the screen to tell you where you will go next if you press ESCAPE.

```
File: COMMON.COMMANDS          REVIEW/ADD/CHANGE          Escape: Main Menu
```

The AppleWorks Environment

Each time you press ESCAPE the prompt changes, indicating the next level up.

1.24 Tip: *You can get help from any AppleWorks environment by typing OPEN APPLE-?.*

If you are new at using AppleWorks or are engaged in a procedure that you perform infrequently, you may be unsure of the exact command to use to bring about a certain effect. Before you resort to the time consuming process of looking through the manual, try accessing the built-in help screen (press OPEN APPLE-?) that is part of each AppleWorks environment.

Whether working with a spreadsheet, a data base, or a word processing document, you must issue this command from the Review/Add/Change menu. You will then be presented with a screen listing all the commands (key combinations) that are appropriate to that particular environment and briefly explaining what each command will do.

If you access the help screen when you are in the Spreadsheet environment, you get the additional bonus of a display of the standard values that currently apply to your spreadsheet. These values are listed at the end of the help screen (use the down arrow to get to them), below the listings for commands.

If, after trying this quick study method, you are still unsure about how to accomplish a specific task, refer to the *AppleWorks Reference Manual* for a more detailed explanation. If you still have problems, no doubt you will find a Tip or a Trap in this book that will help set you straight.

1.25 Tip: *In AppleWorks, important commands are consistent among environments whenever possible.*

One of the aspects of AppleWorks that makes it so easy to learn and use is that its functions are the same in all three environments. Once you learn the basic key commands in one environment, you can usually guess the commands for a similar operation in another environment.

Of course, there are certain operations that are specific to each environment and consequently must be initiated with a unique command. But, in general, consistency prevails.

The following is a list of commands that are effective in all AppleWorks environments. A brief description of each is included here, but you will find that a more thorough explanation of each command and the Tips and Traps associated with them are provided within the appropriate sections of this book.

Common AppleWorks Commands

Command	Function
OPEN APPLE-N	Allows changes to file name
OPEN APPLE-Q	Accesses Desktop Index
OPEN APPLE-S	Quick saves current file
OPEN APPLE-M	Moves data that you highlight
OPEN APPLE-C	Copies data that you highlight
OPEN APPLE-P	Begins printing procedure
OPEN APPLE-?	Accesses help screen
OPEN APPLE-E	Switches between overstrike and insert cursor
OPEN APPLE-D	Deletes characters, lines, or blocks that you highlight
OPEN APPLE-H	Prints hard copy of current screen
OPEN APPLE-F	Finds information that you specify
CONTROL-Y	Erases from cursor position to end of line, cell, or entry

1.26 **Trap:** *Unfortunately, the window feature applies to only the AppleWorks Spreadsheet environment.*

AppleWorks' Spreadsheet environment includes the extremely useful windowing feature. With windowing you can juxtapose two distant areas of your worksheet so that they can be viewed together on your screen. You can make entries in one area of your worksheet while viewing data in another area that you would otherwise be unable to see.

Once you have become familiar with this feature in the Spreadsheet environment, you may find occasions when you would like to use windowing in the Data Base or Word Processor environment. Don't bother trying to figure out how to create a word processing or data base window. At present, AppleWorks is capable of windowing only in the Spreadsheet environment.

1.27 **Tip:** *AppleWorks' Ruler feature works in all three environments to help you move around your work area quickly.*

Whether you are working in the Data Base, Spreadsheet, or Word Processor, and whether your file is 1K or 50K, AppleWorks divides the file into eighths and offers access to each eighth through its built-in ruler. With the AppleWorks Ruler, you can press OPEN APPLE-1 to get to the beginning of a file and OPEN APPLE-9 to get to the end. Pressing OPEN APPLE-2 through -8 moves you through the body of your file by degrees.

When you use the 2 through 8 ruler marks, you cannot be sure of the exact location where you will land. Once there, you may waste a lot of time scrolling up and down trying to find the spot you had set out for. If you run into this frustrating situation often, you will be tempted to refrain from using these in-between ruler marks altogether. Instead of resorting to this extreme, try using the ruler marks to scroll through your file until you locate the position you want.

If you begin with OPEN APPLE-1, which starts you at the top of your file, and next press OPEN APPLE-2, then -3, and so on, you will pass through your file more quickly than you could by any other means. Because you are carrying out this movement progressively from beginning to end, you can maintain a sense of where you are in relation to the location you are seeking. If the location you are searching for is closer to the end of your file than the beginning, use this Tip in reverse, beginning with OPEN APPLE-9 and moving backward progressively.

Disk and File Handling

1.28 Tip: *You have to let AppleWorks know if you are using two disk drives; otherwise, it will assume that you have only one drive and will prompt you to change disks every so often.*

Unless you specify otherwise when you first start up, AppleWorks will assume that you have only one disk drive. This assumption leads to frequent prompts instructing you to place the AppleWorks Program disk in your drive whenever AppleWorks reaches a point at which it needs to read information from that disk. When information is needed from one of your data disks, you will be prompted to replace the Program disk with the data disk.

This bothersome disk-switching process is necessary with a one-drive system. But if you have a second drive from which your data can be read, leaving the first drive available for program information access, you won't have this problem.

However, AppleWorks won't know to read from your second disk drive unless you specify it as the standard location of your data disk.

Do this by selecting option 5, "Other Activities," from the Main Menu. Then choose option 6, "Select standard location of data disk," and specify Drive 2 when the Standard Data Disk screen appears. Once you have done this, your choice will be recorded on the AppleWorks Program disk in Drive 1 and kept as a standard data disk location each time you load the program (unless you change it again in this same way).

You can tell the current drive that AppleWorks considers for your data disk location by looking in the upper-left corner of the Main Menu or any Apple-Works submenu.

1.29 Tip: Through the Other Activities menu you can temporarily change the location of the current drive from which you want your data disks to be read.

In the previous Tip you learned how to specify the disk drive that you wanted AppleWorks to permanently adopt for the location of your data disks. If, for a short-term purpose, you want AppleWorks to read data from a drive other than the specified standard drive, choose option 1, "Change current disk drive or Pro-DOS prefix," from the Other Activities menu (option 5 on the Main Menu).

As long as you are in your current work session, the specified drive will be used, unless you change the specification with the same procedure. However, once you quit your AppleWorks session, this temporary specification will be lost. The next time you load AppleWorks, you will find that your data disks will be read according to the standard location specified from the Other Activities menu (option 6).

1.30 Tip: To avoid bothersome interruptions, load many files from your disk at one time.

As you begin an AppleWorks work session, try to think ahead to all the tasks you expect to accomplish. If these tasks involve working with more than one file, you can save several steps by adding the necessary files at this time, in one operation.

When you choose "Add Files to the Desktop" from the Main Menu and then specify the disk drive where those files are located, a list of all the files on that disk will appear on the screen. You can use the up and down arrow keys to highlight any of these files. When you press RETURN, the file that you highlighted will be loaded onto your Desktop.

You can specify more than one file by moving the highlight to each file you want and using the right arrow key to mark that file for Desktop loading. You can mark up to 12 files in this way. As long as their combined size does not exceed the available Desktop space, they will all be loaded when you press the RETURN key (to indicate that your selection is completed).

When you need to switch from one of these files to another, all you have to do is press OPEN APPLE-Q and specify the file you want from the superimposed Desktop Index on your screen. Think of the time you would have wasted if you had stopped each time to load the file you wanted from disk.

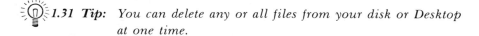 *1.31 Tip: You can delete any or all files from your disk or Desktop at one time.*

The procedure described in the previous Tip can be used when you want to delete or add files to your Desktop. When you choose "Remove files from the Desktop" (Main Menu option 4), a list of your current Desktop files will be displayed on your screen. You can specify one of these files by highlighting it and then pressing RETURN, or you can use the right arrow key to mark any number of files that you want removed from your Desktop.

The removal operation usually involves more steps than the retrieval operation, because AppleWorks requires two confirmations that you really want to go through with it for each file specified that has not been saved since changes were made to it. Specifying all removals at one time is still preferable to carrying them out separately.

The procedure for deleting files from your disk works much the same way. If you choose "Other Activities" (option 5) from the Main Menu, "Delete files from disk" (option 4) will lead you to the following Delete Files screen:

```
Disk: Drive 2                    DELETE FILES          Escape: Other Activities
_____

  I     Main Menu          I_____
  I                        I                                               I
  I   I   Other Activities   I_____I__
  I   I                      I                                                I
  I   I   I   Delete Files      I_____I__
  I   I   I   Disk volume /CHAP1.TIPS has 90K available                        I
  I   I   I     Name        Type of file    Size    Date      Time            I
  I   I   I   ================================================================ I
  I   I   I   Chap1.Intro     Word Processor   1K   10/03/85                   I
  I   I   I   Common.Commands Word Processor  10K   10/10/84                   I
  I   I   I   Desktop         Word Processor  15K   10/10/84                   I
  I   I   I   Disk.File.Hndlg Word Processor  18K   10/10/84                   I
  I   I   I   Printing        Word Processor   1K   10/07/84                   I
  I   I   I   Startup         Word Processor   1K   10/03/85                   I
  I   I   I                                                                    I
  I__I   I                                                                    I
    I   I                                                                    I
    I__I_____I
_____

Use Right Arrow to choose files, Left Arrow to undo              9K Avail.
```

For each file that you mark for deletion from this screen, you will be warned of the severity of your action and asked to confirm your decision. The following illustration shows the AppleWorks warning screen:

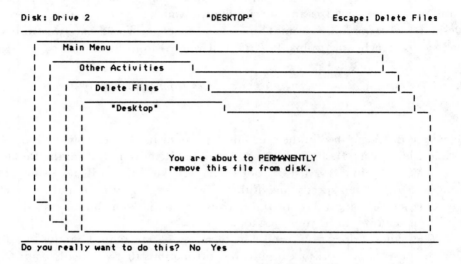

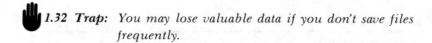

If you choose No, you will be sent back to the Other Activities menu. From there you can press OPEN APPLE-Q and choose the Desktop file that you wish to call to your screen. If you choose Yes, the file that you specified will be permanently deleted from your disk.

1.32 Trap: *You may lose valuable data if you don't save files frequently.*

AppleWorks has many built-in safety features; it is difficult to make inadvertent mistakes. However, there is nothing AppleWorks can do if you fail to follow the basic rule of saving your work frequently and get caught with a power failure or one of numerous possible human failures. Hours of precious time and thoughts can be lost in such situations. To avoid tragedy, save your work at least every half hour—more frequently the more valuable it is. In addition, be sure to keep backup disks that contain duplicates of all your files. Backing up your files ensures that you will always have a copy if something happens to your original disks.

Knowing that disks can be damaged, take the extra precaution of printing a hard copy of any information that would be difficult to replace. If you turn these safeguards into habits, you are bound to be grateful in the end.

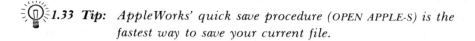 **1.33 Tip:** *AppleWorks' quick save procedure (OPEN APPLE-S) is the fastest way to save your current file.*

You can save the file currently on your screen anytime by pressing OPEN APPLE-S. This feature is a real time saver since the alternative of initiating a save from the Main Menu involves several steps.

1.34 Tip: *AppleWorks' Main Menu option 3 allows you to specify several saves at once.*

The quick save described in the previous Tip is by far the fastest way to save your current Desktop file. However, if you want to save a Desktop file that is not on the screen or if you want to specify more than one file save at once, begin with option 3 from the Main Menu, "Save Desktop files to disk."

When you choose this option, the following Save Files screen displays a list of all the files currently on your Desktop:

```
Disk: Drive 2                  SAVE FILES              Escape: Main Menu

    _____
    I   Main Menu                    I_____
    I   _____      I                                  I
    I   I   Save Files              I_____I__
    I   I   Name              Status         Document type      Size  I
    I   I ================================================================= I
    I   I --> Disk.File.Hndlg  Changed      Word Processor     19K   I
    I   I    Common.Commands    Saved        Word Processor     10K   I
    I   I --> Desktop          Changed      Word Processor     16K   I
    I   I    Printing          Unchanged    Word Processor      1K   I
    I   I    Startup           Unchanged    Word Processor      1K   I
    I   I                                                             I
    I   I                                                             I
    I   I                                                             I
    I   I                                                             I
    I__I                                                             I
        I_____I

Use Right Arrow to choose files, Left Arrow to undo            9K Avail.
```

From this display you can determine whether each file has been changed and if the changed files have been saved. To save any of the files in this list, use the up or down arrows to highlight the appropriate file and press RETURN.

You can mark more than one file for saving by pressing the right arrow key each time you highlight a file that you would like to save. The arrows to the left of the file names in the preceding screen indicate the files that have been marked for saving in this example. The first and third files are marked in this case because the display shows that they had not been saved since changes were made to them.

When you begin a save on a file that has been changed, you must wind your way through two additional levels for each file marked for saving. In the first level, you choose to save files on the current disk drive, and in the second level you specify that you would like to let the new information replace the old.

It is bothersome to have to repeat these steps for each file you want to save, but after doing so, you will be able to quit your session knowing that all your valuable information has been safely stored on disk.

1.35 Trap: *A file save will replace any file on disk with the same file name.*

There are two ways to carry out a file save in AppleWorks: by choosing option 3 from the Main Menu, "Save Desktop files to disk," and by initiating a quick save with OPEN APPLE-S. Whichever save path you take, be aware that the file you are saving will completely replace any other file on your disk that has the same file name.

The save method begun from the Main Menu warns you about this, but the quick-save procedure leaves the entire responsibility up to you. You can always press the ESCAPE key to abort an unwanted save if you act quickly.

Most of the time, such a replacement is exactly what you want. But if, for some reason, you want to retain your original file and still save a new modified file, all you have to do is rename the new file before you save it. See Tip 1.46 for a further explanation of this procedure.

1.36 Tip: *After you save a file, you still have a copy of it in memory until you turn off your computer or choose "Remove files from the Desktop" from the Main Menu.*

When you save a file from your Desktop to disk, you have not moved the information from one place to another. Although your current Desktop file is copied onto your disk exactly in its present form, it is also retained on your Desktop. Once the save is completed, you can return to continue working in your file, adding information and saving every so often to be sure that new data is not lost.

If your save is carried out with OPEN APPLE-S, you will automatically be returned to the location that you occupied in your file when you first initiated the save. If you used Main Menu option 3 to begin your save, you will find the Main Menu on your screen when the save is completed. You need only press ESCAPE to get back to the Desktop file where you began.

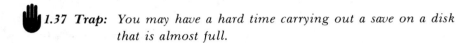*1.37 Trap:* *You may have a hard time carrying out a save on a disk that is almost full.*

Each time you save a file, the newly saved file will replace any disk file with the same name. To be sure that this does not happen inadvertently, AppleWorks allows you to use the ESCAPE key to abort a save while it is in progress.

To make this safeguard possible, it is necessary to make sure that the original disk file with the same name is not deleted until the current save has been carried out. Maintaining two almost identical files on disk uses up almost twice as much disk space.

If you have a 25K file on disk that you are replacing with a 29K file, you should be able to do this with 4K of disk space left, since 25K of the new file would go to replacing the old. But if you attempt a save in AppleWorks under these conditions, you will be confronted with the following screen:

```
Disk: Drive 2              "WP.TIPS.WRTUP2"           Escape: Save Files
_____

    I_____I
    I   Main Menu        I_____
    I   I_____I                                     I
    I   I   Save Files        I_____I__
    I   I   I_____I                                     I
    I   I   I   "WP.TIPS.WRTUP2"    I_____I__
    I   I   I                                                          I
    I   I   I                                                          I
    I   I   I                                                          I
    I   I   I                                                          I
    I   I   I       Insufficient room for your file on this disk.      I
    I   I   I                                                          I
    I   I   I                                                          I
    I   I   I                                                          I
    I   I   I                                                          I
    I  I__I  I                                                          I
    I     I__I                                                          I
    I       I_I                                                         I
    I_____I

Press Space Bar to continue                                   4K Avail.
```

If the data you need to add to complete your current project will overflow to a new disk anyway, you might as well start filling a new disk at this point. However, if you are near the end of a project and are sure that you could fit everything you need on the current disk if it weren't for the redundant file using up your disk space, there is another solution.

If you delete the file in question from your disk and then save its replacement file, you should have ample room to accomplish your mission. To begin this procedure, first escape to the Main Menu and choose "Other Activities" (option 5). The "Delete files from disk" option that you want is number 4 on the Other Activities menu.

Once you specify this option, a Delete Files screen will appear with a list of all your disk files, the size of each one, and the amount of disk space available. From this list you can highlight the file that you want to delete and press RETURN.

You will then be warned of the consequences of this action and asked for confirmation. Once the deletion is completed, you should have plenty of disk space to carry out the save that you had originally intended.

1.38 Trap: *Follow AppleWorks' conventions for naming disks and files, or your name will not be accepted.*

You have to name new disks that you format and new files that you create. AppleWorks will prompt you for a name at the appropriate time when you initiate either of these tasks. However, AppleWorks requires that you follow certain naming conventions for your name to be acceptable.

Each name must begin with a letter and cannot be longer than 15 characters, including spaces. Except for the first character, these 15 characters can be made up of numbers, upper- or lowercase letters, spaces, or periods.

Any characters typed beyond the 15-character limit will not be recorded. If you fail to adhere to any of the other conventions, your entry will be erased when you press RETURN, and you will have to enter another name that meets with AppleWorks' approval.

1.39 Trap: *You'll be in for a lot of confusion if you create disks that are full of unrelated files.*

AppleWorks' integrated package is so useful that you will probably employ it for a variety of business and personal tasks. At first it may seem economical to save files on a disk until it is full. You may have an ingrained sense of thrift that rebels at the idea of storing a few files on one disk and using a new one each time you save other unrelated files.

This is one time when it is to your advantage to sacrifice economics for organization. The price of a few disks is minimal if it means the difference between confusion and knowing exactly which disk to turn to. (If you are using a hard disk, you can get the same advantage by creating subdirectories for files of related information.)

 *1.40 Tip:* *Use descriptive names for disks and files.*

When you give names to the disks you format or the files you create, make sure that the names have some relationship to the information on that disk or within that file. Suppose that you kept records for several businesses. It would be important to keep the records from each company on a separate disk and reasonable to name each disk according to the company name whose records it holds.

Within each disk you might have files related to record keeping, planning and forecasting, and sales and marketing. To have the file names reflect the category that they fall under, you could precede each individual name with a two-letter abbreviation that indicates what type of file it is. The names of the files listed below provide an example of this pattern:

File Name	Indicates
PF.Amortiz	Amortization schedule in Planning and Forecasting category
SM.Inventory	Inventory schedule in Sales and Marketing category
RK.Check.Reg	Check register in Record Keeping category

Perhaps you don't see the necessity for preceding each file name with a category abbreviation. Maybe you would find it more helpful if the company name were somehow indicated in each file related to it. Or you may find that a different pattern works better for you.

In any case, it is helpful to use a system for naming files so that the contents are obvious from the names. The system you design is up to you.

1.41 Tip: *You can use the ESCAPE key to back out of a save while it is in process without losing any data.*

Using AppleWorks' quick save command (OPEN APPLE-S) is a speedy way to save the file you are working on. (Remember, though, that anytime you save a file to disk, it overwrites and replaces any information that was on that disk under the same file name.)

Because the quick save can be carried out so swiftly and does not have any of the built-in safeguards of a save initiated from the Main Menu, you could find yourself in the middle of a save that, on second thought, you don't want to have take place.

The AppleWorks save feature was designed so that a previous disk file with the same name will not be erased until a save of the replacement file has been completed. Furthermore, pressing the ESCAPE key can abort the save procedure midstream and leave you with your original disk file intact. By pressing the SPACE BAR, you can return to your Desktop file with a chance to replan your course of action.

1.42 Tip: *If you are careful to enter the date at the beginning of each AppleWorks session, any files that you create will be labeled with the date that you entered.*

Each time you load your AppleWorks Program disk, you will be presented with a Getting Started screen that prompts you to enter today's date and then press RETURN. Each file saved during your current work session will be labeled with the date entered at this time. AppleWorks provides a chronological record of your disk files that could prove useful for future reference.

To find out the creation date of a disk file, you must first call up the Other Activities menu by specifying option 5 on the Main Menu. From there you choose option 2, "List all files on the current disk drive." The resulting List All Files screen that follows shows the date that each disk file was created — or, more accurately, the date that was entered into the computer when each file was last saved.

```
Disk: Drive 2              LIST ALL FILES        Escape: Other Activities
 _____
|      Main Menu          |                                                 |
|   _____    |
|  |   Other Activities    |                                          |    |
|  |   _____|__  |
|  |  |   List All Files      |                                       |   | |
|  |  |  Disk volume /CHAP1.TIPS has 95K available                    |   | |
|  |  |   Name           Type of file   Size   Date     Time          |   | |
|  |  |  ===========================================================  |   | |
|  |  |  Chap1.Intro     Word Processor   1K   10/03/85               |   | |
|  |  |  Common.Commands Word Processor  10K   10/10/84               |   | |
|  |  |  Desktop         Word Processor  15K   10/09/84               |   | |
|  |  |  Disk.File.Hndlg Word Processor  14K   10/10/84               |   | |
|  |  |  Printing        Word Processor   1K   10/07/84               |   | |
|  |  |  Startup         Word Processor   1K   10/03/85               |   | |
|  |  |                                                               |   | |
|  |__|                                                               |   | |
|     |                                                               |   | |
|     |                                                               |   | |
|    _|                                                               |   | |
|   |  _____ |   | |
 _____
 Use up/down arrows to move through list                        30K Avail.
```

Saving a file from Desktop to disk automatically labels it with the date that AppleWorks has applied to the current session. If you neglected to make the date current for this session, each saved file will be labeled with whatever date was retained from the last session.

1.43 **Tip:** *The List All Files screen tells you the name of the disk in your current drive and the amount of disk space available there.*

When you first format a disk to accept data, you are required to give the disk a name. A great deal of time may pass between that initial christening session and when you need to know the name that you assigned to your disk. (Many such situations are discussed in Chapter 6, "Data Transfer.") Unless you were thoughtful enough to include the exact disk name when you attached your disk label, you may feel like the young queen trying to discover Rumpelstiltskin's true identity.

Fortunately, your problem is easier to solve. All you have to do is access the Other Activities menu from the Main Menu and then choose option 2, "List all files on the current disk drive.'' As you can see from the preceding illustration, the name of the current disk is displayed above the list of files; in this case it is /CHAP1.TIPS.

From this same screen, you can also determine how much disk space you have left. This example shows that disk volume /CHAP1.TIPS has 95K available. Individual file sizes are listed as well, although this information is also available from the Save Files and Remove Files screens.

1.44 Trap: If you turn off your computer at the end of a session without quitting from the Main Menu, you could forget to save valuable data.

The quickest way to end an AppleWorks work session is to turn off your computer, but it is much safer to quit by choosing option 6 from the Main Menu. To make sure that you haven't forgotten anything, you will be asked if you really want to quit and will be warned about unsaved files. The extra thought it takes to respond to this question may be just what you need to remind you to save a file before it is lost forever.

1.45 Tip: OPEN APPLE-CONTROL-RESET quits the current program and loads a new program from Drive 1.

When you want to load a different program into your computer's memory, you can always turn off your system, place the new Program disk in Drive 1, and turn on the computer again to automatically load the new program. But it is faster and easier on your computer to boot the new program by simultaneously holding down the OPEN APPLE, CONTROL, and RESET keys.

Before you use either method, however, be sure that you have saved all the necessary information currently in your computer's memory. Once the new program is loaded, everything associated with the old will, of course, be lost.

1.46 Tip: You can save a new version of a file you already have on disk by first giving the revised file a new name.

If you find that you make frequent changes to your AppleWorks files, you are probably happy to have these changes replace the original disk file when you save to disk. But sometimes you may need to retain a disk file in its original form and save the changed version as well.

To accomplish this, all you have to do is rename the new version before you save it to disk. Whether you are in the Word Processor, Data Base or Spreadsheet environment, the command to use for changing the name of the current Desktop file is OPEN APPLE-N.

Once you give this command a message at the bottom-left corner of the screen will prompt you to "Type filename." Your current file name will be displayed after the prompt and will need to be erased with CONTROL-Y before you can enter the new name. Once the new entry is made, you will be returned to Review/Add/Change and the new file name will be displayed in the upper-left corner of the screen.

Now when you save your newly named file to disk, it will not replace the original, and you will have succeeded in your goal of keeping each file separate and intact.

 1.47 Trap: *You cannot duplicate a disk from AppleWorks.*

AppleWorks' Other Activities option in the Main Menu is your doorway to performing many tasks associated with disk and file handling. However, as you can see from the following illustration of the Other Activities menu, duplicating a disk is not included in these tasks.

```
Disk: Drive 2              OTHER ACTIVITIES          Escape: Main Menu
_____

 I     Main Menu           I_____
 I    _____     I                                        I
 I   I  Other Activities   I_____I_
 I   I                                                               I
 I   I   1.  Change current disk drive or ProDOS prefix              I
 I   I                                                               I
 I   I   2.  List all files on the current disk drive                I
 I   I                                                               I
 I   I   3.  Create a subdirectory                                   I
 I   I                                                               I
 I   I   4.  Delete files from disk                                  I
 I   I                                                               I
 I   I   5.  Format a blank disk                                     I
 I   I___I                                                           I
 I___I   6.  Select standard location of data disk                  I
 I       7.  Specify information about your printer(s)               I
 I_____I

_____
Type number, or use arrows, then press Return              50K Avail.
```

If you have an Apple IIc, you will find this option listed on the System Utilities disk that came with your system. If you have an Apple IIe, you will need to use the ProDOS User's disk to carry out this task.

In either case, you have to leave AppleWorks and reboot your system with the appropriate disk in Drive 1 (press OPEN APPLE-CONTROL-RESET after you have the disk in place). If you choose option 5 on the System Utilities menu that is displayed on your screen, you will be led down the proper path to complete the disk duplication procedure.

Once you have the ProDOS User's disk loaded, choose "F ProDOS Filer" from the menu and then "V - Volume Commands" and "C - Copy a volume" from the two menus that follow. From there it is a matter of responding to the questions presented to you.

You do not have to format a disk that you are duplicating onto. The duplicating process automatically formats before it duplicates.

1.48 Tip: *Copying AppleWorks to a hard disk will speed up the program's performance considerably.*

If you are interested in speeding up your computer's operations, there is no better way than to install a hard disk. A hard disk spinning at about 3500 rpm allows the disk drive head to read from it and write to it much faster than a floppy disk, which spins at about 350 rpm. With a hard disk, your data can be loaded and saved up to ten times faster (depending on your particular system) than with a floppy disk system.

Since speed is your purpose and space isn't a problem, you will benefit from installing the AppleWorks program on a hard disk. As you are performing certain tasks in AppleWorks, the program will need to access the disk for instructions specific to that operation. A hard disk can read these instructions much faster for the same reason that it can read your data faster.

Specific instructions for installing the AppleWorks program on a ProFile hard disk are available in the *AppleWorks Reference Manual,* beginning on page 275. If your hard disk is not a ProFile, the procedure may vary slightly. Seek out an informed source to lead you through the proper steps. One excellent reference is *AppleWorks* by Charles Rubin (Microsoft Press, 1985). Rubin takes you through this process step by step, beginning on page 259.

Printing

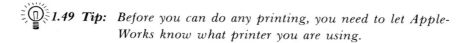**1.49 Tip:** *Before you can do any printing, you need to let Apple-Works know what printer you are using.*

To send the correct messages to your printer, AppleWorks needs to be informed of essential information specific to your printer. If you have an Epson, an Apple, or a Qume printer, all you have to do is access the Add a Printer menu and choose the appropriate option from the list presented there.

To get to this menu, choose option 5, "Other Activities," from the Main Menu and then option 7, "Specify information about your printer(s)." The Add a Printer option in the Printer Information menu will take you to the following screen:

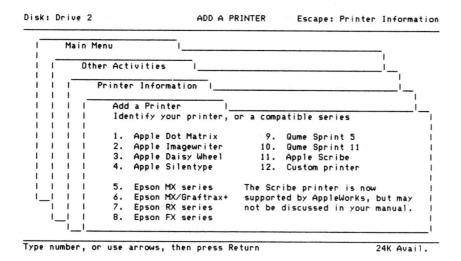

If you have a printer other than the ones specified in this list, choose option 12 from this menu to inform AppleWorks of the idiosyncrasies of your particular printer. Page 281 of the *AppleWorks Reference Manual* gives specific instructions for this procedure. But before you resort to this somewhat lengthy process, refer to Tip 1.51. You may be able to save a great deal of time if you can make this Tip work for you.

🖐 *1.50 Trap:* *If your printer is double spacing against your wishes or*
printing lines on top of each other, you will have to make
adjustments from the Change A Printer menu.

The printer installation process referred to in the previous Tip lets your printer know, among other things, that you would like it to move the page up a line after each line is printed. Some printers are set to do this automatically, so if you end up with double-spaced print when you wanted single spacing, you can assume that your printer is getting the same line feed message twice.

If lines seem to print on top of each other, your printer is not being told to move the page up after each line of print. In either case, you can rectify the situation by specifying the proper printer response from the following Apple-Works' Change a Printer menu:

```
Disk: Drive 2              CHANGE A PRINTER    Escape: Printer Information
_____

|     Main Menu             |_____
|  |_____   |                                       |
|  |   Other Activities   |_|_____|__
|  |  |_____      |                                    |
|  |  |   Printer Information  |_____|__
|  |  |  |_____       |                               |
|  |  |  |   Change A Printer   |_|_____|
|  |  |  |                      |                                  |
|  |  |  |   Printer name: ImageWriter (Port 1)                    |
|  |  |  |                                                         |
|  |  |  |   Printer type: Apple Imagewriter                       |
|  |  |  |                                                         |
|  |  |  |   1.  Needs line feed after each Return      No         |
|  |  |  |   2.  Accepts top-of-page commands           Yes        |
|  |  |  |   3.  Stop at end of each page               No         |
|__|  |  |   4.  Platen width                           8.0 inches |
   |  |  |                                                         |
   |__|  |                                                         |
      |__|_____|

Type number, or use arrows, then press Return              25K Avail.
```

To get to this menu, start by choosing "Other Activities" from the Main Menu (option 5). From here you want option 7, "Specify information about your printer(s)," and then one of the options under "Change printer specifications." At last you will see the preceding menu before you, and you can make whatever line feed adjustments are necessary. As you can see from the other choices in this menu, page commands and platen width adjustments are also available here.

💡 *1.51 Tip:* *Even if you don't have one of AppleWorks' standard print-*
ers, the configuration for one of them could be close
enough to work.

When you first install your printer to work with AppleWorks, you will need to make a choice from the Add a Printer menu. If your printer does not match any of the choices from this menu, you fall under the category of "Custom printer," option 12.

Installing a custom printer takes several steps. It could easily require you to consult your printer manual to find the relevant specifications needed to make it compatible with AppleWorks.

Before you jump into this research problem, however, consider the notion that one of the printers already listed may be compatible with yours. How can you find out? Proceed through the configuration choices by trial and error, printing a test document each time that is filled with as many printer options as you think you will ever use.

If the result is unreadable or does not contain the printer options that you specified, you will know that the choice you made did not match your printer's configuration. Turn the printer off and then on to clear it of its present hieroglyphics and continue testing the other configuration choices on the list.

If you have no luck with this, you will have to enter a custom printer configuration after all. If such is your fate, refer to page 281 of the *AppleWorks Reference Manual,* where specific steps are outlined for selecting a custom printer.

1.52 Tip: OPEN APPLE-H *lets you print a copy of your screen display.*

Use this option when you want to print specific AppleWorks menus for future reference or anytime you want a hard copy of your present screen. Be aware that OPEN APPLE-H will print everything on your screen, including the AppleWorks prompts.

When creating a hard copy of your AppleWorks screen, make sure that the paper in your printer is positioned as far to the left as possible. If you do not take this precaution, the left side of your screen may disappear from the side of your paper.

1.53 Trap: *When you press* ESCAPE *or the* SPACE BAR *to stop or pause printing, you will get a very slow response.*

Anytime you print an AppleWorks document, a message will appear on the screen reassuring you that you can stop the printing procedure by pressing the ESCAPE key or make printing pause with the SPACE BAR. If you have ever tried either of these professed print stoppers, you have probably wondered if there is something wrong with your particular system or program.

Each action eventually brings about the results claimed, but the delay between order and delivery is considerable (much more so if you have a printer buffer than if you don't). If you press ESCAPE as soon as printing starts, it probably will not have any result until it has already printed one page. If you wait 20 seconds, for example, it could print three pages before it finally responds to your command. If your situation calls for a more immediate response, refer to the following Tip.

1.54 **Tip:** *You can turn off your printer if you want to stop printing immediately.*

As described in the previous Tip, there is a considerable response lag when you use the ESCAPE key or SPACE BAR to try to stop or pause AppleWorks' printing. The best way to sidestep this problem is to turn off your printer instead of using either of AppleWorks' print stoppers.

This action will not damage your printer but may result in personal frustration if you forget to turn it on before you attempt to print again. When you turn your printer on again, don't expect printing to resume automatically at the point at which it stopped. To begin printing again, you will need to initiate the print procedure from the beginning.

2

Word Processing

Word processing is a dream come true for anyone who writes. Whether for personal correspondence, business letters, or more lengthy tasks such as term papers or book writing, word processing relieves users of the bothersome and repetitive tasks that inhibit the more important job of producing quality content.

Although word processing programs vary somewhat in sophistication and in the degree of facility they provide, they generally ease the mechanical burden of the writing process. AppleWorks' Word Processor is no different. It provides some features that other word processing programs lack and falls short in some areas where other programs stand out. It is consistently "friendly" to the user: Its functions and commands are used in the same way as those in the Data Base and Spreadsheet environments.

The Tips and Traps presented in this chapter should enhance the usefulness of the program as you follow the various steps involved in word processing with AppleWorks.

Your first task after starting AppleWorks' word processing will be to let AppleWorks know the structural format that you would like to be applied to your document. Refer to the section on "Setting Up" for Tips related to everything from setting tabs to creating stock word processing formats that can be retrieved at your convenience.

Once your setup is complete, you will find that the Tips on getting around and entering and editing will get you off to a good start. Familiarity with the

Tips in the section on word processing commands will help hone your burgeoning expertise to an even sharper edge.

One good test of a word processing program is how well its documents look when printed. Because printing formats are such an integral part of creating a word processing document, a special "Printer Options" section is included in this chapter in addition to the general printing Tips and Traps in Chapter 1.

Although the Tips in this section are laid out in a somewhat progressive order, you may gain the most by absorbing them as you come across the specific problems that they address. Read the Tips and Traps one at a time, from beginning to end, or skip around as much as you like. Either approach can be effective, depending on your style or current need.

Setting Up

2.01 Trap: *The TAB key will not work when you are in Modify Tab Stops mode.*

When you begin a word processing document from scratch, one of the first decisions to make is whether to accept AppleWorks' default tab setting of every five spaces, or to modify the tab stop setting to fit your specific needs.

The tab stops themselves are represented by short vertical lines that cross through the double dotted line at the top of the word processing screen. You can view these tab stops as you are typing a document, but you can change them only by accessing the Modify Tab Stops screen with OPEN APPLE-T:

```
File: Tab Sample            MODIFY TAB STOPS       Escape: Review/Add/Change
=====|====|====|====|====|====|====|====|====|====|====|====|====|====|===
```

```
-----------------------------------------------------------------------
Tab stops:   S: Set   C: Clear   R: Remove all            (Column  1)
```

From here you can set tabs, clear tabs, or remove all current tab settings. To remove all tab settings, you simply press R from any position on the tab line. To set or clear specific tabs, you need to first move your cursor to the tab position that you want to add or remove. Once there, the S key sets a new tab stop for you, and the C key clears the tab stop located at the cursor position.

It would be nice to be able to tab over to tab stops that you wanted to use the Clear feature on, but the TAB key itself is ineffective in this mode. To move to the tab stops that you want cleared, you must use either the SPACE BAR or the right or left arrow key.

When the tabs are set to your satisfaction, you can return to your document in Review/Add/Change by pressing the ESCAPE key. You will find that the TAB key works to take you, one by one, to each tab stop that you have specified. To travel in a left-hand direction tab by tab, press OPEN APPLE in conjunction with the TAB key.

✋ *2.02   Trap: Don't use the OPEN APPLE-S combination instead of the S key when you are setting tab stops, or you will begin the saving procedure.*

Throughout AppleWorks the OPEN APPLE key (actually, either apple key works) is used in conjunction with letter keys to perform numerous built-in functions. In almost every case, this continuity is helpful, but when you are setting tabs, the OPEN APPLE habit can lead you to a lot of frustration.

Although the initial command for changing tab stops is a combination of OPEN APPLE and the T key, the subsequent commands that set tabs (S), clear tabs (C), and remove all current tabs (R) are issued by themselves, without the apple key combination. (See the bottom of the screen in the illustration in Tip 2.01 for a list of the Tab commands.)

If you use AppleWorks frequently, you are more likely than a beginner to use the OPEN APPLE key in conjunction with the S, C, or R key because you have had more time to refine this habit. If you slip into this trap with the C and R keys, no damage will be done. In fact, both operations will be carried out as you had hoped in spite of the superfluous addition of the APPLE key.

Pressing OPEN APPLE-S, however, will begin a save process that could be frustrating. You will lose time and momentum by having to set things right again, and if the save is carried out, it will overwrite an existing file with the same name that you may want to keep intact.

If you think quickly enough, you can keep this from happening by pressing the ESCAPE key immediately to abort the save. Then press the ESCAPE key again to

:eturn to Review/Add/Change. From here OPEN APPLE-T will give you another chance to modify tab stops.

2.03 Tip: *You can increase the width of your screen display by making changes in the right margin or platen width settings or increasing the characters per inch.*

The layout and the physical features of an AppleWorks' word processing document are controlled through the option screen accessed through OPEN APPLE-O:

```
        PW=8.0  LM=1.0   RM=1.0  CI=10  UJ   PL=11.0  TM=0.0  BM=2.0  LI=6  SS
Option:                  UJ: Unjustified     GB: Group Begin     BE: Boldface End
                         CN: Centered        GE: Group End       +B: Superscript Beg
PW: Platen Width         PL: Paper Length     HE: Page Header     +E: Superscript End
LM: Left Margin          TM: Top Margin       FO: Page Footer     -B: Subscript Begin
RM: Right Margin         BM: Bottom Margin    SK: Skip Lines      -E: Subscript End
CI: Chars per Inch       LI: Lines per Inch   PN: Page Number     UB: Underline Begin
P1: Proportional-1       SS: Single Space     PE: Pause Each page UE: Underline End
P2: Proportional-2       DS: Double Space     PH: Pause Here      PP: Print Page No.
IN: Indent               TS: Triple Space     SM: Set a Marker    EK: Enter Keyboard
JU: Justified            NP: New Page         BB: Boldface Begin
```

AppleWorks calls these printer options, because the settings that you specify from this screen let the printer know how to print your document. For the purposes of this Tip, we are concerned with the effect that three of these settings have on the screen display, not on the actual printed material.

The three printer options that can affect the width of your screen display are the right and left margin settings, the platen width, and the characters per inch specification. Unless you specify otherwise, both the right and left margins in your word processing document will be set at 1 inch. The default setting for platen width is 8 inches, and the automatic setting for characters per inch is 10.

This gives you a line width that spreads across about 3/4 of your screen. If you would like to increase this screen display, thereby making a greater portion of your document visible on screen, you can either decrease the right or left margin, increase the platen width, or specify more characters per inch.

The following illustration shows the screen display of the previous paragraph when the default settings for right and left margins (1 inch), platen width (8 inches), and characters per inch (10) are in effect:

```
File: WP.TIPS.WRTUP1          REVIEW/ADD/CHANGE          Escape: Main Menu
================================|=========================================

This gives you a line width that spreads across about 3/4 of
your screen. If you would like to increase this screen
display, thereby making a greater portion of your document
available to your view, you can either decrease the right
and/or left margins, increase the platen width, or specify
more characters per inch.
```

In the next illustration, you can see that changing the right margin setting to 0 has increased the screen width by about 1 inch:

```
File: WP.TIPS.WRTUP1          REVIEW/ADD/CHANGE          Escape: Main Menu
==============================|=========================================
```

```
This gives you a line width that spreads across about 3/4 of your
screen. If you would like to increase this screen display, thereby
making a greater portion of your document available to your view, you
can either decrease the right and/or left margins, increase the platen
width, or specify more characters per inch.
```

Finally, here is the maximum screen width possible:

```
File: WP.TIPS.WRTUP1          REVIEW/ADD/CHANGE          Escape: Main Menu
==============================|=========================================
```

```
This gives you a line width that spreads across about 3/4 of your screen. If
you would like to increase this screen display, thereby making a greater
portion of your document available to your view, you can either decrease the
right and/or left margins, increase the platen width, or specify more
characters per inch.
```

The maximum width can be set in three ways:

1. Set both the left and right margins to 0

2. Set the platen width to 10

3. Change the characters per inch to 13.

The platen width is the distance that your printer head will travel across the paper when the document is printed. Before you actually print a document, make sure that the platen width you have assigned to it corresponds to the printer's platen width that you specify when you choose option 7 — "Specify information about your printer(s)" — from the Other Activities option on the Main Menu. Otherwise, the printhead may move past your paper as it is printing.

Before printing, you should also reset any printer options that you had changed just for display purposes. If you would like the display settings to apply to your printed document as well, you need not make any changes.

2.04 Tip: *Creating "dummy" word processing files formatted with printer options that you find repeated use for can save you the trouble of reinventing the wheel each time you begin a new word processing document.*

AppleWorks assigns certain default formats to each word processing file that you create (margins, platen width, characters per inch, and so on). Any changes that you would like to make in these automatic settings must be repeated each time you begin a new document, even if the formats you create are always the same. This task can become burdensome if more than a few settings are involved, or if you need to change the settings often.

Although you can't change default settings in AppleWorks, you can create dummy word processing files formatted for specific uses and retrieve them when the need arises.

Suppose you write a monthly newsletter that you print at 12 characters per inch, with no right or left margin, and eight lines per inch to fit as much text on one page as possible. You are tired of having to specify the same settings each week and are doubly frustrated when you forget to change one of the settings and don't discover it until the newsletter is printed.

The solution to this problem is to create a word processing file that contains only printer option specifications but no actual text. You begin with the option "Add Files to Desktop" from the Main Menu and then choose to make a new file for the word processor from scratch. When prompted to supply a name for the new file, choose something descriptive, such as Newsletter.

When presented with your new, blank word processing screen, use the OPEN APPLE-O keys to get to the Printer Options screen, where you can specify the options that you would like to apply to the newsletter. Once this is accomplished, you will be ready to save your Newsletter file and can retrieve it, complete with special formats, the next time you want to type your newsletter.

Once your newsletter is complete and you want to save it, be sure to assign it a name that is different from the one you gave your dummy file. Otherwise, saving your file will wipe out your original dummy format and replace it with the completed newsletter.

To be sure that this doesn't happen, rename your dummy file as soon as you load it. Press OPEN APPLE-N to carry out this renaming procedure.

2.05 **Tip:** *Temporary text can act as a placeholder so that custom formats can be specified within the body of your word processing dummy file.*

The previous Tip can be stretched even further if you add text to the dummy file you create. This text could be in the form of an actual heading that you include each time, such as "Cherry Valley School Newsletter." Or it could be meaningless text supplied solely to provide a location where certain formats can be applied.

Word Processing

The following short memo is an example of text that is included each time this weekly memo is printed (the opening paragraph) as well as text that will vary while the formatting remains the same (the date and the agenda items themselves).

```
                      March 24, 1986
   To: All classified staff


   Our weekly staff meeting will be held, as usual, in the
   "blue room" at 3:00 PM. This week's agenda is as follows:

        1. Employee benefits.

        2. Self-esteem workshop.

        3. Playground rules.

        4. Coffee in the classrooms.

        5. Increased break times.
```

To view the actual formats for this file, press OPEN APPLE-Z, and you will be shown the zoomed-in screen:

```
File: MtingMmo2.6t7          REVIEW/ADD/CHANGE              Escape: Main Menu
=====|=====|=====|=====|=====|=====|=====|=====|=====|=====|=====|=====|=====|=====
--------Centered
                    March 24, 1986
--------Unjustified

To: All classified staff


Our weekly staff meeting will be held, as usual, in the
"blue room" at 3:00 PM. This week's agenda is as follows:

--------Left Margin:  2.0 inches
--------Double Space
        1. Employee benefits.
        2. Self-esteem workshop.
        3. Playground rules.
        4. Coffee in the classrooms.
        5. Increased break times.



----------------------------------------------------------------
Type entry or use a commands          Line 1  Column  1      a-? for Help
```

You can retain these formats for subsequent meeting memos by saving the file and its corresponding formats. For next week's memo, you can retrieve the saved file, change the date, add new agenda items, and print without having to make any format changes.

2.06 Tip: *Use descriptive messages that act as placeholders within your dummy file.*

You may want to create a dummy file from the start that looks something like this:

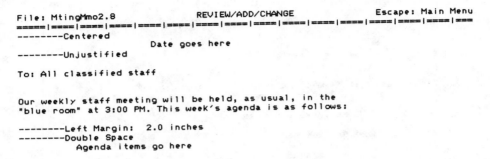

```
File: MtingMmo2.8              REVIEW/ADD/CHANGE              Escape: Main Menu
====|====|====|====|====|====|====|====|====|====|====|====|====|====|====|===
--------Centered
                    Date goes here
--------Unjustified

To: All classified staff


Our weekly staff meeting will be held, as usual, in the
"blue room" at 3:00 PM. This week's agenda is as follows:

--------Left Margin:  2.0 inches
--------Double Space
           Agenda items go here
```

Using such a file maintains the desired text and appropriate formats but holds these formats with a succinct, descriptive message. This short placeholder can be replaced more quickly (press CONTROL-Y, OPEN APPLE-D, or the overstrike cursor) than residual entries from previous memos.

You don't have to worry about the fact that the actual text you want to replace the placeholder with takes up more lines than the dummy text did. Any amount of text can be entered after a specific format, and any subsequent format will be pushed down one line each time a new line is added.

Don't be reluctant to create as many dummy files as you need. They take up very little disk space and can save you a great deal of time.

2.07 **Tip:** *You can create a word processing document from an ASCII (text) file.*

Since this section deals with Tips for setting up word processing files, it would be a blatant omission to leave out the fact that word processing files can be created from ASCII files.

Because this process is covered thoroughly in Chapter 6, "Data Transfer," this chapter does not go into it in detail. But you should know that this option exists once you have chosen "Add files to Desktop" from the Main Menu and then "Make a new file for the word processor."

If you would like to incorporate information into an AppleWorks word processing file that is available from an ASCII file, be sure to familiarize yourself with the steps detailed in Chapter 6.

Getting Around a Word Processing Document

2.08   *Tip:* *Use the* OPEN APPLE *in conjunction with the left arrow to move instantly to the left margin when the cursor is on a blank line.*

AppleWorks' right and left arrow keys move the cursor through lines of text in your word processing document one character at a time. This is fine if you want to hone in on a specific letter within a word, but you would not want to proceed across a whole line at this rate.

AppleWorks has a feature that moves the cursor across a line word by word. Just use the OPEN APPLE along with the right or left arrow to gain this extra travel speed. If you want to move from one line to the next, pressing the down arrow places the cursor a line below the position where you began, and the up arrow a line above. When you travel among lines in this way, your relative position within the line remains constant.

In other words, if you move down a line when your cursor is close to the right margin of the screen, you will end up in the same right-hand position on the line below. This is fine if you are planning to edit a word that is close to the right-hand location. But suppose you want to delete a letter in a word close to the left margin of the same or another line within a document.

The fastest way to move from a right line position to a location near the left margin is to plod along word by word using the OPEN APPLE and left arrow keys. The more occasions you have to cover this distance, the slower the word-by-word method will seem.

One trick that can help you overcome this frustrating pace is to search out blank lines that are near the cursor and use them as speedways to get you to the left margin in an instant. This works well because no matter where the cursor is on a blank line, it instantly moves to the left margin when you press the OPEN APPLE along with the left arrow.

Once the cursor is at the left margin, the up arrow (or down arrow if you have traveled up to a blank line) will get you back to the appropriate line while maintaining the left margin position. Obviously, this method is counterproductive if the number of keystrokes it takes to complete the desired operation exceeds the number of words that you would have to hop to travel to your ultimate destination.

Surprisingly enough, you will probably find yourself in a position in which this trick is a definite advantage quite often. See the next two Tips for additional ways to speed up the process of getting around a word processing document.

2.09 Tip: *Use the* OPEN APPLE *along with the right or left arrow keys when you want to move from the end of one line to the beginning of the next and vice versa.*

The previous Tip can be a great time saver if you have a blank line close at hand and if you begin from a position within a line of text. But if you want to travel quickly between right and left margins within or between lines, you will find the following alternative more effective.

You know that the right arrow moves you to the right one character at a time and that the left arrow does the same in a left-hand direction. Suppose you are already positioned at the left margin and then press the left arrow key. You might assume that this action would get you nowhere since your cursor is already as far left as it can go. But, in fact, the wraparound feature built into AppleWorks' word processor steps in to wrap your cursor around to the right margin of the previous line. This same feature works to move you from the right margin to the left margin of the next line when you press the right arrow.

Unfortunately, you are not able to move forward from the left margin to the right margin. Nor can you move backward from the right margin to the left. However, once you have achieved your move from one margin extreme to the other, it is a simple matter to use the up and down arrows to move you quickly to whatever line you choose.

Although moving through a document in this manner takes some practice to get used to, it is worth the effort. The alternative of traveling through 10 to 12 words to change right and left margin positions verges on cruel punishment.

When you have become thoroughly comfortable with this method, you will probably find that you can save time by using it even when the position that you want to move to or from is not at the extreme right or left of a line. Traveling along for several words is still preferable to transversing an entire line a word at a time.

2.10 Tip: *The* TAB *key sends the cursor quickly to the beginning or the end of a line if you remove all tab stops.*

The TAB key moves the cursor right one tab stop at a time. To move to the left in these same increments, use the OPEN APPLE and TAB keys in conjunction. The distance between tab stops determines the distance that the cursor will move each time you tab to the right or to the left.

AppleWorks' default setting for tab stops is every five spaces, which is an excessive number for most purposes. You can specify tab stops at whatever intervals you like by accessing the Modify Tab Stops screen through OPEN APPLE-T and using the Tab commands to set (S), clear (C), or remove all tab stops (R) (see Tip 2.01).

If you use the R command to remove all tab stops, you will create a situation in which the TAB key will instantly rocket the cursor to the right margin of the line; the OPEN APPLE-TAB combination will move it to the left margin just as fast.

Since AppleWorks does not make allowances for traveling quickly from one margin to the other, using the tabs to achieve this can save you from having to move across a line a word at a time. You may want to add a tab at the middle of your line as well so that words in the middle range of a document are more accessible for editing.

These tabs are so helpful in overcoming this significant AppleWorks flaw that you may want to operate with them on a regular basis whenever possible. If you need more tab stops for certain sections of a document, you can change the settings for those sections.

2.11 Tip: *AppleWorks' built-in ruler moves the cursor through a word processing file in increments that you specify.*

AppleWorks divides each file into eight equal sections. These sections offer proportional access to a word processing document. Pressing OPEN APPLE-1 instantly moves the cursor to the beginning of a document, and OPEN APPLE-9 places the cursor at the end of the document.

OPEN APPLE-2 through -8 move the cursor proportionally through the rest of the document by eighths. Where you will actually end up when you use the 2 through 8 ruler positions is a guess. It can sometimes take more time than it saves to figure out where you will be once you are placed in one of these in-between positions.

For this reason, you will find it most useful to stick with positions 1 and 9 on the AppleWorks ruler. However, the longer your document is, the more viable it becomes to make use of the other ruler marks, since the only other alternative, scrolling page by page, can be time consuming.

You can use the Ruler feature itself to achieve a kind of super-scrolling by beginning with OPEN APPLE-1 and going systematically through OPEN APPLE-2, -3, -4, and so on, until the cursor ends up at the desired destination.

You will find that the more you use the AppleWorks ruler, the better you become at judging the proportional distances that it sends the cursor across. By all means, use it as frequently as you find it helpful. You will probably find that its usefulness rises in direct proportion to frequency of use.

*2.12 **Tip:** You can set markers at various points within a word processing document and use the Find feature to send you to these points whenever you want.*

One of the options available from the Printer Options screen (OPEN APPLE-O) is "Set a Marker," option code: SM. With this feature you can tag any position(s) within a document that you need to refer to often and use the Find feature to move to them.

Here's how it works. Begin by moving to the spot within your document where you want to place the marker. From there press OPEN APPLE-O and type in **SM** (set a marker) from the option code. When you press the RETURN key, a prompt will appear asking you for a number. The number you enter (any number between 0 and 254 is allowed) will be assigned to the marker you are currently placing and will be used by the Find feature to identify it. You can specify up to 254 markers in any one word processing document.

Once the marker has been set, use the ESCAPE key to get back to your document. The next time you need to refer to the section you have tagged with a marker, you won't need to waste time scrolling through the document in search of the right location.

Instead, you can issue the Find command (OPEN APPLE-F) and choose "Marker" from the options shown:

```
------------------------------------------------------------------------
Find?  Text  Page  Marker  Case sensitive text  Options for printer
```

When asked for the marker number, enter the number you assigned to the marker when you first set it:

```
------------------------------------------------------------------------
Marker number?                                              32K Avail.
```

Once you press RETURN, the section of text that you tagged with the specified marker will zoom onto your screen. Because the Find command searches both forward and backward in a file when you ask it to find a marker, you can initiate this procedure from any point in a document.

The following illustration shows the marker 1 location that the Find command has found:

```
File: WP.TIPS.WRTUP1                 FIND            Escape: Review/Add/Change
=================================|===============================================




--------Set a Marker: 1

One of the options that is available to you from the Printer
Options screen (OPEN APPLE - O) is "Set a Marker", option
code: SM. With this feature you can tag any position(s)
within your document that you need to refer to often and use
the Find feature to move you to them upon request.



------------------------------------------------------------------------

Find next occurrence? No  Yes
```

It is unlikely that you have set another marker 1, so you will probably answer No
to "Find next occurrence?" Now you are back in Review/Add/Change, but you
may be distracted by formatting features such as the marker tag and the carriage
return rectangles that appear on the screen.

To hide them from view, press OPEN APPLE-Z. This same command will make
them visible whenever you wish. These formatting markers are never included
when you print a document.

2.13 Tip: *Use the Find command to get you to your current work
area when you first load your file or when you want to
move within a document.*

When you load a word processing file, you are always positioned at its beginning.
Rarely is this where you want to be. If you are adding new material to the end of a
file, you will want to use OPEN APPLE-9 to transport you there instantly.

If you have marked an area somewhere in the midst of a long document, you
can gain access to it by using OPEN APPLE-F to find the marker (see the previous
Tip).

Another practice that can be helpful is to adopt a habit of leaving prompts
for yourself throughout a document. A notation such as "edit spot" can be left in
places that you know need revision but don't want to bother with on a first draft.

When you are ready to put the final polish on a document, move to the beginning (use OPEN APPLE-1 to get you there quickly). The Find command only searches for text below the spot at which it is initiated, so if you are positioned below the area that you want it to search, your specified text will never be found.

From the beginning of a document, you can be sure that the Find command will search the entire document, so you can begin the procedure by typing OPEN APPLE-F. When the Find options are presented, the appropriate choice for your current need is "Text." Since you want to find the text prompt(s) "edit spot" that you sprinkled throughout your first draft, type **edit spot** when asked "Find what text?"

Your first edit spot prompt quickly appears on the screen. But before you can actually work on screen, you must specify whether or not you want to "Find next occurrence." If this isn't the edit spot that you want to work on at this time, your answer will be Yes, and you will instantly be presented with the next edit spot.

If you would like to make revisions in this edit spot before moving on, choose No, and the screen will be at your disposal. Once you have completed the revisions, erase your edit spot prompt and issue the Find command again to make your move to the next edit spot.

This time you don't even need to enter the text that you want to be found. AppleWorks has maintained your previous entry just in case; you can accept it by pressing RETURN and move to the next spot more quickly than ever.

2.14 Trap: *Don't expect to be able to use the Find command to send you to specified page numbers within your document unless you have already formatted it with page numbers.*

The two previous Tips looked at ways in which the Find command can help speed travel through a word processing document. Another Find option available is "Page." Especially in a long document, being able to move to a specific page, whether for rereading or editing purposes, could be a real time saver.

However, before the Find command can perform a page find, you need to make sure that your document is formatted with pages. You can do this easily by issuing the Calculate Page Breaks command with OPEN APPLE-K, which leads you to the following screen:

```
File: WP.TIPS.WRTUP1              CALCULATE MENU        Escape: Review/Add/Change
==========================|=================================================




                    Which printer will be used when
                    the file is actually printed?

                    1.  Apple DMP

                    2.  ImageWriter

                    3.  SAMPLE (disk)

                    4.  A text (ASCII) file on disk




        -----------------------------------------------------------------------
        Type number, or use arrows, then press Return               28K Avail.
```

Once you use this screen to specify which printer you will use, your document can be calculated for page numbers. If there are more than a few pages involved, AppleWorks will warn, "This may take some time" and count off the page numbers as it formats them into your document. Once this is done, you are returned to the spot at which you initiated the command.

The Find command will respond to any page find request that you make, searching forward and backward in your file until it locates the page that you specified.

You will find that AppleWorks saves any page formats that you have made whenever you save a file, so you can locate by page number as soon as you load your document. As you add to a file, be sure to reformat for pages (OPEN APPLE-K) if you plan to use a page find on the additional material. Be aware that certain editing procedures will delete page calculations, making it necessary for you to use OPEN APPLE-K when you want these calculations performed again. (See Trap 2.50.)

Entering and Editing

 2.15 Trap: If you press RETURN at the end of each line of type, AppleWorks' built-in justification feature will be ineffective.

Anyone who has been using a typewriter for years and has recently switched to word processing on a computer has a tendency to end each line of type with a carriage return. Because of the word wrap feature available in AppleWorks and most other word processing programs, this added effort is not only unnecessary but downright destructive.

Word wrap allows you to continue to enter text without pausing at the end of a line. When you reach the line's end, this feature breaks your line at the space closest to the right margin and wraps your next word around to the beginning of the following line. In other words, it treats your text as one long, continuous line until you press RETURN to begin a new paragraph.

Automatic adjustments are made for additional letters or words entered at any point within this continuous line. This is called automatic rejustification, and it is one of AppleWorks' handiest features.

The RETURN key formats a carriage return in text wherever it is used. This tells AppleWorks, "Begin a new line after this point, and maintain this new line position as long as a carriage return is present." When you have reached the end of a paragraph, this is exactly the message you want to convey. But within a paragraph, you want the text you enter to display in a continuous flow without inappropriate spaces or gaps between words.

If you press the RETURN key at the end of each line, the next word that you enter will not be brought up to fill a gap on the previous line should subsequent editing create one.

If you add text to a line punctuated with a carriage return, the wraparound feature moves the last word, including the carriage return, down to the next line. Any text that had occupied that line (text that, in fact, should follow right after the word in question) will be sent to the next line.

Thus, using the RETURN key inappropriately creates gaps that make your text unpresentable. To remove the gaps, you must determine exactly where the unwanted carriage returns are located.

OPEN APPLE-Z zooms all your document's formats into view. The carriage returns are displayed as rectangular blocks. Once you have located them, move your cursor to the space just to the right of each return that you want to erase and press the DELETE key. Once the carriage returns are gone, the automatic justification feature will take over, and the unsightly gaps will disappear.

2.16 **Tip:** *Use the RETURN key to insert blank lines within your document.*

In almost every document you type, you will find a need for blank lines. The most frequent use of blank lines is between paragraphs, but they are also often used at the beginning of a document to place the text lower on the page during printing. Blank lines within a letter, a term paper, or a book chapter serve to set off important sections from the rest of the text.

You can insert a blank line at any location by moving the cursor to the left-most position on the screen and pressing the RETURN key. If you do this when you have completed a paragraph and find yourself at the beginning of a new empty line, you will create one blank line between the last line of text and the next for each press of the RETURN key. Pressing RETURN from any position within a blank line automatically inserts a new blank line and moves the cursor to the left margin of that new line.

You can also insert spaces between adjacent lines of text by pressing the RETURN key when your cursor is on top of the first character in the lower line. Each time you press RETURN from this position, a new blank line will be inserted above the line from which you began the procedure.

Anytime you press RETURN from a position within a line of text, the character at your cursor position and all of the characters following it will be moved down to the next line beginning at the left margin. This provides a great way of breaking unwieldy paragraphs in two:

```
You can also insert spaces between adjacent lines of text by
pressing the RETURN key when your cursor is on top of the
first character in the line. Each time you press RETURN from
this position, a new blank line will be inserted above the
line from which you began the procedure. Any time you press
RETURN from a position within a line of text, the character
at your cursor position and all of the characters following
it will be moved down to the next line beginning at the left
margin. This provides a great way of breaking unwieldy
paragraphs like the following in two:
```

It is obvious that this paragraph is better broken into two. Since you want the second paragraph to begin with *Any,* move the cursor to the first letter of that word—*A*—and press RETURN. You will then see the following:

```
You can also insert spaces between adjacent lines of text by
pressing the RETURN key when your cursor is on top of the
first character in the line. Each time you press RETURN from
this position, a new blank line will be inserted above the
line from which you began the procedure.
Any time you press RETURN from a position within a line of
text, the character at your cursor position and all of the
characters following it will be moved down to the next line
beginning at the left margin. This provides a great way of
breaking unwieldy paragraphs like the following in two:
```

Any and all the words following it are transported to the next line beginning at the left margin and are automatically rejustified with the words originally occupying that position. If you press the RETURN key one more time, a blank line will separate the two paragraphs.

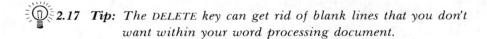

2.17   Tip: *The* DELETE *key can get rid of blank lines that you don't want within your word processing document.*

Anytime you press the RETURN key within a word processing document, it tells AppleWorks, "Don't allow any characters on this line past this point." Thus blank lines are created (see the previous Tip).

But the DELETE key erases the message that the RETURN key implants and with it removes the blank line that was a result of that message. When you press the DELETE key from any position on a blank line, that line disappears and all the lines below it move up one line. In the following illustration, there are two short paragraphs separated by two blank lines:

```
Hey diddle diddle, the cat and the fiddle. The cow jumped
over the moon.


The little dog laughed to see such sport. And the dish ran
away with the spoon.
```

This is what happens if you move to the blank line above the second paragraph and press DELETE:

```
Hey diddle diddle, the cat and the fiddle. The cow jumped
over the moon.

The little dog laughed to see such sport. And the dish ran
away with the spoon.
```

If the line above the deleted one is also a blank line, as it is in the preceding illustration, this operation will place the cursor at the left margin of that line. From this position pressing DELETE will erase that line as well, positioning the cursor to the right of the carriage return that signifies the end of that paragraph. In the following example, the return symbol is to the right of the period following the word *moon*. The cursor is to the right of the return symbol.

```
Hey diddle diddle, the cat and the fiddle. The cow jumped
over the moon.
The little dog laughed to see such sport. And the dish ran
away with the spoon.
```

Pressing the DELETE key erases the carriage return and merges the two paragraphs as shown in the following illustration:

```
Hey diddle diddle, the cat and the fiddle. The cow jumped
over the moon.The little dog laughed to see such sport. And
the dish ran away with the spoon.
```

Use the Zoom feature (OPEN APPLE-Z) to be sure that the cursor is correctly positioned when you want to accomplish a paragraph merge. This feature zooms all of the normally invisible document formats into view, including carriage returns represented by dotted rectangles. Now you can position the cursor to the right of the hard carriage return in question and carry out the intended deletion. Press OPEN APPLE-Z again to banish the formats from your screen when you no longer need to view them.

2.18 Tip: *You will be able to perform all operations within your document whether document formats are zoomed in or out of screen view.*

The Zoom feature (OPEN APPLE-Z), which brings your document's format features into view, does not affect your ability to continue entering text into the document or use the word processing commands. Although you may find the visible formats somewhat distracting, you can leave them on the screen all the time if you wish.

2.19 Tip: *The insert cursor and the overstrike cursor affect existing text in different ways.*

The insert cursor could be considered the default cursor. It is in effect unless you use OPEN APPLE-E to switch to the overstrike cursor (the same key combination is used to switch back). The two cursors are different in both appearance and function.

Each time you type a character, the insert cursor, represented by a blinking bar, pushes the characters to its right over one space. The overstrike cursor, a flashing solid rectangle, replaces characters as it goes without changing their positions.

When you are entering text for the first time, you will probably use the default insert cursor. During editing, each specific situation determines which cursor choice is most effective.

Be sure that you do not inadvertently erase valuable text with the overstrike cursor when you meant to be using the insert cursor.

2.20   Trap: *Don't expect the overstrike cursor to strike over existing carriage returns.*

Though its function is to replace characters as it strikes, the overstrike cursor meets its match when it confronts the powerful carriage return. If you observe from a zoomed-in position, you will note that striking over a carriage return with the overstrike cursor simply pushes the carriage return ahead of it until it finally wraps around at the end of the line.

2.21   Trap: *Using the SHIFT key when CAPS LOCK is down will not shift you to lowercase.*

In some programs the SHIFT key takes on a reverse role, changing from upper- to lowercase, when it is used while the CAPS LOCK key is in effect. This does not occur in AppleWorks. When CAPS LOCK is on, all letter characters are typed in uppercase, whether the SHIFT key is used or not. The only way to get back to lowercase is to take off the CAPS LOCK. However, any special character (e.g., $, *, #) that is the upper partner on a two-character key will only be typed when the SHIFT key is used, whether or not the CAPS LOCK key is down. If the shift key is not used, the lower character will be typed.

2.22   Tip: *CONTROL-Y can speed up deletions in your word processing document.*

When you press CONTROL-Y from any position in a line of text, all characters from the cursor position to the end of the line are erased. At the same time, any text that was on the following line is pulled up to close the gap created by the deletion.

This feature comes in handy when you want to get rid of a few words at the end of a line. In fact, when you want to erase a whole paragraph, you may find that it takes longer to use the Delete command than to position the cursor at the beginning of the paragraph and repeat CONTROL-Y until the entire paragraph is erased.

2.23 *Trap:* *Word wrap may separate words that should print on the same line.*

Suppose you are entering the date June 6, 1986, near the end of a line of type. You can see that only June will end up on the current line and that the next line will begin with 6, 1986—a rather awkward placement. To assure that meaningful word groups such as this are not placed on separate lines, AppleWorks has included a special formatting feature that it calls "sticky spaces."

A sticky space is created by using the OPEN APPLE in conjunction with the SPACE BAR whenever you are spacing between words that you want to remain together. When you use a sticky space, a small caret is placed on screen to represent the sticky space. This caret will not be printed in the document.

The same caret symbol is used for other word processing formats. You can determine the format that a particular caret represents by placing your cursor on top of the caret symbol and reading the identifying prompt displayed at the bottom of the screen.

Word Processing Commands

2.24 *Tip:* *The Delete, Copy, and Move commands all affect the area that you highlight.*

You can instruct these commands to act on as little as one character, as much as an entire file, or any percentage of text in between.

Whenever you issue one of these commands, the character at the cursor position is highlighted, and a prompt at the bottom of the screen instructs you to "Use cursor to highlight block then press Return."

The same tricks that you use for getting around a document in various increments are effective when you want to highlight sections to be moved, deleted, or copied:

1. The arrow keys highlight one character at a time in the direction of the arrow. Once you have moved in one direction, the opposite arrow will erase your

highlight, so don't try to start in the middle of a word that you want highlighted and move in both directions.

2. The OPEN APPLE-arrow combination highlights one word at a time.

3. The down arrow highlights from the cursor position to the end of the line. When you highlight with the up arrow, the same rules apply except that the highlight extends from the cursor position to the beginning of the line. Each time you use the up or down arrow key again, another line is included in the highlight.

4. Use the OPEN APPLE with the up or down arrow key when you want to highlight from the cursor position to the top of the screen (up arrow), or from the cursor position to the bottom of the screen (down arrow).

5. The Ruler feature allows you to highlight an entire document by degrees. No matter where the cursor is, you can press OPEN APPLE-1 to highlight the area from the cursor position to the beginning of the file. OPEN APPLE-9 highlights the area from the cursor position to the end of the file. The other ruler marks (2-8) respond by degrees but are harder to judge, and therefore not as useful.

2.25 Trap: Pay attention to the formats that are displayed whenever you issue the Delete, Copy, or Move commands, or you could be in for some frustrating surprises.

You may wonder why formats are zoomed onto the screen without your requesting them each time you begin a delete, move, or copy procedure. AppleWorks is trying to save you grief by including this automatic feature.

If any of the formatting characters are included in text that you are deleting, the format they represent will be deleted as well, and strange things that you do not understand may happen to your document. The same thing happens with the Move command. Any formatting characters that are included in the area you highlight to be moved will go along with the moved text, adding the format to the new location and erasing it from the old.

Although the Copy command does not erase the format from its original location if it is highlighted along with the text to be copied, it does add it to the copied text's new position. If this is what you want, the Zoom feature will ensure that you include the appropriate formats; if it is not, you will, instead, be assured of avoiding them.

The most frustrating aspect of this Trap is not knowing why it happens. Once you are aware of the reason, it is easy to repair. Simply access the formats by pressing OPEN APPLE-O, and reissue any formats that you have mistakenly destroyed or misplaced.

2.26 Tip: *Use the Delete command to get rid of unwanted formats.*

You can always access the option screen (OPEN APPLE-O) and counteract any formats that you no longer want in your word processing document. However, it is much faster and easier to get rid of these undesirables with the Delete command.

First zoom in the formats with OPEN APPLE-Z and place the cursor on the format that you want erased. When you press OPEN APPLE-D, the entire format line will be highlighted, and the RETURN key will delete it all.

When you delete a format, the previous format in the document will gain jurisdiction over the new area.

2.27 Tip: *The Replace command automatically adjusts for length discrepancies between the text that was replaced and that which replaced it.*

The Replace command is a valuable feature in AppleWorks. It enables you to make consistent changes throughout a document in one operation.

You probably have one word (or more) that you misspell with frustrating consistency. Sometimes you don't discover the error until you have completed a body of writing. To scan back through the entire document looking for the misspelled culprits could take a great deal of time, and there is no assurance that you would catch all the misspellings.

The Replace command is ideal for this situation. When you issue it with OPEN APPLE-R, the following prompt appears:

```
-------------------------------------------------------------------
Replace?  Text  Case sensitive text
```

If you want to make a distinction between upper- and lowercase when the word is being searched for, choose "Case sensitive text." If it doesn't matter, choose "Text."

Next you will be asked "Replace what?" Enter the text that you would like replaced exactly as it appears in the document. "Replace with what?" is the next question. Text entered here will replace the text entered at the previous prompt.

We have mentioned using this feature to correct misspelled words, but it is also useful for replacing one or more words with one or more other words that improve your document's style, meaning, or clarity. In such cases, the length of the replaced and replacing text usually differs. But because of the built-in justification feature included in the Replace command, we do not have to give this discrepancy a thought.

This feature assures that gaps are automatically closed when longer text is replaced with shorter text and that accommodations are automatically made for longer text that needs to fit in a space previously occupied by shorter text. Neither the replaced nor replacing text can be more than 30 characters long, but this limitation is rarely a problem.

✋ 2.28 Trap: *Be sure to choose the "One at a time" option if you want to replace specific occurrences of a certain string of text but want to leave other occurrences as is.*

Once you have issued the Replace command (OPEN APPLE-R) and have entered the replaced and replacing text, you will be able to choose whether you want this replacement carried out on every occurrence of the text that you first entered, or whether you want to make each choice individually. If you choose the former, all of the replacements will be conducted in one operation.

If your choice is "One at a time," you will be moved to each occurrence of the specified text, and at each stop you will be asked to choose, first, whether you want to make a replacement at that location, and then whether you want to move on to find the next occurrence of the specified text. At the next occurrence, the same choices will be available. The pattern continues until all of the occurrences have been found or you choose not to search for the next occurrence.

If you are sure that you want a certain string of text replaced each time it occurs, it is faster to specify the All option. But, if you are too trigger-happy and this choice leads you to replace text that you really did not want replaced, you will end up with a situation that could be very time consuming to rectify.

💡 2.29 Tip: *Speed up entry by using abbreviations for frequently used words or phrases and then using the Replace command to restore them to their full length later.*

Using the Replace command to replace all occurrences of a specific string of text

```
George Bliss
tms
Thomas Rd.
Ridge, N.H.


Dear George,


Thank you for your recent letter on the failing enrollment
at tms. I was saddened to find out that the future of tms
could be threatened by this state of affairs.

You asked if those of us on the West Coast who had attended
tms would be interested in forming a scholarship fund in
order to help make it possible for a West Coast student to
attend tms. Though I have not had a chance to contact the
other West Coast alumni of tms, my response to this idea is
very positive.

The experience that tms provides for students that are
fortunate enough to attend, is valuable beyond measure. It
is unfortunate that students with limited financial
resources should be denied this experience.

Still, I know that money is what is needed to pay electric
bills, upgrade tms buildings, and retain the quality staff
that has always been a part of tms. And so I will be happy
to do all I can to get the word out to other alumni from tms
as well as try to tap the financial resources of the wider
population.

Thank you for all of the time you have devoted to tms and
for your specific efforts in this area.

                              Keep up the good work,

                                 Janet
```

Figure 2-1. Letter using abbreviations

is quick and effective. This makes it very practical to abbreviate words or groups of words that you use often in your document.

Consider the letter shown in Figure 2-1. The school name, The Meeting School, is repeated frequently throughout the letter. To save entry time, the abbreviation tms was used when the letter was first written. Once the document was complete, all occurrences of the characters *tms* were replaced with the words *The Meeting School,* and the final letter was printed without abbreviations, as shown in Figure 2-2.

```
George Bliss
The Meeting School
Thomas Rd.
Ridge, N.H.


Dear George,


Thank you for your recent letter on the failing enrollment
at The Meeting School. I was saddened to find out that the
future of The Meeting School could be threatened by this
state of affairs.

You asked if those of us on the West Coast who had attended
The Meeting School would be interested in forming a
scholarship fund in order to help make it possible for a
West Coast student to attend The Meeting School. Though I
have not had a chance to contact the other West Coast alumni
of The Meeting School, my response to this idea is very
positive.

The experience that The Meeting School provides for students
that are fortunate enough to attend, is valuable beyond
measure. It is unfortunate that students with limited
financial resources should be denied this experience.

Still, I know that money is what is needed to pay electric
bills, upgrade The Meeting School buildings, and retain the
quality staff that has always been a part of The Meeting
School. And so I will be happy to do all I can to get the
word out to other alumni from The Meeting School as well as
try to tap the financial resources of the wider population.

Thank you for all of the time you have devoted to The
Meeting School and for your specific efforts in this area.


                          Keep up the good work,


                          Janet
```

Figure 2-2.   Finished letter

✋2.30 Trap: *Use spaces to assure that words specified for replacement are not found and replaced within other words.*

Suppose you wanted to change all occurrences of the word *Ms.* within a document to *Mrs.* If you specify Ms. as the text to be replaced without regard to upper-

or lowercase, the Replace command will include in its replacement every combination of the characters *ms.* If you ask that this replacement be carried out for all occurrences, you will find that ms. has been replaced with Mrs. even within words such as *chums* or *plums* when they appear at the end of a sentence, followed by a period.

In this particular case, you could have prevented this catastrophe by specifying case sensitive text when you entered the text to be replaced. The case sensitive specification would assure that only when the *M* in *Ms.* is capitalized would it be included in the replacement operation. Since the *M* from the *Ms.* combination you are replacing is never capitalized when it is within a word, you have avoided this Trap.

Often you do not have a situation in which capitals provide this handy distinction, however. In such cases, you need another way to make it clear to the Replace command that you do not want the word that you specified for replacement to be replaced when it is found within another word.

Since words are always set off by spaces, if you enter a space before and after the word that you are asking AppleWorks to replace, no occurrences within words will be found.

2.31 Trap: *You can end up with words that run together if you are inconsistent in your use of spaces when specifying replaced and replacing words.*

When you tell the Replace command what you would like to replace, it takes you literally. If you enter a space before the word you are specifying for replacement, you can be sure that the Replace command will not inadvertently replace letter combinations within words that are identical to the word that you entered. (See the previous Tip.)

It is important to realize, however, that in entering this space, you have instructed the Replace command to get rid of it along with the other characters that you entered. This is fine, as long as you also include a space before the word or groups of words that will be the replacing text. Without this replacing space, the new word(s) will not be separated from the word on the left.

2.32 Tip: *You can use the Replace command to delete occurrences of specific text.*

When you issue the Replace command, you have an opportunity to specify both the text that you want to be replaced and the text that will take its place. Suppose that you would like a certain word deleted from your document without replacing it.

The Replace command will carry out this deletion if you enter the unwanted word when you are asked "Replace what?" and enter nothing (press RETURN) when you are asked "Replace with what?"

This sort of deletion is best carried out if you include a space either before or after the word(s) that you specify to be replaced, unless the specified word is the last in the sentence. Since all other words are defined by a space on either side, deleting only the word itself means that two spaces will be left when the replacement is completed. If one of these spaces is deleted along with the undesirable word, the final product will be properly spaced.

2.33 Tip: *The Find command follows the same procedure as the Replace command when searching for text that you specify.*

The spacing tricks outlined in Tips 2.30 and 2.31 are important to keep in mind when you are asking the Find command to locate certain occurrences of text. Like the Replace command, it conducts its search literally, according to your specifications. If you do not include a space in that specification, characters within other words that match the text that you entered will be included in the search.

2.34 Trap: *You will not be able to make any changes in text found by the Find command until you return to Review/Add/Change.*

The Find command can be useful for locating text that you would like to apply formats to (such as boldfacing or underlining) or make other changes to. Once you issue the Find command (OPEN APPLE-F) and specify the text that you want to be found, the search is conducted with great speed, and the "found" text is highlighted on screen.

Gratefully, you begin to make the appropriate changes you had in mind, but nothing happens. If you look at the bottom of the screen, the following prompt tells you that the command has not released you yet:

```
----------------------------------------------------------------------
Find next occurrence?  No  Yes
```

To get back to Review/Add/Change, where you will actually be able to effect some changes, you must either press ESCAPE or answer No (just press N) to the question "Find next occurrence?"

This procedure is a bit of a pain, especially since you may want to find the next occurrence once your changes have been completed, and to do so means initiating the Find command all over again. The only saving grace is that the last entry that you specified for a find is retained and can quickly be accepted again with the RETURN key. If you do not want the same entry used for the next find, just delete it with CONTROL-Y.

2.35 Tip: *The Find command can locate both pages and specific markers within a word processing document.*

Special tricks associated with these Find command options are outlined in the section "Getting Around a Word Processing Document." Refer to Tips 2.12 and 2.14 for these helpful techniques.

2.36 Trap: *AppleWorks does not accept wildcard characters when you are doing a replace or a find.*

Some programs allow you to use a wildcard character such as a * or ? to stand for another character in a text string that you are specifying in a replace or find operation. Using the wildcard feature, you could be sure, for instance, that all instances of Anderson would be found whether it was spelled Anderson or Andersen.

When asked for the text to find or replace, you would enter the appropriate word, and the wildcard character would take the place of any character in that word that might vary, such as Anders?n.

Now that you know about this useful feature, do not expect to be able to use it when you are conducting a find or replace operation in AppleWorks. Unfortunately, it was not included in these AppleWorks commands.

2.37 Trap: *If the Find or Replace commands do not seem to be locating text that you know is there, check to see where the cursor is.*

When asked to locate text, both the Find and Replace commands conduct their search only on the area of a document that is below the position of the cursor when the command is issued. If you forget to move above the appropriate area before issuing either of these commands, you will be confronted with the disappointing message, "Not found, press Space Bar to continue."

The easiest way to make sure that this does not happen is to use the OPEN APPLE-1 combination to move the cursor quickly to the top of the file before you issue either of these commands.

Of course, there are times when you do not want the find or replacement to be conducted on the entire document. In such a case, cursor placement can be an important factor in helping you localize the impact of these commands.

2.38 Trap: *Don't begin a move, copy, or delete without placing the cursor on the appropriate text.*

All three of these commands rely on the cursor highlights that you provide to get their instructions as to which group of text to act on. Once the command is initiated, all your cursor movements will be included in the highlight. This means that before you begin the command, you have to be sure that the cursor is either at the beginning or the end of the text that you want included in a highlight.

If you have forgotten this rule, just press the ESCAPE key to get back to Review/Add/Change, move your cursor to the proper place, and issue the appropriate command again.

2.39 Tip: *Choose "Within document" when you are issuing a move or a copy that will not occur again.*

Whenever you use the Move or Copy command, you are given these three choices:

```
---------------------------------------------------------------------------
Move Text?  Within document  To clipboard (cut)  From clipboard (paste)
```

Moving or copying text to the Clipboard is most advantageous when you know that you will want to copy that text from the Clipboard several times, or when you want to be able to switch to another file on the Desktop and copy or move from the Clipboard into it. (Note: Tips that discuss both copies and moves involving the Clipboard are included in Chapter 6, "Data Transfer.")

Many times when you want to move text within a document or copy a section from one area to another, you do not need the Clipboard. In this case, your first step is to move the cursor to the position where you want to begin the move or copy (see the previous Trap).

Once correctly positioned, give the Move (OPEN APPLE-M) or Copy command (OPEN APPLE-C), select within the document, and follow the direction "Use cursor to highlight block, then press Return." Next, move the cursor (now independent of the highlight) to the new spot where you want the text to be placed. Once there, press RETURN, and the move or copy will be carried out for you.

2.40 Tip: *Automatic rejustification makes the necessary adjustments when you carry out a move or a copy.*

Whenever you move text out of one section of a word processing document, the potential gap that is created is immediately closed by the built-in rejustification feature.

Similarly, when you move text to an already occupied location, the original occupants are moved to the right, and the newcomers are squeezed in between.

Rejustification saves you from having to make adjustments after you reposition text. But do keep in mind spaces on boundaries of the "move from location" and the "move to location" if you want to avoid gaps or words that run together.

If you include a space at the beginning of the section of text that you have highlighted for a move or a copy, make sure that you position the cursor on a space when you indicate the new position for the text to occupy. This tells AppleWorks, "Move this space over, along with the other words, to make room for the space I am transferring with my text."

You can also save steps by planning your highlights and cursor placements so that you end up with one, and only one, space between the end of the moved group and the accommodating text. If you take the time to consider spacing before you move or copy, you will save time in the long run. You will also find that making these allowances automatically soon becomes second nature.

Printer Options

2.41 Trap: *Printer options specified will not be applied to the entire document unless you move to the top of the document before specifying the option.*

Printing options that control margins, characters per inch, spacing, and how your document is justified exercise this control over only the area below the position in the document where they were entered. If you want a certain portion of a document to have centered text, just move to this area and choose CN from the Printer Options screen (accessed through OPEN APPLE-O).

When such a format is embedded within a word processing document, it is applied to all subsequent text (whether already entered or to be entered) until another embedded format informs it, "I'll take over from here." These new formats serve to turn off those that are no longer appropriate.

The flexibility this provides when you want to apply various formats within different sections of a document can be invaluable. However, this very flexibility can trip you up if you don't remember to move to the top of the document when you want the format(s) you specify to apply to an entire document.

Be aware that formats issued at the beginning of a document are applied to the entire document if no other format overrules it later in the document. In other words, if you have formatted a certain portion of text to be centered but later decide that you would like the entire document to be unjustified, it is not enough to move to the top of the document and specify UJ from the printer options. You must also remove the centered format from the point you had placed it within the document (simply delete it with OPEN APPLE-D).

2.42 Trap: *Printer options that you apply to specific lines within a paragraph will be adopted by the whole paragraph.*

Printer options that control the layout of a document on the page (spacing, print density, justification, and margin settings) are applied to the entire paragraph no matter where you are within that paragraph when you choose the format.

Suppose that you have a line within a paragraph that you would like to set off from the rest of the paragraph by centering it. You move to that line, access the printer options (OPEN APPLE-O), enter the center option, CN, and then press RETURN.

When you escape back to Review/Add/Change, you expect to find centering beginning at the line that you specified. But instead, the whole paragraph is centered. When you zoom in (OPEN APPLE-Z) to find out where the centering format has been placed, you are surprised to see it at the top of the paragraph instead of in the location that you specified.

In AppleWorks the last carriage return acts as a beginning boundary marker for these types of formats. Therefore, to make sure that the format that you specify is applied to specific lines within a paragraph, first set these lines off with a carriage return.

You can do this by pressing RETURN at the end of the line, right before the one that you want to apply the specific format to. Unless your formatted line(s) fall at the end of the paragraph, you will need to repeat this procedure to embed the option that will turn off the specific line(s) format.

 2.43 Trap: *The Indent option creates hanging paragraphs only.*

Indenting within a paragraph is a helpful technique for setting off certain sections of text. When you choose the Indent option from AppleWorks' Printer Options screen, it will indent the number of spaces that you specify, beginning at the second line of the paragraph within which you specify Indent (IN).

This creates what is called a hanging paragraph. The following paragraph is such an example:

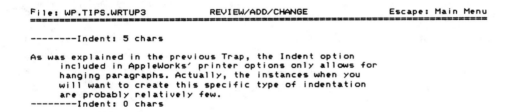

```
File: WP.TIPS.WRTUP3          REVIEW/ADD/CHANGE          Escape: Main Menu
=========================================================================

--------Indent: 5 chars

As was explained in the previous Trap, the Indent option
        included in AppleWorks' printer options only allows for
        hanging paragraphs. Actually, the instances when you
        will want to create this specific type of indentation
        are probably relatively few.
--------Indent: 0 chars
```

You can specify the indent format at any point within the paragraph, and the format will be applied to the entire paragraph (see the previous Trap).

To turn off the indent format, return to the Printer Options screen (OPEN APPLE-O), specify Indent again (IN), and enter zero for the number of characters you want indented.

2.44 Tip: *Use the left margin to help you create indentations when you do not want hanging paragraphs.*

As was explained in the previous Trap, the Indent option included in AppleWorks' printer options only allows for hanging paragraphs. Actually, the instances when you will want to create this specific type of indentation are probably relatively few.

The best way to achieve the standard type of indentation in which all lines are indented equally is to format the area that you wish to be indented with wider left margins. As you can see from the zoomed-in format display in the following illustration, a left margin of two inches is embedded at the beginning of this paragraph:

```
File: WP.TIPS.WRTUP3          REVIEW/ADD/CHANGE          Escape: Main Menu
===========================================================================

As was explained in the previous Trap, the Indent option
included in AppleWorks' printer options only allows for
hanging paragraphs. Actually, the instances when you will
want to create this specific type of indentation are
probably relatively few.
--------Left Margin:  2.0 inches

        The best way to achieve the standard type of
        indentation in which all lines are indented
        equally is to format the area that you wish to be
        indented with wider left margins. As you can see
        from the zoomed-in format display, we embedded a
        left margin of 2 inches at the beginning of this
        paragraph.
--------Left Margin:  1.0 inches

Using this format places all the text that follows it two
inches in from the left margin. Since the rest of the
---------------------------------------------------------------
Type entry or use ⌂ commands        Line 103   Column 62      ⌂-? for Help
```

Using this format places all the text that follows it two inches in from the left margin. Since the rest of the document is formatted at one inch, the result is a one-inch indentation. Do not forget to reset the margins (to match the rest of the document) at the end of the area to be indented.

2.45 *Tip:* *Use CONTROL-B and CONTROL-L as shortcuts to specify boldfacing and underlining in a word processing document.*

Display enhancements such as boldfacing, underlining, and subscripting and superscripting can be formatted to apply to one or more characters anywhere in a word processing document. One way to achieve this is to move to the exact position where you want the format to begin, access the printer options, and enter the appropriate option code; then you must return to the document (press ESCAPE), position the cursor at the end of the text that you are formatting, access the printer options again, and specify the option code designed to end that particular format.

This is a very lengthy process, especially if you want to apply these formats in several locations throughout a document. Thank goodness for the shortcuts AppleWorks has provided for boldfacing and underlining.

These shortcuts can be issued without having to access the printer options. Simply move the cursor to the first character of the group that you want to underline or display in boldface print. From this point press CONTROL-B for boldfacing or CONTROL-L for underlining. A small caret (^) will appear, indicating the beginning of the format. (This caret will not appear when the document is printed.)

Now move to the end of the area to which you want either of these formats to apply, and type CONTROL-B or CONTROL-L again. Another caret will tell you that the format has been stopped at that point.

AppleWorks will consider the location where you first issue one of these commands to be the point at which you want the format to begin. Because of this, you must make sure that you issue the commands in order. First specify the point where you want the format to begin, and then indicate where you want it to end.

If you feel unsure about whether you have embedded the proper formats in the right places, you can check to see which format each caret represents. Move the cursor to the caret symbol in question, and read the identifying prompt at the bottom of the screen. It will say, for example, "Boldface (or Underline) Begin" or "Boldface (or Underline) End."

If you would like a section of your document to be both boldfaced and under-lined, simply embed these two formats as a pair before and after the section. In this case, two carets will be displayed at beginning and ending locations to let you know that both formats are in force.

2.46 Tip: *You can control the size of your print through several different printer options.*

The printer options that control the actual size of the type your document will be printed in are Characters per inch (CI), Proportional-1 (P1), and Proportional-2 (P2). (Note: some printers are not capable of Proportional-1 or Proportional-2 printing or have problems with justification when it is used.)

Figure 2-3 gives examples of various print sizes achieved with these different options. As you can see, the fewer characters per inch that you specify, the larger the print size. The opposite is, of course, also true. The exact characters per inch limits you are allowed in either direction depend on the capabilities of your specific printer. Through experimentation you can discover what these boundaries are for your printer.

Both Proportional-1 and Proportional-2 make your print size considerably smaller than standard, but you can print more characters per line with Proportional-1 than Proportional-2.

The same number of characters per line are printed when you apply Proportional-1 printing and when printing is done with 15 characters per inch. But if you look closely at Figure 2-3, you will see that there is a difference in

---

PRINT SIZES

Four characters per inch:

This is an example of the
print size achieved when
four characters per inch
are specified. The lower
the number of characters
per inch, the larger the
print size.

Fifteen characters per inch:

This is an example of the print size achieved when 15 characters per inch are specified.
The greater the number of characters per inch, the smaller the print size.

Proportional-1

This is an example of printing done with a Proportional-1 format. This option prints more
characters per line than Proportional-2.

Proportional-2

This is an example of printing done with a Proportional-2 format. This option
prints fewer characters per line than Proportional-1.

Figure 2-3.   Print size examples

proportional spacing between Proportional-1 and a specification of 15 characters
per inch.

When you choose either proportional option, characters are spaced according
to individual width. Nonproportional spacing (standard) means that each
character — narrow or wide — is given the same amount of space when printed. It
is good to be aware of these differences so you can specify the one that appeals to
you most.

When you want to return your document to the standard print format, access
the Printer Options screen (OPEN APPLE-O) and then enter **CI** (characters per inch)
and **10**.

2.47 Trap: *You could end up with unsightly gaps in a document if
you are not careful when you use the New Page option or
the Group Begin and Group End options.*

To print a document page by page, the continuity of the printing must be broken at each page. A built-in feature of AppleWorks makes sure that this break does not occur at a point that leaves less than two lines of a paragraph at the beginning or the end of a page.

You can also control the point at which page breaks occur. This control could be important if you want to be sure that a specific portion of text is not broken during printing, or if you want to ensure a break at an appropriate location, such as the beginning of a new chapter.

To format for the first situation, sandwich the text you wish to keep together between the Group Begin (GB) and Group End (GE) options from the Printer Options screen. To create this sandwich, first move the cursor to the first part of the text you are formatting, access the printer options (OPEN APPLE-O), and type **GB** followed by RETURN. Next escape back to Review/Add/Change, move to the end of the group you are sandwiching, and repeat the procedure using GE as your option code this time.

In the second situation, you simply move to the line that you want to be at the beginning of a new page and specify NP once you have gained access to the Printer Options screen.

Handy as these controls are, they do come with a built-in Trap that is important to keep in mind. To keep a group of text together on a page, AppleWorks will push the entire group to the next page if there is not enough room on the current page for all of it to print. If there is lots of text included in this group, this could create a large blank space in the page where the grouped information was pushed from.

A New Page format could result in the same blank spaces unless it is entered relatively close to the bottom of a page. If the new page begins a new chapter or a different section of a report, this gap will not be a detraction. In fact, you are most likely to resent these gaps when they occur as a result of using the grouping option. But keep them in mind to avoid hard copy surprises.

2.48 Tip: OPEN APPLE-K *will calculate page breaks for you.*

AppleWorks figures out where it will break each page according to formats such as top and bottom margins and lines per inch. It is important to know the position of these page breaks before you print the document if you are applying formats that are affected by them. (See the previous Trap for an example.)

Normally, AppleWorks calculates page breaks after you have issued the Print command. If you want page breaks displayed before you print, all you have to do is type OPEN APPLE-K. Page calculations will be performed and entered into the document display so that you can take them into account when you are applying certain formats.

Once this calculation has been performed, it is automatically saved the next time you save your file. (Unless it somehow gets erased — see Trap 2.50.) However, you must reissue the command as you enter new data into the file if you want pages beyond the last calculation point to be included.

As with other formats, the calculated page break markings will not be displayed when the document is actually printed.

2.49 Trap: *"Print from" specifications may be misread unless you first calculate pages in the document with OPEN APPLE-K.*

When you first issue OPEN APPLE-P for printing, you are asked to choose whether you want printing to start from the Beginning of the document, "This page" (meaning the beginning of the page where your cursor is), or right at the Cursor position. For printing to proceed correctly from the choices of "This page" or "Cursor," you will probably need to perform a page calculation (OPEN APPLE-K) before you issue the Print command.

If printing never seems to begin from the point at which you specified, this is probably your problem. Go back and calculate with OPEN APPLE-K; then try printing again — you will be pleasantly surprised.

2.50 Trap: *Page calculations will be erased, and headers, footers, and page numbers that depend on them nullified if certain commands are used after page calculations have been made.*

Once you have calculated pages with OPEN APPLE-K, you will see dotted lines and page numbers throughout the document. They represent the locations where page breaks will occur. These page calculations must be made before headers, footers, and page numbers will print.

However, if certain commands or formats are applied to a document after you have already calculated pages, the calculations will be erased. Specifically, these page break destroyers are (1) the DELETE key, (2) the Delete command, (3) the Move, Replace, and Copy commands, (4) CONTROL-B and CONTROL-L, (5) a sticky space (OPEN APPLE-SPACE), (6) the Printer Options command, OPEN APPLE-O, and (7) anytime insertions are made in existing text.

Unless you realize this and repeat the Calculation command again before you print your document, no headers, footers, or page numbers will print, even though they are still displayed as formats within the document.

2.51 Tip: *The EK option can get around AppleWorks' mail merge omission.*

There is nothing like a mail merge feature if you are printing form letters that are identical except for the specific names, addresses, and dates that vary from letter to letter. With this feature you can have the letters printed with the appropriate variable information merged into each letter as it prints. What a time saver!

Though AppleWorks does not have this marvel, it does have a feature that accomplishes the same thing with a little more trouble on your part.

You can embed the EK format at any number of points throughout a document to let the printer know that you want to be able to enter information from the keyboard at certain locations.

You have probably received a letter similar to the one shown in Figure 2-4. You can print a form letter of this type with AppleWorks by creating a special kind of word processing file. If you look at the formats on the screen display in Figure 2-5, you will see how this works.

As you can see, the letter was typed as usual until locations were reached where variable information needed to be entered. The first such location in this example is the date that will be entered right below the Winner's Circle address.

After moving to this spot, printer options were accessed with OPEN APPLE-O. By typing **EK** and then pressing RETURN, you can embed the "Enter from keyboard" message into your document at the position where you want to be able to type the appropriate date. This embedded format is indicated on screen by a small caret (^) shown just below the I in ID.

The next EK format was needed for the name and address, which vary with each letter. The three carets on the left margin just below the unjustified format show the three separate formats that were entered to allow for each line of the address.

It is important that you specify a separate format for each address line. When your letter is being printed, the whole printing operation will be halted at each caret location. You can enter as many or as few characters as you like each time this pause occurs. The RETURN key is the printer's cue to begin printing again.

Since the printer assumes that you are finished with your current keyboard entry as soon as you press RETURN, it will continue with the rest of the letter

```
                         The Winner's Circle
                           13 Scam Lane
                          Sting, ID 12121


                         January 10, 1986


Mrs. Janet McBeen
112 Lost Cause Blvd.
Seneca, CA 99999


Dear Mrs. McBeen,


This is to inform you, Mrs. McBeen, that you are the lucky winner of
one of the fabulous prizes listed at the bottom of this letter. I
know, Mrs. McBeen, right now you're wondering, " How much is this
going to cost me? "

Well, Mrs. McBeen, here's the amazing part - there is no cost to you.
That's right, Mrs. McBeen, this fabulous prize will be given to you
absolutely free of charge!

All you have to do is present yourself at our ranch-like paradise,
which we have aptly named The Winner's Circle, not later than midnight
on April 10, 1986 and listen to a fifteen hour presentation and slide
show about the horse shares that we are offering to a select and elite
group of people.

Now don't tell me, Mrs. McBeen, that you don't know what a horse share
is. Why, a share in one of our remarkable horses means that you or any
member of your immediate family owns the pleasure of a day's ride
through our ranch with your horse on a once-a-year basis for the next
two years.

Don't delay now, Mrs. McBeen. This offer is only good for 90 short
days and we are so looking forward to presenting you with one of the
fabulous prizes listed below. Call us soon, now.......


                                   Yours truly,



                                   I. M. Crooked

ONE OF THESE FABULOUS PRIZES WILL BE YOURS, MRS. MCBEEN:

1. An all-expense paid trip around the world.

2. A brand-new car - you choose make and model, Mrs. McBeen.

3. A toenail polishing kit.
```

Figure 2-4.   Form letter printout

```
--------Centered

                    The Winner's Circle
                       13 Scam Lane
                      Sting, ID 12121


--------Unjustified

  ^
  ^
  ^

Dear ^,

This is to inform you, ^, that you are the lucky winner of one of the
fabulous prizes listed at the bottom of this letter. I know, ^, right
now you're wondering, " How much is this going to cost me? "

Well, ^, here's the amazing part — there is no cost to you. That's
right, ^, this fabulous prize will be given to you absolutely free of
charge!

All you have to do is present yourself at our ranch-like paradise,
which we have aptly named The Winner's Circle, not later than midnight
on ^ and listen to a fifteen hour presentation and slide show about
the horse shares that we are offering to a select and elite group of
people.

Now don't tell me, ^, that you don't know what a horse share is. Why,
a share in one of our remarkable horses means that you or any member
of your immediate family owns the pleasure of a day's ride through our
ranch with your horse on a once-a-year basis for the next ^ years.


Don't delay now, ^. This offer is only good for ^ short days and we
are so looking forward to presenting you with one of the fabulous
prizes listed below. Call us soon, now........


                              Yours truly,



                              I. M. Crooked

^ONE OF THESE FABULOUS PRIZES WILL BE YOURS, ^:^

1. An all-expense paid trip around the world.

2. A brand-new car — you choose make and model, ^.

3. A toenail polishing kit.
```

Figure 2-5. EK formats displayed within form letter

unless another EK format embedded in the next line causes it to pause there so you can make an additional entry. This is exactly what was done in the three address lines in the Winner's Circle letter.

The entries in the remainder of the letter are much shorter and are carried out within a sentence. The same rules apply to entries made in this fashion. Whenever a ^ is encountered during the printing process, the printer stops and you are invited to make an entry from the keyboard. When you are finished with your entry, pressing RETURN causes the printer to begin again, first typing the characters that you entered from the keyboard, and then continuing with the letter until it meets another ^.

When you are entering from the keyboard, the RETURN key does not send you to the next line as it does when you are typing from Review/Add/Change. If your keyboard entry is too long to fit on one line, built-in word wrap will move it to the next line down, just as it does when you are typing in normal mode.

As your letter is being printed, the lines of print are displayed on screen. Each time you reach a keyboard entry position, a screen highlight pinpoints the location where your entry will be printed. The entry that you make will not be displayed on the screen; it will be sent directly to the printer.

2.52 Tip: *AppleWorks displays your keyboard entry on screen as you type it so you have a chance to view and edit it before it is printed.*

When your printer pauses to let you enter information from the keyboard, you will see the following prompt at the bottom of the screen:

```
You can type information to be placed
at the point marked above.

-----------------------------------------------------------------------
Information?                                                  24K Avail.
```

As you type in the characters from the keyboard, they are displayed on the bottom of the screen. Always scrutinize your entry closely before you press RETURN to signal the printer to print your entry. Until RETURN is pressed, you can make any spelling corrections or other changes needed to assure a perfect printed copy.

2.53 Trap: *You have to escape back to Review/Add/Change each time you want to place another EK format within the document.*

The EK option embeds its "Enter from keyboard" message into your document at the exact point where your cursor is positioned when you specify the format. This means that before you access the printer options (OPEN APPLE-O) to specify the EK format, you must make sure that the cursor is positioned in the exact spot where you want the information that you enter from the keyboard to begin.

It also means that to indicate subsequent EK formats, you must repeatedly move the cursor to the next position. You cannot do this while the printer options are on screen, which means that you must use the ESCAPE key to get back to Review/Add/Change in between each EK format that you place in your document.

2.54 Tip: *When printing form letters, enter the number of copies that you want printed when you issue the Print command for the first time.*

When you first issue the Print command, you can choose how many copies of the letter you want printed. If you are printing form letters, it is wise to choose multiple copies at this point. This will save you from having to reissue the Print command each time you want to begin another letter. As each letter prints, the embedded EK formats enable you to make the appropriate changes that distinguish each letter from the others.

2.55 Tip: *The quickest way to get rid of printer formats that you no longer want in a document is to erase them with the Delete command.*

It is possible to undo most printer formats by placing an opposite format just below the original. For instance, formatting with unjustified (UJ) just below a center format (CN) would assure that the center format no longer had any effect on the text that followed.

However, this procedure means accessing the printer options, which requires several steps. It is much faster to move to the line that contains the unwanted format and delete it with OPEN APPLE-D. Once this deletion is carried out, the previous format (or default) will gain jurisdiction over the new area.

Usually, this is exactly what you want to happen. If, instead, you want that area to take on a different format entirely, you might as well use an overruling format from the Printer Options screen in the first place. (If you are short on file space, make sure that you delete the superfluous format.)

✋ *2.56* **Trap**: *You have three "Print from" choices in document print-*
ing but no "Print to" choices.

The following illustration shows the printing choices that you are presented with
when you initiate the printing procedure with OPEN APPLE-P:

```
-----------------------------------------------------------------------------
Print from?  Beginning  This page  Cursor
```

If you choose to print from the beginning, your document will be printed starting
at the beginning of your file and going to the end.

In order for either of the other choices ("This page" or "Cursor") to work
correctly, you must make sure that you have already calculated page breaks (OPEN
APPLE-K). Without this page calculation, AppleWorks won't know at what point
to begin printing, and you are likely to get print that you didn't ask for (see Trap
2.49).

If you choose "This page," your document will be printed beginning at the
top of the page where the cursor was positioned when you issued the Print command. Do not expect "This page" to mean that printing will stop at the end of
the specified page. It will continue from "This page" to the end of the file.

The third choice, "Cursor," allows you to position the cursor at any point
within a document as a signal for AppleWorks to begin printing from that point.
In this case also, printing continues from the specified point to the end of the file.

In fact, there is no built-in way, short of disabling the printer, to specify a
position for printing to stop before the end of the file — but there is a trick that
works well. See the next Tip.

💡 *2.57* **Tip**: *Make the EK command or the "Pause Here" option cause*
printing to stop at any point you want before the end of
the file.

Although you can use the cursor to specify a particular starting point for your
printer, AppleWorks does not provide a way for you to specify a stop-printing
point before the end of the file. If you want to print only a portion of a document
within your file, your frustration with this flaw could, understandably, run quite
high.

But there are two ways to get around this problem. The first is to move one
space beyond the point in the document where you want printing to stop. Call up

the Printer Options screen with OPEN APPLE-O, and supply the code for Enter from Keyboard (EK), followed by pressing RETURN. An escape back to the document will reveal that a small caret (^) has been placed at the point that you specified.

This is an indication that the EK format is embedded here. It means that printing will stop at this point so that you can enter information directly from the keyboard. If you do this and then press RETURN, printing will continue. But if you press ESCAPE instead, the whole printing procedure will be aborted, and you will be returned to your document in Review/Add/Change, free to gloat over your ingenuity.

The second way to stop the printing operation at a particular location is to specify the "Pause Here" option (enter PH from the Printer Options screen) at the point where you want printing to stop. A ------ Pause Here format will be displayed on screen, and printing will stop when it gets to this point. If you press RETURN, printing will resume, but if you press ESCAPE, you will be sent back to Review/Add/Change.

2.58 Tip: *You can find out the format represented by a caret (^) by reading the message displayed when the cursor is on one.*

AppleWorks uses the caret symbol to indicate a variety of word processing formats. When you see one of these little characters on screen, it could mean that you have formatted for boldfacing, underlining, or many other things.

To find out which particular format each caret stands for, move the cursor on top of the caret in question, and read the revealing message at the bottom of the screen. If you look at the caret positioned between the *a* and *m* in the following illustration, you will see an example of such a message that unveils the caret's true identity — a sticky space.

```
To find out which particular format each caret stands for,
simply move your cursor on top of the caret in question and
read the revealing message at the bottom of your screen. If
you look at the caret positioned between the a and m in the
following illustration, you will see an example of such
a^message that unveils the caret's true identity - a sticky
space!


--------------------------------------------------------------
Type entry or use a commands         Sticky Space         a-? for Help
```

2.59 Tip: *Before you print a document, use the Find feature to help you check your printer options.*

When you initiate the Find command (OPEN APPLE-F), you are presented with the following five choices:

```
------------------------------------------------------------------------
Find?  Text  Page  Marker  Case sensitive text   Options for printer
```

This chapter has discussed all but the last choice, "Options for printer," in previous Tips. When you specify the option for printer choice, the Printer Options screen appears, allowing you to enter any of the codes listed there. Once you have done this, the search begins immediately, and you are taken to the appropriate option within your document. As with the other Find options, you then have the opportunity to choose whether or not to find the next occurrence.

You will want to continue searching if this was not the particular instance of the format that you were looking for. When you find it, you will need to press ESCAPE before you can actually move within the document again or make changes to the format.

It is important to remember that when you use the Find command in this way, it searches the area of the document below the point where the cursor was positioned when the command was issued. If you do not seem to find options that you know are there, move to the beginning of the document (OPEN APPLE-1 will get you there quickly) and try again.

2.60 Trap: *Depending on the options that you have formatted into the document, you could get printed copy that is different from the screen display.*

To a large degree, the display that you see on screen will match what you get when you print a document. However, some print enhancements and formats that you embed within a document do not show up on screen, although they are displayed when the document is printed.

On the other hand, format symbols and messages present on your screen are not included during printing. A list of the features that fall into these two categories follows:

Printed but not Displayed on Screen

- Double and triple spacing
- More than 12 characters per inch
- Proportional printing (1 or 2)
- Justified print (aligned on both right and left margins)
- Superscript and subscript
- Boldfacing and underlining
- Headers and footers on each page.

Displayed on Screen but not Printed

- Format messages preceded by dashed lines (e.g., --------Unjustified)
- Carets (^) representing embedded formats
- Rectangles indicating carriage returns
- The cursor line.

3

The Data Base

A data base organizes information just as a list does. But because it is an electronic list, it can also maintain numerous facts about each item that is listed. For example, your grocery lists probably include items such as milk, bread, yogurt, lettuce, and apples. In a data base, you could also have categories to indicate food type (dairy, vegetable, fruit, and so on), the store that has the lowest price for each item, and the purchase quantity for each item. AppleWorks' Data Base even has mathematical capabilities that can calculate how much each item will cost and give you a grand total of what you will spend on groceries if you buy all the items on the list.

Not only that, but if you are going to buy only vegetables, it can extract a sublist of vegetables from your main list and give you a subtotal of what they will cost.

That's the good news. The bad news is that you have to enter the information that AppleWorks stores and manipulates. Because entering information takes time, you want to be sure that the time investment will be worthwhile.

If you buy groceries for a single family, creating a data base would probably not be time well spent. However, a restaurant or a food-buying co-op might save both time and money by acting on the information provided by data base manipulations.

Even after you have determined that using a data base is worthwhile, you can choose to venture into this electronic process by degrees.

The smallest commitment is to enter and view the data you are concerned with. At this point, you could benefit from the Tips in this chapter on "Setting Up," "Using a Single-Record Layout," and "Using a Multiple-Record Layout."

The next step will probably be precipitated by the need to make changes in the setup of your records or to begin using the data base commands to manipulate the information you have previously been storing. The Tips in the "Using Change Record Layout" and "Data Base Commands" sections will further enhance the power that this step offers.

Once you have come this far, you will probably want to see your information in the form of hard copy. To achieve this in the smoothest way possible, refer to the Tips in Chapter 4, "Data Base Reporting."

Above all, don't be intimidated by this powerful tool. Start small. Refer to the *AppleWorks Reference Manual* and the Tips and Traps in this book, and adopt a learn-as-you-go attitude that assumes you will soon be an expert.

Setting Up

3.01 Trap: *The claim that an AppleWorks data base file can hold up to 1350 records is a bit misleading.*

In theory, AppleWorks can hold up to 1350 records. In actuality, these records would have to be so small that they would be impractical. If you have 128K of memory, a more reasonable number of records to maintain in one file is about 750. This depends upon the amount of information in each record and can therefore vary greatly. (Various memory expansion cards are available to increase memory capacity if you find the existing limits inhibiting.)

If you don't have enough memory to add more records to your data base, you can easily divide the data base into two files, thereby doubling the capacity to store more information.

To accomplish this, load the data base file and delete the second half. (Break it at some appropriate halfway mark—probably determined alphabetically or numerically within an important category.) Rename the first half and save it as a new file.

Next, load the original file a second time and delete the first half of the records. Rename and save the remaining second half as a new file (or save it under its original name, if you like). The last step is to delete the now superfluous original file. You are left with plenty of room for records in the two new files.

The Data Base

 3.02 Trap: *Keep the length of category names and entries in the data base to a minimum to save space and avoid truncation.*

Although at times it is helpful to use long descriptive names for data base category headings or entries, doing this may cause problems down the road.

Since AppleWorks won't allow you to move beyond the width of the screen to view off-screen data base categories, the narrower the category columns, the more you can see of the data base at one time. You can make long entries into categories or choose long names for the headings and still narrow the columns to make maximum use of the screen display.

However, in this case the record entries will be truncated to such an extent that they may be difficult to understand. If your original rationale for creating long category names or entries was to enhance meaning and clarity, you may be left with the feeling that you have sunk your own ship.

3.03 Tip: *When you create category headings for a data base, choose names that are descriptive of the information in that category.*

The single record displayed in the following illustration shows category headings created by following the lead presented by AppleWorks in suggesting Category 1 as the name for the first category in a new data base.

```
File: Food List              REVIEW/ADD/CHANGE              Escape: Main Menu

Selection: All records


Record 1 of 1
===============================================================================
Category 1: Fruit
Category 2: Orange
Category 3: .49
Category 4: 50
Category 5: Food City
```

You can either accept this suggestion or type in your own category names. Consider a single record with the same category entries, but with headings that describe the information that they categorize.

```
File: Food List              REVIEW/ADD/CHANGE          Escape: Main Menu

Selection: All records


Record 1 of 1
=============================================================================
Food Type: Fruit
Food Name: Orange
Max. Purchase Price: .49
Purchase Quantity: 50
Store Name: Food City
```

There are several advantages to the second method. Not only are the screen display and printed report clearer and more informative with headings that describe the category's contents, but the process of data entry is greatly facilitated when there are no ambiguities about which type of information to enter into which category.

 3.04 Trap: *If you use the word* Date *when setting up data base category headings, be aware of the conventions that you must follow within this format.*

As handy and straightforward as AppleWorks' technique for dealing with dates seems, there are several potential Traps to keep in mind.

The most basic guideline to follow when entering dates in AppleWorks is to keep within the options that can be converted to the standard date format. In actuality, AppleWorks offers so many entry options for dates that it would be difficult to come up with an unacceptable style. If you have any doubts, refer to the options listed on page 63 of the *AppleWorks Reference Manual*.

At times, however, varying the form of date entry can get you into trouble later. For example, look at the following data base used by a small food-buying co-op:

```
File: Food List            REVIEW/ADD/CHANGE    Escape: Restore former entry

Selection: All records


Food Type      Food Name      Price    Unit      Quantity  Order Date
=============================================================================
veg.           cabbage        .19      lb.       25        Jun 15
Fruit          Oranges        .49      lb.       50        Jun  7
veg.           mushrooms      1.19     lb.       18        Jun 21 85
bev.           Ap. juice      2.00     gal.      10        May 85
cheese         Edam           2.79     lb.       12        Jun 10 85
```

Since the tasks in the co-op are divided among all members, several people often collect information about the various food items to be ordered and enter the collected data in the Food List data base as it becomes available. Each person uses a different form for entering the date by which the food item needs to be ordered so that it will be available for the July buyers' meeting.

The cabbage and orange buyers, assuming that it was obvious that the year was 1985, simply entered the month and day when their items needed to be ordered. The mushroom and cheese buyers adopted the convention that they used at work and entered month, day, and year. The person who ordered the bottled apple juice didn't have to be concerned with spoilage but was assured a special price if it was ordered before June 1. The most appropriate entry in this case seemed to be May 85.

Since AppleWorks can accept all these conventions and convert them to date format, there seems to be little problem. However, when the co-op coordinator used the Arrange command to sort the records so they would be listed from earliest order date to latest, the May date seemed out of place, as shown in the following illustration:

```
File: Food List          REVIEW/ADD/CHANGE          Escape: Main Menu

Selection: All records


Food Type      Food Name      Price   Unit    Quantity  Order Date
================================================================================
Fruit          Oranges        .49     lb.     50        Jun  7
veg.           cabbage        .19     lb.     25        Jun 15
bev.           Ap. juice      2.00    gal.    10        May 85
cheese         Edam           2.79    lb.     12        Jun 10 85
veg.           mushrooms      1.19    lb.     18        Jun 21 85
```

This Trap arises because of the way AppleWorks reads date entries. The order dates for oranges and cabbage are read as Jun 7 00 and Jun 15 00. The order date for the apple juice is read as May 00 85 and thus is placed below the previous dates, in mathematical order. Although the fact that May comes before June seems like enough of a tip-off for correct placement, in this case you cannot depend on such logic.

3.05 Tip: You must let AppleWorks know if the time you are entering is not during regular business hours.

AppleWorks' time schedule works in 12-hour sections signified by Am and Pm. It converts 24-hour time into the Am/Pm format and allows you to make casual entries such as 3, which it converts to 3:00 Pm, or 1105, which it displays as 11:05 Am. If you do not specify otherwise, it will be assumed that the time you are entering is within regular business hours. If this is not the case, use *a* or *p* with the entry to let AppleWorks know that the time falls beyond the business hour range.

3.06 Tip: *When you are setting up a data base, it is helpful to include a blank record at the end.*

When you are using a multiple-record layout, it is impossible to venture below the last record in the file. This can be a handicap in several situations.

Suppose that you wanted to move or copy one of the records in the data base to a position just below the last record. To copy from the Clipboard, you must move the cursor to the spot at which you want the copied record to be placed. But if you try to move beyond the last record to indicate the desired placement, you will be beeped at incessantly.

Likewise, all efforts at inserting a new record at the end of the data base will be thwarted by this access limitation. Since the Insert command places the new record above the cursor point (or in front of the current record in a single-record layout) and you cannot get below the current last record, it seems that the best you can do is to insert records just above the last one in the list.

The easiest way to get around this limitation is to create a dummy record in the data base when you first set it up. If you don't realize the need until later, you can add the extra record at any time by following the procedure presented in Trap 3.29.

The following illustration shows how a blank record looks at the end of a simple data base:

```
File: Food List              REVIEW/ADD/CHANGE           Escape: Main Menu

Selection: All records


Food Type      Food Name      Price    Unit     Quantity  Order Date
================================================================================
Fruit          Orange          .49     lb.       50       Jun  7
veg.           cabbage         .19     lb.       25       Jun 15
bev.           Ap. juice      2.00     gal.      10       May 85
cheese         Edam           2.79     lb.       12       Jun 10 85
veg.           mushrooms      1.19     lb.       18       Jun 21 85
-              -               -        -         -        -
```

Through this blank record, you can specify the correct placement of records that you want positioned below the last real record of the data base file.

Problems can arise from this trick, however. If you use the Arrange command (OPEN APPLE-A) to sort the records in the data base, you will find that a blank entry is given a value of less than zero in a numeric sort and before A in an alphabetical sort. This means that anytime you arrange records numerically from 0 to 9 or alphabetically from *A* to *Z*, the blank record at the end will be sorted to the top, and all the access advantage that it provided will be lost.

To keep this from happening, use the letter *z* as a placeholder in each category in the false record:

```
File: Food List           REVIEW/ADD/CHANGE           Escape: Main Menu

Selection: All records


Food Type      Food Name      Price    Unit     Quantity  Order Date
===================================================================
Fruit          Orange         .49      lb.      50        Jun  7
veg.           cabbage        .19      lb.      25        Jun 15
bev.           Ap. juice      2.00     gal.     10        May 85
cheese         Edam           2.79     lb.      12        Jun 10 85
veg.           mushrooms      1.19     lb.      18        Jun 21 85
z              z              z        z        z         z
```

The *z* is evaluated above 9 in a numeric sort and beyond Z in an alphabetical sort. You will not have any further problems unless, for some reason, you need to sort in descending alphabetical or numeric order.

3.07 Tip: *Use the structure of a current data base to quickly create a new one with the same category headings but different record entries.*

The following illustration shows the data base used by a small food-buying co-op:

```
File: Food List           REVIEW/ADD/CHANGE     Escape: Restore former entry

Selection: All records


Food Type      Food Name      Price    Unit     Quantity  Order Date
===================================================================
veg.           cabbage        .19      lb.      25        Jun 15
Fruit          Oranges        .49      lb.      50        Jun  7
veg.           mushrooms      1.19     lb.      18        Jun 21 85
bev.           Ap. juice      2.00     gal.     10        May 85
cheese         Edam           2.79     lb.      12        Jun 10 85
```

Every month different foods are ordered, depending on which fruits and vegetables are in season and what prices are available. At the beginning of each month a new file is created for the current monthly order. Since the categories in each monthly file remain the same, it is expedient to create each new file by loading last month's file, deleting the old records, and adding the current month's items in the same structure. In this way, you skip the step of creating category names each time you create a new monthly file.

Unfortunately, there is one catch in this process that requires a little extra effort to sidestep. You will find that when you try to delete all the records from the old data base before entering the current records, there will be one persistent record that refuses to be deleted. Several ways to get rid of it are presented in Trap 3.28.

3.08 Tip: *If you are adding records that share a great deal of category information with previous records, it may be faster to use OPEN APPLE-C to copy the previous record and make necessary changes later.*

The time-saving trick discussed in the previous Tip can be used when you are adding records in a file that are similar to existing records.

To illustrate this, let's refer to the data base created by the food-buying co-op. The co-op orders all beverages from the same company. In most cases, the price per gallon for the various juices is a standard $2.00. The date by which the juices have to be ordered is consistent among juice types. Since the food type is obviously the same, the only variables are Food Name and Quantity.

Rather than individually entering each record for juice type, the co-op juice person begins with one juice entry as shown in the following illustration:

```
File: Food List          REVIEW/ADD/CHANGE          Escape: Main Menu

Selection: All records


Food Type      Food Name      Price   Unit    Quantity  Order Date
================================================================================
cheese         Edam           2.79    1b.     12        Jun 10 85
veg.           mushrooms      1.19    1b.     18        Jun 21 85
Fruit          Oranges        .49     1b.     50        Jun  7
veg.           cabbage        .19     1b.     25        Jun 15
bev.           Ap. juice      2.00    gal.    10        May 85
```

Then she uses AppleWorks' Copy command (OPEN APPLE-C) to duplicate that record to match the number of different juices that were ordered.

```
File: Food List                REVIEW/ADD/CHANGE              Escape: Main Menu

Selection: All records


Food Type        Food Name      Price    Unit      Quantity  Order Date
=========================================================================
cheese           Edam           2.79     lb.       12        Jun 10 85
veg.             mushrooms      1.19     lb.       18        Jun 21 85
Fruit            Oranges         .49     lb.       50        Jun  7
veg.             cabbage         .19     lb.       25        Jun 15
bev.             Ap. juice      2.00     gal.      10        May 85
bev.             Ap. juice      2.00     gal.      10        May 85
bev.             Ap. juice      2.00     gal.      10        May 85
bev.             Ap. juice      2.00     gal.      10        May 85
```

The final step is to quickly go through the records and adjust the juice names and quantities to fit the actual order.

```
File: Food List                REVIEW/ADD/CHANGE              Escape: Main Menu

Selection: All records


Food Type        Food Name      Price    Unit      Quantity  Order Date
=========================================================================
cheese           Edam           2.79     lb.       12        Jun 10 85
veg.             mushrooms      1.19     lb.       18        Jun 21 85
Fruit            Oranges         .49     lb.       50        Jun  7
veg.             cabbage         .19     lb.       25        Jun 15
bev.             Ap. juice      2.00     gal.      10        May 85
bev.             Rasp.-Ap.juice 2.00     gal.       6        May 85
bev.             Ap.-Straw. juice 2.00   gal.      12        May 85
bev.             Grpfrt. juice  2.00     gal.       8        May 85
```

You can save time using this duplicate entry method as long as the changes are minor.

3.09 Tip: *Any changes made in the Change Name/Category screen will automatically be reflected in all other layouts within the current file.*

When you use AppleWorks' Name Change command (OPEN APPLE-N), you can change the name of the current file and any category headings within it.

Any changes made to the file name or category headings are automatically reflected in the single- and multiple-record layouts of the Review/Add/Change screen as well as the Change Record Layout and Report Format screens.

3.10 Tip: *To revert to the original structure of a file quickly, ask AppleWorks to add the original file to the Desktop.*

Suppose you are working with the Food List data base depicted in the previous illustrations. Every time you enter data in the Food Type category, you wonder why you need this category at all. After all, it must be obvious to everyone that an orange is a fruit. You decide to save everyone time by deleting this category.

No sooner do you complete this task than it occurs to you that the food-buying co-op using this list divides its monthly ordering responsibilities among group members according to the food type ordered. Your first thought is that you will have to re-create the Food Type category and then enter data into that category for every record in the file. Then you realize that a copy of the original list is still intact on your disk. You simply delete the changed file from the Desktop, add the original file in its place, and breathe a sigh of relief.

Using a Single-Record Layout

3.11 Tip: *Make data entry more efficient by customizing the single-record layout to match data input forms.*

This seemingly obvious Tip is often ignored. The people from Survey Services, Inc., realized this only after they wasted many precious hours.

In conducting a survey of downtown shoppers in Tanguy Heights, Pennsylvania, Survey Services personnel asked shoppers to fill out the simple questionnaire in Figure 3-1. Figure 3-2 shows a completed survey form. As you can see in the following illustration, the survey information from that form has been entered in a data base used at the company's home office:

```
File: Tanguy Heights          REVIEW/ADD/CHANGE              Escape: Main Menu

Selection: All records


Items purchased    X per wk.    Store name          Happy-Y/N   Other stores
================================================================================
pool cleaner       1            Life of Riley       Y           shoe
counselling        1            Close Encounters    Y           laundry
groceries          2            Lentz Health Foods  Y           -
```

After several hours of staring at survey forms, the data entry operator found

Dear Downtown Shopper,

Survey Services, Inc., has been asked by the Tanguy Heights
Chamber of Commerce to conduct a survey of downtown shoppers
and their shopping preferences to compare with a similar
survey to be conducted at the nearby shopping mall drawing
from the same customer base. In this way we hope to be able
to supply the downtown merchants with a picture of their
future business possibilities in their present location.

Your cooperation in answering the following questions is
requested in order to compile the necessary information for
this survey:

Name of downtown stores where you shop:	How many times/wk?	What do you buy there?	Are you happy with service?	Other stores needed

We at Survey Services would like to express our appreciation
to you for taking the time to complete this important
survey. It is our greatest hope that the results of our
survey will bring increased service to you.

Sincerely,

Harry Bleecher

Harry Bleecher
Public Relations

Figure 3-1. Survey form letter

that she had made numerous errors of the same type. She had repeatedly entered
the store name in the column where items purchased should have gone. This was
an easy mistake to make. Since the first column on the survey form was the name
of the store, it was natural to supply it first during data entry.

Dear Downtown Shopper,

Survey Services, Inc., has been asked by the Tanguy Heights Chamber of Commerce to conduct a survey of downtown shoppers and their shopping preferences to compare with a similar survey to be conducted at the nearby shopping mall drawing from the same customer base. In this way we hope to be able to supply the downtown merchants with a picture of their future business possibilities in their present location.

Your cooperation in answering the following questions is requested in order to compile the necessary information for this survey:

Name of downtown stores where you shop:	How many times/wk?	What do you buy there?	Are you happy with service?	Other stores needed
Life of Riley	*1*	*pool cleaner*	*yes*	*shoe store*
Close Encounters	*1*	*counselling service*	*yes*	*laundry*
Lentz Health Foods	*2*	*groceries*	*yes*	

We at Survey Services would like to express our appreciation to you for taking the time to complete this important survey. It is our greatest hope that the results of our survey will bring increased service to you.

Sincerely,

Harry Bleecher

Harry Bleecher
Public Relations

Figure 3-2. Completed survey form

Cleverly, she realized that changing the layout of the data base to match the order of the survey questions (see the following illustration) would save time and minimize entry errors.

```
File: Tanguy Heights          REVIEW/ADD/CHANGE            Escape: Main Menu
Selection: All records


Store name           X per wk.   Items purchased   Happy-Y/N   Other stores
================================================================================
Life of Riley        1           pool cleaner      Y           shoe
Close Encounters     1           counselling       Y           laundry
Lentz Health Foods   2           groceries         Y           -
```

You can save even more time, of course, if you apply this Tip when you first create a data base that stores information from a related form.

*3.12 **Tip:*** *Use AppleWorks' ruler in a single-record layout to move quickly between widely dispersed records.*

You can move from the current record displayed in a single-record layout to the next record by using the OPEN APPLE and down arrow keys and move to the previous record by using the OPEN APPLE and up arrow keys. This works well if you are traveling through one or two records, but it takes too long if you need to move between records that are far apart.

AppleWorks speeds up this process by dividing each file into eighths and offering access in increments with OPEN APPLE-1 through -9. OPEN APPLE-1 takes you to the beginning of the file, while OPEN APPLE-9 speeds you to the very end. If you know the relative location of the record you want, you can also use ruler stops 2 through 8.

However, since fractional savvy is quite unlikely, using anything but the two extremes (and perhaps the middle: OPEN APPLE-4) will be approximate. Even approximate placement can be a time saver, though, especially if you know the direction you want to move in from your approximate position toward the actual destination.

You will find that you get better at judging placement the more you do it. Being aware of the relative locations of records in a data base can save time.

*3.13 **Tip:*** *Viewing and entering data base information in a single-record layout can sometimes be preferable to using a multiple-record layout.*

A multiple-record layout lets you view up to 15 records at a time, while in a single-record layout, the data base records are displayed one at a time. Unfortunately, if you have more than six or eight categories in a data base, you won't be able to see all of them on the screen in a multiple-record layout. The categories that are not seen cannot be brought into view, nor can new data be entered into them in a multiple-record layout unless time consuming adjustments are made to the record layout (see the last part of Tip 3.16).

Because of this, it is often better to choose a single-record layout if you want to view, enter, or edit information in a data base of any size.

Another viewing advantage that the single-record layout has over the multiple-record layout is that all category entries can be seen in their entirety. In a multiple-record layout, category entries longer than the width of the category column are truncated to display within the column; meaning is sometimes lost in the process. If you have any questions about a category entry because you can't read all of it in a multiple-record layout, use OPEN APPLE-Z to zoom into a single-record layout where you can view the unexpurgated version.

Finally, you may find it advantageous to choose a single-record layout if you are entering information from a series of forms that contain category information for a single record. In this case, designing a single-record layout to match your entry form can speed entry tremendously (see Tip 3.11).

✋3.14 Trap: *Don't expect the changes you make to the order of categories in a single-record layout to be reflected in a multiple-record layout.*

When an AppleWorks data base is first created, each category that you specify is automatically applied to single- and multiple-record layouts in the exact order that you specify. The layouts of categories in both multiple- and single-record layouts match, as shown in Figure 3-3.

However, if you later change category names in a single-record layout, they will not be reflected in a multiple-record layout, and vice versa.

Although you may at first wonder about this apparent inconsistency, you will probably find that most of the time it works to your advantage. Whereas the order that a single-record layout takes is often designed around the data source form from which you are entering, the layout of multiple records should be designed to allow you to display the categories that you refer to most often. (You don't have access to off-screen categories in a multiple-record layout.)

✋3.15 Trap: *In single-record layout, you do not have access to the Clipboard.*

The Data Base

```
┌─────────────────────────────────────────────────────────────────────┐
│  File: Food List              REVIEW/ADD/CHANGE        Escape: Main Menu │
│                                                                         │
│  Selection: All records                                                 │
│                                                                         │
│                                                                         │
│  Food Type       Food Name      Price    Unit     Quantity  Order Date  │
│  ═══════════════════════════════════════════════════════════════════   │
│  veg.            cabbage         .19      lb.        25      Jun 15      │
│  fruit           oranges         .49      lb.        50      Jun  7      │
│  veg.            mushrooms      1.19      lb.        18      Jun 21 85   │
│  bev.            ap. juice      2.00      gal.       10      May 85      │
│  cheese          Edam           2.79      lb.        12      Jun 10 85   │
│                                                                         │
│                                                                         │
│                                                                         │
│  File: Food List              REVIEW/ADD/CHANGE        Escape: Main Menu │
│                                                                         │
│  Selection: All records                                                 │
│                                                                         │
│                                                                         │
│  Record 1 of 5                                                          │
│  ════════════════════════════════════════════════════════════════════ │
│  Food Type: veg.                                                        │
│  Food Name: cabbage                                                     │
│  Price: .19                                                             │
│  Unit: lb.                                                              │
│  Quantity: 25                                                           │
│  Order Date: Jun 15                                                     │
└─────────────────────────────────────────────────────────────────────┘
```

Figure 3-3. Matching layout order for multiple- and single-record layouts

In a multiple-record layout, you can move or copy records to the Clipboard and retrieve and reposition them in a record lineup. This feature is not available in a single-record layout, since you can't access the Clipboard.

You can, of course, copy the current single record by using OPEN APPLE-C, but you cannot then manipulate it using the Clipboard.

Luckily, you can copy or move records in a multiple-record layout, and they will be applied to all records in a single-record layout. The end result is the same.

Using a Multiple-Record Layout

3.16 Tip: Sometimes using a multiple-record layout has advantages over using a single-record layout for entering, editing, and viewing records.

Since a multiple-record layout displays many records on the screen at one time, it gives you a wider perspective of the information in a data base. This advantage is obvious when you are comparing information in two records and want to view both simultaneously.

Being able to see records in a group might lead you to decide to make entries into categories from a multiple- instead of single-record layout. Since AppleWorks was designed so that new records would be inserted from Insert New Records, which displays a single-record format, it takes a bit of juggling to bring this about.

When you create a new data base from scratch, you will be placed in the Change Name/Category screen, where you can then enter the category names that you have chosen for the data base. This done, you will be led to Insert New Records, which invites you to enter information into each category in the single-record format presented.

To make entries in a multiple-record layout, use the RETURN key to speed through each category within the first record, thus creating a blank record as the first record of the data base. Next, duplicate the blank record by using OPEN APPLE-C. Create as many blank records as you think you will need in the completed data base.

Now, if you switch to a multiple-record layout, you will see that the screen is full of blank records that you can fill by entering data either column by column or row by row. (See Tip 3.18 to learn how to adjust the cursor to proceed through columns or rows.)

You will run into trouble if all of the data base categories do not fit on the screen. Since you cannot move beyond the screen display in a multiple-record layout, you will not be able to enter data into categories that are off the screen.

The only way to get around this is to first enter data into each record in the categories that are on the screen, and then adjust the placement of the off-screen categories so they are positioned on screen and available for data entry.

To make this adjustment, get to the Change Record Layout screen (OPEN APPLE-L), and move all the off-screen categories to the left using OPEN APPLE-< until they take the places of the previous on-screen categories. Now, press ESC to return to a multiple-record layout and continue entering category information into the now available categories in the multiple display.

3.17 Trap: *The up and down arrow keys in combination with the OPEN APPLE key have a different effect in a single-record layout than in a multiple-record layout.*

If you are used to working in a single-record layout and have used the OPEN APPLE-arrow key combinations to move to either the next or the previous record,

The Data Base

you may be surprised that they have different functions in a multiple-record layout. There the OPEN APPLE key used with the up arrow moves the cursor to the top of the currently displayed screen. Used again, it moves the cursor up another entire screen. The OPEN APPLE used with the down arrow key has the opposite effect. It moves the cursor down one screen each time, until it reaches the end of the data base.

3.18 Tip: *You can change the direction (to the right or down) that the cursor will move when you press RETURN in a multiple-record layout.*

The standard direction that the entry cursor will move when you press RETURN in a multiple-record layout is down to the next record within the same category. If you are setting up a data base in a multiple-record layout, as described in Tip 3.16, or you are entering or editing information in several categories in one or more records, it is more convenient to have the cursor move to the right after each category entry is completed.

You can make this adjustment in cursor direction easily. First press OPEN APPLE-L. You are now in the Change Record Layout screen. If you press the ESC key, you can choose one of two options presented in the following screen:

```
File: Personnel          CHANGE RECORD LAYOUT     Escape: Review/Add/Change




===============================================================================



                  What direction should the cursor
                  go when you press Return?

                       1.  Down (standard)
                       2.  Right

         ----------------------------------------------------------------
```

Choose option 2, Right, and you are back in business.

3.19 Tip: *AppleWorks has several built-in features that allow you to get around multiple records quickly.*

Use the right and left arrow keys to move past characters within a category in a multiple-record layout. You will not be able to move from one category to another using these keys—you need the TAB key for that.

Use the up and down arrow keys to move through records. Holding the key down moves the cursor faster in the arrow's direction. Using the OPEN APPLE key in conjunction with the up and down arrow keys takes you through the file still faster by moving a screen at a time. But the fastest way to move through multiple data base records is by using AppleWorks' built-in ruler.

The ruler divides the entire file into eight equal parts and gives you access to any part by using the OPEN APPLE key along with a number from 1 through 9. OPEN APPLE-1 speeds you to the beginning of the file and OPEN APPLE-9 to the end. The exact placement that you achieve by using any of the numbers in between is more difficult to predict. Still, if your file is large, you will probably find that it saves time to use the ruler to get to the approximate vicinity of where you want to go and then use the arrow keys to get to the precise place.

To switch between multiple- and single-record layouts, use OPEN APPLE-Z.

✋ 3.20 Trap: *The main disadvantage of a multiple-record layout is that you do not have access to categories within records not displayed on the screen.*

The following illustration shows the first record of a construction company's personnel data base:

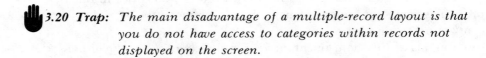

```
File: Personnel              REVIEW/ADD/CHANGE              Escape: Main Menu

Selection: All records


Record 1 of 5
===================================================================================
F. Name: Dustin
L. Name: Rascon
Street: 56 First St.
City: Sonoma
Zip: 94476
Soc.Sec. #: 543-12-7776
Emp. Date: Jan 20 82
Pay Rate: 6/hr.
```

Note that there are eight categories within this data base ranging from F. (First) Name to Pay Rate.

If you switch to the multiple-record display of this same data base, as shown in the following illustration, you can see that only five of these categories fit within the width of the screen.

The Data Base

```
File: Personnel              REVIEW/ADD/CHANGE            Escape: Main Menu

Selection: All records


F. Name        L. Name       Street        City          Zip
=================================================================
Dustin         Rascon        56 First St.  Sonoma        94476
Gabe           Brueske       126 Moss Ave. Santa Rosa    92354
Shannon        Bean          1732 Fox Ave. Petaluma      93456
Earl           Horn          8 Short St.   Cotati        96632
John           Wright        25 Lee Ct.    Kenwood       92236
```

Wouldn't it be nice if you could use the right arrow to move to the off-screen categories? Sorry. This is not possible in AppleWorks. When operating from a multiple-record layout, what you see is what you get.

The only saving grace is that you have some control over what you see. If you look at the multiple-record layout in the previous illustration, you will notice that several columns are wider than they need to be for you to comfortably view the information in them.

If you move from a multiple-record layout in Review/Add/Change to Change Record Layout (OPEN APPLE-L), you can use the OPEN APPLE and left arrow keys to narrow the columns that are excessively wide and thereby bring more categories onto the screen. The following illustration shows that this adjustment brought two more categories into view: Soc. Sec. # and Emp. Date.

```
File: Personnel              REVIEW/ADD/CHANGE            Escape: Main Menu

Selection: All records


F. Name    L. Name    Street        City        Zip     Soc.Sec. #  Emp. Date
==============================================================================
Dustin     Rascon     56 First St.  Sonoma      94476   543-12-7776 Jan 20 82
Gabe       Brueske    126 Moss Ave. Santa Rosa  92354   145-76-8904 Sep 15 85
Shannon    Bean       1732 Fox Ave. Petaluma    93456   556-76-1234 Oct 19 75
Earl       Horn       8 Short St.   Cotati      96632   233-88-5487 Apr 16 81
John       Wright     25 Lee Ct.    Kenwood     92236   029-34-1986 Sep  3 80
```

Unfortunately, the Pay Rate category is still not visible, and it is essential to see in deciding who to use for an upcoming low-budget job. Other categories that are irrelevant in this decision don't need to be visible at this time.

You can sacrifice unwanted categories to gain visibility of the Pay Rate category in three ways. All are achieved from the Change Record Layout screen. The first method involves choosing currently irrelevant categories and narrowing them as much as you can; that is, so that only one character remains visible. The following illustration shows that the F. Name and Emp. Date columns were narrowed, which gained enough room to display the Pay Rate category.

```
File: Personnel              REVIEW/ADD/CHANGE          Escape: Main Menu

Selection: All records


F L. Name      Street          City        Zip     Soc.Sec. # E Pay Rate
==========================================================================
D Rascon       56 First St.    Sonoma      94476   543-12-7776 J 6/hr.
G Brueske      126 Moss Ave.   Santa Rosa  92354   145-76-8904 S 12/hr.
S Bean         1732 Fox Ave.   Petaluma    93456   556-76-1234 O 15/hr.
E Horn         8 Short St.     Cotati      96632   233-88-5487 A 18/hr.
J Wright       25 Lee Ct.      Kenwood     92236   029-34-1986 S 8/hr.
```

You can also move the Pay Rate category from its position as the last column to a position that will place it on screen when you return to a multiple-record layout. You accomplish this move from the Change Record Layout screen (OPEN APPLE-L) by using OPEN APPLE-< to move the Pay Rate category to the left five columns, placing it well within view to the right of the L. Name category, as shown in the following illustration:

```
File: Personnel              REVIEW/ADD/CHANGE          Escape: Main Menu

Selection: All records


F. Name         L. Name        Pay Rate     Street          City
==========================================================================
Dustin          Rascon         6/hr.        56 First St.    Sonoma
Gabe            Brueske        12/hr.        126 Moss Ave.   Santa Rosa
Shannon         Bean           15/hr.        1732 Fox Ave.   Petaluma
Earl            Horn           18/hr.        8 Short St.     Cotati
John            Wright          8/hr.        25 Lee Ct.      Kenwood
```

Finally, you can bring categories that are off screen in Review/Add/Change into an on-screen position by using the Delete command (OPEN APPLE-D) while in Change Record Layout. This command removes categories specified by the position of the cursor at the time the Delete command is issued and places them in Insert a Category. You can access this environment at any time with the Insert command (OPEN APPLE-I), and any categories held there can be reinserted into the lineup in Change Record Layout (this is also reflected in a multiple-record layout of Review/Add/Change).

You can make this feature work in one of two ways when you want to view off-screen categories in a multiple-record layout. One way is to simply go to Change Record Layout (OPEN APPLE-L) and delete categories that are superfluous to your current needs. The space left by these deletions will be filled by the off-screen categories, which you can view on a multiple-record screen. When you don't need to see the newly displayed categories anymore, you can reinsert the banished categories at any time by issuing the Insert command (OPEN APPLE-I).

But suppose you want to exchange the categories currently on screen for categories off screen, thereby at least keeping them all accessible through a single-record layout. You begin the same way, by first deleting the current on-screen categories from Change Record Layout. Next use the right arrow key to move to the right of the data base layout on the Change Record Layout screen. Now you can reposition the deleted categories by issuing the Insert command (OPEN APPLE-I). Placing them in this rightmost position means that they will be off screen in the multiple-record layout, replaced by the categories that moved up to their on-screen positions when they were deleted.

If your data base includes relatively few records, you will probably find it easier to review, edit, and enter category information not available to you in a multiple-record layout by passing through record displays in a single-record layout, where all the categories for a single record are displayed in one screen (see Tip 3.13).

If you are working with a data base containing many records and want to be able to view entries within a certain category in relation to all your data base records, you will find that the adjustments outlined in this Tip are well worth making.

3.21 Trap: *When entering or editing category data in a multiple-record layout, be aware that your entry will be affected by the width of the category column.*

You can change column widths in a multiple-record layout so that they range from 1 to 78 characters. Just press OPEN APPLE-L (you are now in Change Record Layout), and then use the OPEN APPLE in conjunction with the arrow keys to increase or decrease the width of the column that the cursor is on. Once this is done, the ESC key takes you back to a multiple-record layout, where the new column width is displayed.

If you begin typing a long entry into a column that is not wide enough to hold it all, you will hear a beep when you reach the edge. This is a subtle way of telling you that no more characters will be accepted into this column until it is widened.

If you know ahead of time that you will be making long entries into a certain category, it is expedient to widen that column to an appropriate width before you begin the entry procedure or use a single-record layout for that entry.

Sometimes once the entries are made, it is advantageous to shrink the columns back to their original width. This is especially likely if you want to see categories that have been pushed off the screen by a widened column. If you narrow a column to the point at which a large portion of its entry is truncated, the characters that are no longer visible are not erased. You can widen the column at any time and bring the original characters into view.

By the same token, when you make long entries from a single-record layout, although the entire entry will be accepted there, you will find that when you switch to a multiple-record layout, the entry has been clipped to fit within the category column. Again, the nonvisible characters are not lost and can be regained at any time if you widen the column where they are stored.

3.22 Tip: *It is easier to make entries in many records within one category from a multiple-record layout than from a single-record layout.*

Look at the following Book List data base: Of particular concern is the category Avail., which tells whether a book is presently on the library shelves. As you can see, all five books listed are available at this time except Tim May's *No Nonsense*. Availability is a condition that changes often and must be updated frequently.

```
File: Book List              REVIEW/ADD/CHANGE          Escape: Main Menu

Selection: All records


Title                Author              Publisher      Year    Avail.
===============================================================================
No Nonsense          May, Tim            Guidelines     1976    NA
Christopher John     Collins, Mary       Cross          1972    A
Thinking Thrift      Manende, Carmella   Lightfoot      1974    A
Lastest Thing        Brook, Jena         Early          1976    A
Never Slow Down      Burke, Taylor       M & B          1977    A
```

The updating procedure could be conducted from a single-record layout, where a change could be made in each necessary record. This is a time consuming process, however, since you can access only one record at a time, and records that do not need to be changed must be passed through on the way to those that do.

A better course is to make the necessary changes from a multiple-record layout. There you can use the RETURN key to go quickly from record to record within the Avail. category, making changes as you go. Do not forget to press the RETURN key to lock in each change that you make. If you try to move somewhere or initiate an OPEN APPLE command without doing this, you will be reprimanded with a beep. If you press ESC before RETURN, your change will be erased and the original entry reinstated.

Using this method, you will find that you can update category information with a multiple-record layout in about a third of the time it would take from a single-record layout. You also have a wider view of which books are available.

Using Change Record Layout

3.23 *Tip:* *When you are changing the order of categories in a single-record layout, think of the OPEN APPLE and right or left arrow combination as a push-pull machine.*

The following illustration shows a display of Change Record Layout in single-record form with category headings ordered from Food Type through Order Date:

```
File: Food List              CHANGE RECORD LAYOUT    Escape: Review/Add/Change

                    Return or arrows     Move cursor
                    ∂ and arrows         Move category location
================================================================================
Food Type: veg.
Food Name: cabbage
Price: .19
Unit: lb.
Quantity: 25
Order Date: Jun 15
```

The members of the food co-op who use this form have realized that data entry could be speeded up if the single-record layout were designed to match the order forms sent to members.

This means moving quite a few categories around. Place the cursor on the first character of the category to be moved, and then use OPEN APPLE in conjunction with the arrow keys to push that category out of its original position and pull it into a new one.

It is likely that this operation will take several steps, because the new position is probably still occupied by a category that needs replacement before its space can be taken.

The best way to avoid confusion is to first push all the categories to be repositioned over to the right of the original list, as shown in the following illustration:

```
File: Food List              CHANGE RECORD LAYOUT    Escape: Review/Add/Change

                    Return or arrows     Move cursor
                    ∂ and arrows         Move category location
================================================================================
                    Food Type: veg.
                    Food Name: cabbage
                    Price: .19
                    Unit: lb.
                    Quantity: 25
Order Date: Jun 15
```

Then one by one each category can be pulled into its final resting place. The first of the two illustrations that follow shows this final placement half completed; the second depicts the new layout order.

```
File: Food List            CHANGE RECORD LAYOUT      Escape: Review/Add/Change

                    Return or arrows    Move cursor
                    ð and arrows        Move category location
===============================================================================
Food Name: cabbage
Food Type: veg.
Quantity: 25        Price: .19
                    Unit: lb.

Order Date: Jun 15
```

```
File: Food List            CHANGE RECORD LAYOUT      Escape: Review/Add/Change

                    Return or arrows    Move cursor
                    ð and arrows        Move category location
===============================================================================
Food Name: cabbage
Food Type: veg.
Quantity: 25
Unit: lb.
Price: .19
Order Date: Jun 15
```

✋ *3.24 Trap: Do not expect to be able to move up and down within data base records when you are changing a multiple-record display in Change Record Layout.*

When you move to Change Record Layout from a multiple-record layout, you will see a screen similar to the one in the following illustration.

```
File: Food List              CHANGE RECORD LAYOUT       Escape: Review/Add/Change



===================================================================================
                  --> or <--    Move cursor
                    >  a  <      Switch category positions
                  --> a <--      Change column width
                    a-D          Delete this category
                    a-I          Insert a previously deleted category

----------------------------------------------------------------------------------

Food Type       Food Name       Price       Unit        Quantity  Order Date
------------    -------------   ---------   ----------   --------- ------------
veg.            cabbage          .19         lb.          25        Jun 15
Fruit           Orange           .49         lb.          50        Jun 7
veg.            mushrooms        1.19        lb.          18        Jun 21 85


-------------------------------------------------------------------- More --->
Use options shown above to change record layout              14K Avail.
```

Though you can see the first few records of the data base on the screen, you will notice that the cursor remains on the line displaying category headings. Anytime that you attempt to move down through the data base records, you will hear a beep.

Although you can use the right and left arrow keys, you will find that they make the cursor jump from column to column and do not offer access to any characters in the category heading line that they travel on. Thus, you cannot make changes to category headings (but you can do this from Change Name Category) or entries from Change Record Layout (but you can do this from Review/Add/ Change).

You can, however, use the right and left arrow keys to move back and forth through categories and change column widths as you go by pressing the OPEN APPLE key in conjunction with either the right arrow key (to widen) or the left arrow key (to narrow). Note that in this mode you can access off-screen categories denied to you in Review/Add/Change.

Besides being able to delete categories (OPEN APPLE-D) and reinsert them (OPEN APPLE-I), you can move an entire category to a new column position by specifying it with the cursor and using the OPEN APPLE key in conjunction with either the right or left arrow key to point it in the right direction, column by column.

3.25 Tip: *The Delete and Insert commands work like magic in Change Record Layout.*

The Delete command (OPEN APPLE-D) performs a marvelous disappearing act in all data base format areas. But it deserves the most applause for the additional reappearing feat it achieves in Change Record Layout.

The position of the cursor at the time that the Delete command is initiated serves as a pointer that specifies where the deletion will occur. In Change Record Layout the cursor can only travel from category to category, never leaving the category heading line to venture into the records themselves.

Under these restrictions, any deletions that are specified apply to the entire category (and all its entries) specified by the cursor. Thus, pressing OPEN APPLE-D in Change Record Layout eliminates a whole category and repositions the remaining categories to fill the resulting gap.

The following illustration shows the Change Record Layout of a children's book data base kept by a librarian:

```
File: Book List           CHANGE RECORD LAYOUT      Escape: Review/Add/Change



================================================================================
              --> or <--  Move cursor
                >  ⌂  <   Switch category positions
              --> ⌂ <--   Change column width
              ⌂-D         Delete this category
              ⌂-I         Insert a previously deleted category

    --------------------------------------------------------------------
    Title                Author               Publisher        Year     Avail.
    --------------------  --------------------  ---------------  --------  ---------
    No Nonsense          May, Tim             Guidelines       1976      NA
    Christopher John     Collins, Mary        Cross            1972      A
    Thinking Thrift      Manende, Carmella    Lightfoot        1974      A

    ------------------------------------------------------------- More --->
    Use options shown above to change record layout              52K Avail.
```

For her current purposes, the librarian does not need to know the publisher or the year that the books were published. She can just move the cursor to the Publisher category using the right arrow key and press OPEN APPLE-D. Instantly, the entire Publisher category disappears, and the next category to the right, Year, moves up to take its place. If she uses the Delete command again, the Year category will disappear as well, leaving her with the layout depicted in the illustration that follows.

```
File: Book List          CHANGE RECORD LAYOUT    Escape: Review/Add/Change




==========================================================================
             --) or <--  Move cursor
              >  @  <     Switch category positions
             --) @ <--    Change column width
              @-D         Delete this category
              @-I         Insert a previously deleted category

-------------------------------------------------------------------------

Title                   Author              Avail.      M
-------------------     ------------------  ----------- A
No Nonsense             May, Tim            NA          R
Christopher John        Collins, Mary       A           G
Thinking Thrift         Manende, Carmella   A           I
                                                        N
-------------------------------------------------------------------------
Use options shown above to change record layout           52K Avail.
```

Pressing ESC twice gets the librarian back to a multiple-record layout in Review/Add/Change, where she can see the deletions just made in Change Record Layout reflected, as shown in the following illustration:

```
File: Book List          REVIEW/ADD/CHANGE        Escape: Main Menu

Selection: All records


Title                   Author              Avail.
==========================================================================
No Nonsense             May, Tim            NA
Christopher John        Collins, Mary       A
Thinking Thrift         Manende, Carmelia   A
Lastest Thing           Brook, Jena         A
Never Slow Down         Burke, Taylor       A
```

Later, when she is ordering new books, she realizes that it is important to know the publisher and year of publication. No problem. The Insert command (OPEN APPLE-I) can bring those categories back in a minute. Not only that, but it can place them in any new position.

Once back in Change Record Layout, she places the cursor on the category that she wants to the right of the inserted category, and she presses OPEN APPLE-I. The screen switches to Insert a Category (shown in the following illustration) and presents a list of all the categories that were previously deleted, allowing the librarian to choose which one to reinsert.

```
File: Book List              INSERT A CATEGORY   Escape: Change record layout


===========================================================================
  1.  Publisher
  2.  Year
```

She chooses Year and presses RETURN; then she gives the Insert command again
and chooses Publisher to complete the insertions.

As you can see in the following illustration, the reinserted categories have a
new spot in the category layout:

```
File: Book List              CHANGE RECORD LAYOUT   Escape: Review/Add/Change



===========================================================================
            --> or <--   Move cursor
              >  ∂  <     Switch category positions
            -->  ∂  <--   Change column width
              ∂-D         Delete this category
              ∂-I         Insert a previously deleted category


--------------------------------------------------------------------------
Publisher     Year         Title              Author              Av
-----------   ----------   ----------------   --------------      --
Guidelines    1976         No Nonsense        May, Tim            NA
Cross         1972         Christopher John   Collins, Mary       A
Lightfoot     1974         Thinking Thrift    Manende, Carmella   A
- --------------------------------------------------------- More --->
Use options shown above to change record layout       52K Avail.
```

This happened because the librarian gave the Insert command while the cursor
was on the Title category. By doing this she told AppleWorks, "The category I
specify should be reinserted to the left of this category."

Since she wanted the final layout order to have the Publisher category in the
far left position followed by Year, Title, and so on, she inserted the Year category
first, which placed it to the left of Title. The cursor, formerly on the Title category, went to the newly inserted Year category, which usurped Title's position.
Since the librarian wants the next inserted category (Publisher) to the left of the
Year category, she does not have to reposition the cursor before using OPEN APPLE-
I to get to Insert a Category. Once there, she presses RETURN to specify the insertion of the last remaining category.

Data Base Commands

 3.26 Tip: *The Delete and Insert commands affect both multiple- and single-record layout displays no matter which layout you enter the command from.*

If you are in a single-record layout, the Delete command (OPEN APPLE-D) erases the record that is on the screen at the time the command is issued. This erasure, though carried out in a single-record layout, also affects the multiple-record display.

If you are in a multiple-record layout when you issue this command, the record that the cursor was pointing to when you pressed OPEN APPLE-D will be highlighted. You can delete this single record by pressing RETURN, or you can use the arrow keys to highlight any number of records contiguous to it and then press RETURN to erase them all. Again, any records that you delete from a multiple-record layout will also disappear from single-record display.

Deleting records from either of these formats erases them from Change Record Layout as well. This deletion is irreversible, so don't expect to be able to reinsert deleted records later, as you can with deleted categories when you are in Change Record Layout.

When you are in either layout of Review/Add/Change (single- or multiple-record) the Insert command (OPEN APPLE-I) serves only to insert a new record, not replace formerly deleted ones.

If you issue the Insert command from a single-record layout, the new record will be inserted before the record that was on screen at the time the command was given. If you issue it from a multiple-record layout, the new record will be inserted before the record that the cursor was on when OPEN APPLE-I was used.

Whether you insert from a multiple- or single-record layout, you will be sent to the Insert New Records screen to enter the new record information.

```
File: Food List              INSERT NEW RECORDS      Escape: Review/Add/Change


Record 1 of 6
=================================================================================
Food Name: -
Food Type: -
Quantity: -
Unit: -
Price: -
Order Date: -
```

AppleWorks Tips and Traps

Once done, you have an opportunity to insert any number of additional records or use the ESC key to get back to the layout where the Insert command was initiated. From there you can see that the new records have been integrated into the data base.

3.27 Tip: *When you want to delete a series of records that are not adjacent in the data base, set up a record selection rule that will extract the desired records so that you can carry out the deletion quickly.*

The following illustration shows part of a food co-op's Food List data base. The records are arranged in the random order in which they were entered.

```
File: Food List              REVIEW/ADD/CHANGE            Escape: Main Menu

Selection: All records


Food Type        Food Name        Price    Unit     Quantity  Order Date
===========================================================================
bev.             Ap. juice        2.00     gal.     10        May 85
bev.             Ap.-Straw. juice 2.00     gal.     12        May 85
veg.             cabbage          .19      lb.      25        Jun 15
cheese           Edam             2.79     lb.      12        Jun 10 85
bev.             Grpfrt. juice    2.00     gal.     6         May 85
veg.             mushrooms        1.19     lb.      18        Jun 21 85
Fruit            Oranges          .49      lb.      50        Jun  7
bev.             Rasp.-Ap.juice   2.00     gal.     6         May 85
```

The co-op coordinator has just received a call from the juice supplier saying that they are changing warehouses and will not be filling juice orders for the next two months. In order to update the data base, all juice records must be deleted. Since there is only one instance where juice records are in adjacent positions, this would mean issuing the Delete command (OPEN APPLE-D) three times.

Although this would not be a problem in a small data base like this, it could entail a great deal more work in a large data base in which records are spread out. Luckily, AppleWorks' Record Selection feature offers the perfect solution to this problem. Try it on the co-op Food List.

Give the Record Selection command (OPEN APPLE-R) from a multiple-record layout. This takes you to the following Select Records screen.

```
File: Food List            SELECT RECORDS       Escape: Review/Add/Change
Selection:

================================================================================
  1.  Food Type
  2.  Food Name
  3.  Price
  4.  Unit
  5.  Quantity
  6.  Order Date
```

Press RETURN while the cursor is on category one, Food Type, indicating that you want to select records according to the entries in that category.

Once this selection is made, you are presented with options that help you focus on specific records in the Food Type category, as follows:

```
File: Food List            SELECT RECORDS       Escape: Review/Add/Change
Selection: Food Type

================================================================================
  1.  equals
  2.  is greater than
  3.  is less than
  4.  is not equal to
  5.  is blank
  6.  is not blank
  7.  contains
  8.  begins with
  9.  ends with
 10.  does not contain
 11.  does not begin with
 12.  does not end with
```

Since you want to extract all bev. entries in Food Type, choose option 8, "begins with," and then press B when you are asked to "Type comparison information."

Next, a screen displaying the choices "and," "or," or "through," gives you the opportunity to hone the selection criteria even further. In this case, all records in Food Type that begin with *B* will give you exactly what you want, so indicate that your rule is complete by pressing ESC. Presto— all bev. records are displayed on the Review/Add/Change screen, as the following illustration shows.

```
File: Food List                  REVIEW/ADD/CHANGE              Escape: Main Menu

Selection: Food Type begins with B


Food Type      Food Name        Price      Unit      Quantity  Order Date
==============================================================================
bev.           Ap. juice        2.00       gal.      10        May 85
bev.           Ap.-Straw. juice 2.00       gal.      12        May 85
bev.           Grpfrt. juice    2.00       gal.      8         May 85
bev.           Rasp.-Ap.juice   2.00       gal.      6         May 85
```

Now you can carry out the deletion in a few short steps. First, press OPEN APPLE-D, and use the cursor to highlight all records on the screen (OPEN APPLE-9 does this in one step). With one press of the RETURN key, the bev. records are deleted, and you are placed back in Review/Add/Change, where the data base is displayed minus the deleted records.

```
File: Food List                  REVIEW/ADD/CHANGE              Escape: Main Menu

Selection: All records


Food Type      Food Name        Price      Unit      Quantity  Order Date
==============================================================================
veg.           cabbage          .19        1b.       25        Jun 15
cheese         Edam             2.79       1b.       12        Jun 10 85
veg.           mushrooms        1.19       1b.       18        Jun 21 85
Fruit          Oranges          .49        1b.       50        Jun 7
```

The Find Command can also be used to extract records for deletion, although the simple criteria it offers is more limiting than record selection rules.

3.28 Trap: *AppleWorks always leaves one record in the data base, even if you instruct it to delete all the records.*

Suppose you are setting up a personnel file with employee names, addresses, and phone and Social Security numbers. You have gotten through ten names when you discover that you are working off an old list and have entered the names of employees who no longer work at your company.

All you can do is delete all the erroneous records and begin again with the correct list. You go to the first record in a multiple-record layout, give the Delete command (OPEN APPLE-D) and press OPEN APPLE-9 to specify that you want all records in the file erased. But when you press RETURN, you see that although the other records have been deleted, the first one is still there. No matter how many times you try to delete the last record, it hangs on with tenacious determination.

You have several alternatives. You can use the Insert command (OPEN APPLE-I) to add a blank record above the remaining record and then delete the offender, leaving only the blank record, which can be filled with new information. You can replace the old information with the new by typing directly over it in either the single- or multiple-record layout. Or you can temporarily ignore it, enter the new data, and delete it anytime your data base is filled beyond the one-record-minimum mark.

Of course, if you had followed Tip 3.06 and included a blank record at the end when you first created the data base, you never would have had this problem.

 3.29 Trap: *You won't be able to insert a record past the end of a file.*

There's another reason to follow Tip 3.06 and include a blank record at the end of a data base when you create it. Without this placeholder, you will not be able to move the cursor beyond the last data base record, a restriction that is especially inhibiting when you want to insert new records at the end of the data base.

The Insert command (OPEN APPLE-I) places the new records it inserts above the cursor position when the command is given. If the cursor cannot go beyond the last full record in the file, the inserted record cannot be placed after the last record.

If you were unaware of the need to keep an empty record at the end of a data base and need to add records beyond the last current one, you can solve the problem with the following procedure.

Begin from a single-record layout (OPEN APPLE-Z gets you there if you are in a multiple-record layout), and use the OPEN APPLE and down arrow combination to get past all the records in the data base. When you get past the last record, you will see the following message:

```
        You are now past the last record
        of your file and can now start
        typing new records at the end.

----------------------------------------------------------------
Do you really want to do this?  No  Yes
```

Choose Yes (just press the Y key), and you will be presented with the following Insert New Records screen:

```
File: Food List           INSERT NEW RECORDS     Escape: Review/Add/Change


Record 5 of 5
================================================================
Food Type: —
Food Name: —
Price: —
Unit: —
Quantity: —
Order Date: —
```

```
File: Book List            REVIEW/ADD/CHANGE          Escape: Main Menu

Selection: All records


Author            Title              Publisher       Year
==============================================================================
May, Tim          No Nonsense        Guidelines      1976
Collins, Mary     Christopher John   Cross           1972
Manende, Carmella Thinking Thrift    Lightfoot       1974
Brook, Jena       Lastest Thing      Early           1976
Burke, Taylor     Never Slow Down    M & B           1977
```

Figure 3-4.   Book List data base

Entering data into the categories displayed in this screen creates a new record at the end of the data base. When this record is completed, you can repeat the procedure to add as many new records as you like.

3.30 Tip: *The Copy command can be a time saver when you are entering records that have a lot of category information in common.*

Figure 3-4 shows the childrens' Book List data base discussed earlier in the chapter. Figure 3-5 shows a list of new Tim May books that need to be added to the Book List file.

The author and the publisher are the same for all the books to be added to this list. Because you already have one record in the file with this author and publisher, you can avoid having to enter the information again by copying the existing record three times (the number of new records that you have to enter). The following illustration shows the Book List file with four copies of the original Tim May record:

```
File: Book List            REVIEW/ADD/CHANGE          Escape: Main Menu
Selection: All records


Author            Title              Publisher       Year
==============================================================================
May, Tim          No Nonsense        Guidelines      1976
May, Tim          No Nonsense        Guidelines      1976
May, Tim          No Nonsense        Guidelines      1976
May, Tim          No Nonsense        Guidelines      1976
Collins, Mary     Christopher John   Cross           1972
Manende, Carmella Thinking Thrift    Lightfoot       1974
Brook, Jena       Lastest Thing      Early           1976
Burke, Taylor     Never Slow Down    M & B           1977
```

The Data Base

```
Memo to: Children's librarian, Rose Valley branch



Please add the following Tim May books (all published by
Guidelines Publishing) to your Book List file.


1. Your Esteem is My Esteem, 1979

2. Miss Cue Reads On, 1980

3. Footnote One, Footnote Two, 1982
```

Figure 3-5.   Books to be added to the Book List data base

Next, replace the erroneous entries in the Title and Year categories with the correct information from the memo shown in Figure 3-5. The best way is to move to the appropriate category, erase the old entry by pressing CONTROL-Y, and then enter the new information.

The first of the following two illustrations shows this operation partially completed. In the second illustration, you can see the completed file with the necessary entries reshaped to match the list in the memo.

```
File: Book List            REVIEW/ADD/CHANGE            Escape: Main Menu

Selection: All records


Author               Title                  Publisher       Year
==================================================================================
May, Tim             No Nonsense            Guidelines      1976
May, Tim             Your Esteem is My Esteem  Guidelines   1979
May, Tim             Miss Cue Reads On      Guidelines      1980
May, Tim             No Nonsense            Guidelines      1976
Collins, Mary        Christopher John       Cross           1972
Manende, Carmella    Thinking Thrift        Lightfoot       1974
Brook, Jena          Lastest Thing          Early           1976
Burke, Taylor        Never Slow Down        M & B           1977
```

```
File: Book List              REVIEW/ADD/CHANGE           Escape: Main Menu
Selection: All records


Author               Title                      Publisher       Year
======================================================================
May, Tim             No Nonsense                Guidelines      1976
May, Tim             Your Esteem is My Esteem   Guidelines      1979
May, Tim             Miss Cue Reads On          Guidelines      1980
May, Tim             Footnote One, Footnote Two Guidelines      1982
Collins, Mary        Christopher John           Cross           1972
Manende, Carmella    Thinking Thrift            Lightfoot       1974
Brook, Jena          Lastest Thing              Early           1976
Burke, Taylor        Never Slow Down            M & B           1977
```

 3.31 Trap: *The only way to copy a group of two or more records in one operation is to use the Clipboard.*

If you want to copy a group of adjacent records from one part of a data base to another, you have to issue the Copy command (OPEN APPLE-C) and choose "To Clipboard (cut)." Use the cursor to highlight the records that you want copied, and press RETURN. The specified records are placed in the Clipboard and will remain there until you copy or move other records to the Clipboard or move them from the Clipboard with OPEN APPLE-M. To achieve this, place the cursor on the record just below the line where you want the records in the Clipboard to be repositioned (pasted). Then press OPEN APPLE-M and choose "From Clipboard (paste)." The copied records instantly appear in the spot that you specified for them.

If you want to make copies of several groups of records that are not contiguous, you must perform the procedure described above for every group of adjacent records that you want copied.

The procedure for making one or more copies of a single record within a file is more straightforward. Just press OPEN APPLE-C and choose "Current Record." Then specify the number of copies you want. When you press RETURN, the current record will be duplicated the number of times that you specified. Be aware that this duplication is in addition to the original record, so if you want to end up with four copies, for instance, make sure to note that the current record should be copied only three times.

You can make copies of the current record from a multiple- or single-record layout, but only a multiple-record layout gives you the access to the Clipboard that is necessary to carry out a copy on a group of adjacent records in one operation.

You can also make copies of single records by first copying to the Clipboard and then pasting from the Clipboard. The only time this is an advantage over the simpler copy of the current record is when you want the copy to be placed in a different spot when it is pasted back into the other records.

3.32 Tip: *AppleWorks' Ditto command (OPEN APPLE-″) lets you copy single-category entries from one record to another.*

Tip 3.30 explained a trick for using the Copy command to add records to a data base that had quite a bit of category information in common.

Look again at the original file in Figure 3-4. As you recall, the librarian's task is to add the books listed in the memo shown in Figure 3-5. With Apple-Work's Ditto command, you can accomplish this without having to re-enter any information that the new records have in common with the Tim May record already listed in the file.

The first step is to insert three blank records below the record you want to ditto (*No Nonsense* by Tim May). Move the cursor to the second record in the file (Christopher John) and give the Insert command (OPEN APPLE-I). The cursor immediately moves to the Insert New Records screen.

From there, you create a blank record each time you press the OPEN APPLE and down arrow key combination. Since you want three blank records, do it three times, and then press ESC to get back to Review/Add/Change, where you will see the three blank records just where you wanted them:

```
File: Book List            REVIEW/ADD/CHANGE           Escape: Main Menu

Selection: All records


Author            Title            Publisher     Year
=================================================================
May, Tim          No Nonsense      Guidelines    1976
-                 -                -             -
-                 -                -             -
-                 -                -             -
Collins, Mary     Christopher John Cross         1972
Manende, Carmella Thinking Thrift  Lightfoot     1974
Brook, Jena       Lastest Thing    Early         1976
Burke, Taylor     Never Slow Down  M & B         1977
```

Now you are ready to put the Ditto command to work. Position the cursor in the Author category, just below the entry that you want to ditto (May, Tim), and press OPEN APPLE-″. Like magic, the entry from the above category is duplicated in the second record, and the cursor moves down to the next record within the Author category.

Use the Ditto command two more times, filling all three blank entries in the Author category with May, Tim.

```
File: Book List              REVIEW/ADD/CHANGE          Escape: Main Menu

Selection: All records


Author               Title               Publisher      Year
===================================================================================
May, Tim             No Nonsense         Guidelines     1976
May, Tim             -                   -              -
May, Tim             -                   -              -
May, Tim             -                   -              -
Collins, Mary        Christopher John    Cross          1972
Manende, Carmella    Thinking Thrift     Lightfoot      1974
Brook, Jena          Lastest Thing       Early          1976
Burke, Taylor        Never Slow Down     M & B          1977
```

Then tab over to the Publisher category, and repeat the same procedure until the blank entries in this category are replaced with Guidelines.

```
File: Book List              REVIEW/ADD/CHANGE          Escape: Main Menu

Selection: All records


Author               Title               Publisher      Year
===================================================================================
May, Tim             No Nonsense         Guidelines     1976
May, Tim             -                   Guidelines     -
May, Tim             -                   Guidelines     -
May, Tim             -                   Guidelines     -
Collins, Mary        Christopher John    Cross          1972
Manende, Carmella    Thinking Thrift     Lightfoot      1974
Brook, Jena          Lastest Thing       Early          1976
Burke, Taylor        Never Slow Down     M & B          1977
```

Now type in the appropriate entries for Title and Year.

One note of caution when you are using the Ditto command: If you issue it from a category entry that is not blank, it will erase the information that was entered there and replace it with the data copied from the record above. Sometimes this is exactly what you want to happen. But if it is not, be sure to insert blank records before using the command.

✊ *3.33 Trap: The Move command only works when you are in a multiple-record layout.*

The only way to move records from one position in a data base to another is to use the Clipboard as a sort of intermediate transfer station. Since you do not have access to the Clipboard from a single-record layout, the Move command can only be issued from a multiple-record display.

As with the other commands, the cursor position at the time the command is issued indicates which record(s) will be moved. Once you move to this position and issue the command (OPEN APPLE-M), you can highlight adjacent records to be moved by moving the cursor up or down from its original point. When you press RETURN, you must choose "To Clipboard (cut)" — just press T. This removes the records that you highlighted from the file and sends them to the Clipboard.

Now you can move to the new position in the file where you want the transitory records to return. From there, give the Move command again, and choose "From Clipboard (paste)" — press F. Your original records will be pasted back into the file in the new position indicated.

As with the Copy command, the Move command works on groups of records only when they are adjacent to each other. The only way to get around this is to use the Find command (OPEN APPLE-F) or Record Selection command (OPEN APPLE-R) to extract certain records from the file and then move them to the Clipboard and back again to a new position. See Tip 3.27 for a thorough explanation.

3.34 Tip: *AppleWorks' Arrange command (OPEN APPLE-A) enables you to rearrange the order in which records are listed.*

The category in which the cursor is positioned when you press OPEN APPLE-A is the category that AppleWorks will evaluate when it is assigning the arrange criteria that you specify. The criteria options are presented as soon as you issue the Arrange command.

```
File: Sales              ARRANGE (SORT)       Escape: Review/Add/Change

Selection: All records


==============================================================================

                    This file will be arranged on
                    this category: Total Sales

                    Arrangement order:

                        1.  From A to Z
                        2.  From Z to A
                        3.  From 0 to 9
                        4.  From 9 to 0
```

If you use the Arrange command on a Date category, you choose your criteria from a slightly different screen, which also includes a chronological sort option.

Once you lock in one of these choices with the RETURN key, you are returned to the Review/Add/Change screen where you began (either multiple- or single-record layout) and are presented with a new arrangement of data base records according to your specifications.

This versatile feature allows you to group and regroup records in the data base file according to your current needs.

✋ *3.35 Trap: Be aware of the order of precedence that AppleWorks applies to all characters, or you may get results that you don't expect when you rearrange records.*

To arrange data base records in a certain order, AppleWorks must have a system for rating the value of each entry in the sort category. In an ascending sort, alphabetical entries are evaluated from *A* to *Z* (uppercase and lowercase letters have the same value) and numeric entries from 0 to 9.

To find out the order of precedence assigned to characters that fall outside the range of alphabetical or numeric, refer to the list on page 72 of the *AppleWorks Reference Manual*.

In most circumstances, you will not need to include special characters in data base entries. But there may be times when a space at the beginning of a category entry can change the order of an entire sort, either on purpose or by accident.

If you have any blank records in data base (as suggested in Tip 3.06) an ascending sort will place them at the top of the list of records. This can be quite frustrating if the reason for including a blank record was to provide an accessible spot at the end of the data base. Tip 3.06 also suggests a solution to this problem.

✋ *3.36 Trap: You can't arrange (sort) records by more than one category at a time with AppleWorks.*

Suppose that the following illustration shows a data base of people who have asked to be on the waiting list for the preschool that you manage.

```
File: Waiting List              REVIEW/ADD/CHANGE              Escape: Main Menu

Selection: All records


Child's Name        Child's Age Girl/Boy  Date       Parent's Name      Phone Num
================================================================================
Close, Karen        3           G         Jun  7 85  Close, Kay         255-3456
Durney, Lewellyn    4           G         Mar 16 85  Durney, Carol      255-7664
Kortum, Julie       4           G         Feb  9 85  Kortum, Bill       254-5544
Likong, Alfonso     4           B         Jun  6 85  Likong, Richard    255-9962
Lyons, Tony         3           B         Dec 13 84  Lyons, Tami        255-8312
Meyers, Robin       3           B         Jul 14 85  Meyer, Ken         254-6678
Randolph, Missy     4           G         Apr  7 85  Newhauser, Sue     255-1145
Walker, Brenda      4           G         Apr 18 85  Fenelli, Julia     256-3034
```

An opening has just come up for a four-year-old girl, and you want to offer the position to the child whose name has been on the list longest.

It would be helpful to rearrange the records of all the girls according to age and, within age, according to the date they were added to the waiting list.

In some programs you can accomplish such a three-pronged sort by specifying primary, secondary, and tertiary sort criteria that the program then carries out in one operation. Although AppleWorks' Arrange command does not offer this level of sophistication, you can achieve the same results by repeating the command several times.

Let's begin with the previous data base illustration and take it step by step. The data base records in the Waiting List file are arranged in alphabetical order according to Child's Name. Since you are looking for four-year-old girls and the date they were added to the list, the current order is meaningless.

When you are planning more than one sort, it is best to start by sorting within the category that has the most variables, in this case the Date category. To accomplish this, you use the TAB key to move to the Date category (TAB moves you to the right category by category, and OPEN APPLE-TAB moves you to the left). Once there, you issue the Arrange command (OPEN APPLE-A) and are presented with the options for arrangement order. When you choose option 5, "Chronological," you are placed back into the newly arranged data base as shown in the following illustration:

```
File: Waiting List              REVIEW/ADD/CHANGE              Escape: Main Menu

Selection: All records


Child's Name        Child's Age Girl/Boy  Date       Parent's Name      Phone Num
================================================================================
Lyons, Tony         3           B         Dec 13 84  Lyons, Tami        255-8312
Kortum, Julie       4           G         Feb  9 85  Kortum, Bill       254-5544
Durney, Lewellyn    4           G         Mar 16 85  Durney, Carol      255-7664
Randolph, Missy     4           G         Apr  7 85  Newhauser, Sue     255-1145
Walker, Brenda      4           G         Apr 18 85  Fenelli, Julia     256-3034
Likong, Alfonso     4           B         Jun  6 85  Likong, Richard    255-9962
Close, Karen        3           G         Jun  7 85  Close, Kay         255-3456
Meyers, Robin       3           B         Jul 14 85  Meyer, Ken         254-6678
```

The next step is to move to the category Child's Age, and press OPEN APPLE-A to access the arrange options. By choosing option 3, 0 to 9, you will find yourself back in Review/Add/Change with the records arranged as shown in the following illustration:

```
File: Waiting List          REVIEW/ADD/CHANGE          Escape: Main Menu

Selection: All records


Child's Name      Child's Age Girl/Boy  Date      Parent's Name    Phone Num
============================================================================
Lyons, Tony       3           B         Dec 13 84 Lyons, Tami      255-8312
Close, Karen      3           G         Jun  7 85 Close, Kay       255-3456
Meyers, Robin     3           B         Jul 14 85 Meyer, Ken       254-6678
Kortum, Julie     4           G         Feb  9 85 Kortum, Bill     254-5544
Durney, Lewellyn  4           G         Mar 16 85 Durney, Carol    255-7664
Randolph, Missy   4           G         Apr  7 85 Newhauser, Sue   255-1145
Walker, Brenda    4           G         Apr 18 85 Fenelli, Julia   256-3034
Likong, Alfonso   4           B         Jun  6 85 Likong, Richard  255-9962
```

At this point the records show four-year-olds distinguished from three-year-olds, and they are ordered by date.

For the final refinement, move to the last category to be sorted: Girl/Boy. Choosing an alphabetical sort, from A to Z, gives you the result you want, as shown in the following example:

```
File: Waiting List          REVIEW/ADD/CHANGE          Escape: Main Menu

Selection: All records


Child's Name      Child's Age Girl/Boy  Date      Parent's Name    Phone Num
============================================================================
Lyons, Tony       3           B         Dec 13 84 Lyons, Tami      255-8312
Meyers, Robin     3           B         Jul 14 85 Meyer, Ken       254-6678
Likong, Alfonso   4           B         Jun  6 85 Likong, Richard  255-9962
Close, Karen      3           G         Jun  7 85 Close, Kay       255-3456
Kortum, Julie     4           G         Feb  9 85 Kortum, Bill     254-5544
Durney, Lewellyn  4           G         Mar 16 85 Durney, Carol    255-7664
Randolph, Missy   4           G         Apr  7 85 Newhauser, Sue   255-1145
Walker, Brenda    4           G         Apr 18 85 Fenelli, Julia   256-3034
```

It is obvious from this illustration that the preschool position should be offered to Julie Kortum, the four-year-old girl who was the first to be placed on the waiting list.

3.37 Tip: *With AppleWorks' Record Selection command (OPEN APPLE-R), you can extract groups of records that are related in specific ways.*

Tip 3.36 used the Arrange command to sort a preschool waiting list so that four-year-old girls were grouped and arranged in order of the date they were added to the list. You can achieve this same result if you set up record selection rules that extract all the records of four-year-old girls from the rest of the data base records.

Here's how to create these rules. First press OPEN APPLE-R and choose the first category where you will assign criteria. The following illustration shows the list of categories:

```
File: Waiting List          SELECT RECORDS        Escape: Review/Add/Change

Selection:


=============================================================================
  1.  Child's Name
  2.  Child's Age
  3.  Girl/Boy
  4.  Date
  5.  Parent's Name
  6.  Phone Number
```

If you choose Child's Age, you are presented with a list of logical qualifiers:

```
File: Waiting List          SELECT RECORDS        Escape: Review/Add/Change

Selection: Child's Age


=============================================================================
  1.  equals
  2.  is greater than
  3.  is less than
  4.  is not equal to
  5.  is blank
  6.  is not blank
  7.  contains
  8.  begins with
  9.  ends with
 10.  does not contain
 11.  does not begin with
 12.  does not end with
```

Now you want to specify that Child's Age should equal 4, so you choose "equals" from the list and enter the number 4 when you are asked to type comparison information.

That takes care of one criterion. Since you still have one more rule to specify, choose "and" from the three options (and, or, through) presented next. This sends you back through the cycle started in the first illustration in this Tip. This time choose the third category, Girl/Boy, and "equals" again from the list of logical qualifiers. You want all the records selected to equal G in the Girl/Boy column, so enter a *G* this time when you are asked for comparison information.

You can repeat the cycle one more time, but in this case you have made all the necessary selection specifications. Press ESC to get to the following screen:

```
File: Waiting List          REVIEW/ADD/CHANGE           Escape: Main Menu

Selection: Child's Age equals 4
   and      Girl/Boy equals G

Child's Name        Child's Age Girl/Boy  Date     Parent's Name     Phone Num
================================================================================
Durney, Lewellyn    4           G         Mar 16 85  Durney, Carol    255-7664
Kortum, Julie       4           G         Feb  9 85  Kortum, Bill     254-5544
Randolph, Missy     4           G         Apr  7 85  Newhauser, Sue   255-1145
Walker, Brenda      4           G         Apr 18 85  Fenelli, Julia   256-3034
```

As the message in the upper-left corner under File indicates, this selection was made based on "Child's Age equals 4 and Girl/Boy equals G."

This is a neat trick, but we still do not have the records ordered according to when they were added to the waiting list. Our old friend, the Arrange command, can take care of that in no time. Just tab over to the date category, press OPEN APPLE-A, and choose "Chronological" from the menu of choices presented. You are back to the selected records with the list of four-year-old girls arranged by date:

```
File: Waiting List          REVIEW/ADD/CHANGE           Escape: Main Menu

Selection: Child's Age equals 4
   and      Girl/Boy equals G

Child's Name        Child's Age Girl/Boy  Date     Parent's Name     Phone Num
================================================================================
Kortum, Julie       4           G         Feb  9 85  Kortum, Bill     254-5544
Durney, Lewellyn    4           G         Mar 16 85  Durney, Carol    255-7664
Randolph, Missy     4           G         Apr  7 85  Newhauser, Sue   255-1145
Walker, Brenda      4           G         Apr 18 85  Fenelli, Julia   256-3034
```

To get back the complete data base from the screen of selected records, press OPEN APPLE-R again, and choose Yes when asked if you want to select all records. You are now viewing a screen of the entire Waiting List file:

```
File: Waiting List          REVIEW/ADD/CHANGE           Escape: Main Menu

Selection: All records


Child's Name        Child's Age Girl/Boy  Date     Parent's Name     Phone Num
================================================================================
Lyons, Tony         3           B         Dec 13 84  Lyons, Tami      255-8312
Kortum, Julie       4           G         Feb  9 85  Kortum, Bill     254-5544
Durney, Lewellyn    4           G         Mar 16 85  Durney, Carol    255-7664
Randolph, Missy     4           G         Apr  7 85  Newhauser, Sue   255-1145
Walker, Brenda      4           G         Apr 18 85  Fenelli, Julia   256-3034
Likong, Alfonso     4           B         Jun  6 85  Likong, Richard  255-9962
Close, Karen        3           G         Jun  7 85  Close, Kay       255-3456
Meyers, Robin       3           B         Jul 14 85  Meyer, Ken       254-6678
```

As you can see, the records are arranged chronologically. This is because the last command that you gave was a chronological sort on the Date category. Although at the time you saw the results of this sort carried out on the selected records that you were viewing, it affected the entire data base.

When using record selection rules, be sure to consider the logical qualifier that best suits your need for each specific case. You will often see several ways to use the qualifiers and yet achieve the same results.

3.38 Tip: *Use the Find command when you want to find all records*
that match the conditions that you specify.

The Find command works much as the Record Selection command does in that it extracts records based on a criterion that you specify. However, the Find command is much more limiting than the Record Selection command, because you can have only one qualifier when you are making this specification, and you cannot choose what the qualifier will be.

The following screen is where OPEN APPLE-F leads you:

```
File: Waiting List          FIND RECORDS        Escape: Review/Add/Change
Find all records that contain


==========================================================================



----------------------------------------------------------------------
Type comparison information:                          14K Avail.
```

The automatic qualifier, "contain," that this command assigns to all the records it finds is shown below the file name in the upper-left corner of the screen. You can type in comparison information, to make the command find all records that contain a certain number or group of numbers, or a certain letter or group of letters.

At the same time that the Find command limits your choice of qualifying selectors, it expands the area that it searches for criterion matches. The find search is not category specific as in the record selection search. Each category is searched for matching criteria, and all records that contain a match in any category are extracted. Thus, if you search a sales data base for records that contain 24, it might find one record with a July 24 date of sale, another with a quantity order of 24, and still another with a price of $240.

You will find instances when this kind of search locates just what you need. At other times a situation calls for the more specific qualifiers available by using record selection. Being aware of each command's specific abilities tunes you in to the appropriate use of each.

3.39 Tip: *You can issue other data base commands on the selected records that have been extracted by the Find command or record selection criteria.*

Both the Find command (OPEN APPLE-F) and the Record Selection command (OPEN APPLE-R) present a group of records that match the specific criteria you gave. Once this subgroup is collected, you can act upon it with four other data base commands: Move, Copy, Delete, and Arrange.

Move (OPEN APPLE-M) and Copy (OPEN APPLE-C) give you the opportunity to move or copy one or more extracted records to the Clipboard. If you move the records, they will also be moved from the main body of records and can be re-entered there in any position at your request. The Copy command sends a copy of the records you specify to the Clipboard but leaves the originals in place.

When you use the Delete command (OPEN APPLE-D) on one or more extracted records, it will also be erased from the data base at large.

You will find it particularly handy to combine these "selection" and "act" commands when you want to delete, move, or copy records that are not contiguous and you do not want to have to repeat the command many times. You can specify criteria that can be used by the Record Selection or Find command to extract the records you want to affect with further commands. Then the task can be completed in one operation by issuing the command and specifying with the highlight that it should apply to all extracted records.

3.40 Tip: *Assign standard values in your data base whenever possible to save entry time.*

The partial data base that follows was created from a list of books available at a small town library:

```
File: Book List              REVIEW/ADD/CHANGE           Escape: Main Menu

Selection: All records


Author            Title                    Publisher        Year
===================================================================
May, Tim          No Nonsense               Guidelines       1976
May, Tim          Your Esteem is My Esteem  Guidelines       1979
May, Tim          Miss Cue Reads On         Guidelines       1980
May, Tim          Footnote One, Footnote Two Guidelines      1982
Collins, Mary     Christopher John          Cross            1972
Manende, Carmella Thinking Thrift           Lightfoot        1974
Brook, Jena       Lastest Thing             Early            1976
Burke, Taylor     Never Slow Down           M & B            1977
```

As we can see, there are quite a few entries for Tim May books published by Guidelines.

You saved a great deal of entry time when you set up this data base by assigning standard values to the Author and Publisher categories so that May, Tim would automatically be entered in the Author category, and Guidelines would automatically be entered in the Publisher category for each additional record.

To make this time saver possible, you issued the standard Value command (OPEN APPLE-V) as soon as you were ready to begin entering Tim May's books. Presented with the Set Standard Values screen shown in the following illustration, you entered May, Tim next to Author and Guidelines next to Publisher:

```
File: Book List          SET STANDARD VALUES      Escape: Review/Add/Change



Record
===================================================================
Title: -
Author: May, Tim
Publisher: Guidelines
Year: -
```

Each new record already had the current information entered in the Author and Publisher categories. All you had to fill in was Title and Year. When you finished entering the Tim May books, you erased the Standard Values by using OPEN APPLE-V to get back to the Set Standard Values screen and then used the CONTROL-Y combination to erase the standard entries in both the Author and Publisher categories. The records entered from then on contained no standard entries.

AppleWorks Tips and Traps

Of course, if you had not wanted to bother undoing the standard values or thought that they might have applied again soon, it would have been easy enough to replace that value with another at the time of entry, either by erasing it with CONTROL-Y or using the overstrike cursor (OPEN APPLE-E) to type over it.

Another set of standard values can be specified at any time, such as when you come across several more books that have the same author and publisher. Any new set of standard values that you call for will apply to records entered after that time. The records that are already a part of your data base will not be affected.

4

Data Base
Reporting

The Tips and Traps in this chapter are designed to help you generate data base reports. They offer valuable information about creating report formats as well as hints that can help you decide when to use a label- or table-style report. This chapter also contains Tips and Traps that you can use when you create each report style.

Also included are techniques for printing reports that contain calculated categories and group totals, as well as Tips that can help you gain the skills necessary to create data base reports that are aesthetically pleasing and present valuable information in an easy-to-use manner.

Setting Up

 4.01 Trap: *Unless you create a report format for your data base, you will not be able to print the information in your data base file.*

When you want to print any information that you have accumulated in a data base file, you issue AppleWorks' standard Print command (OPEN APPLE-P). When you are printing data base records, however, this is only the beginning. To print specific records in the order you want, with the right column width and category placement, AppleWorks requires that you create a report format that it can refer to in shaping the report to your specifications.

The first choice to make when creating these specifications is presented to you in the Report menu shown in Figure 4-1 immediately after you indicate a desire to print with OPEN APPLE-P. There you choose whether to print a label-style or table-style report. (Examples of printed reports in both of these styles are shown in Figure 4-2.)

The choice you make depends entirely on the purpose of your current report. If you are creating a mailing list, you will want the vertical listing of one record at a time that the label-style report offers. But if you want to use the data base information to create a phone and address list to be distributed among the listees, you will want the consolidated, horizontal format that a table-style report provides.

The procedures for setting up either report style are similar to those used in shaping multiple- and single-record layouts. See specific Tips for each of these report styles in the following sections entitled "Label-Style Reports" and "Table-Style Reports."

```
File: Personnel              REPORT MENU        Escape: Review/Add/Change
Report: None




========================================================================

             1.  Get a report format
             2.  Create a new "tables" format
             3.  Create a new "labels" format
             4.  Duplicate an existing format
             5.  Erase a format
```

Figure 4-1. Report options

(a)

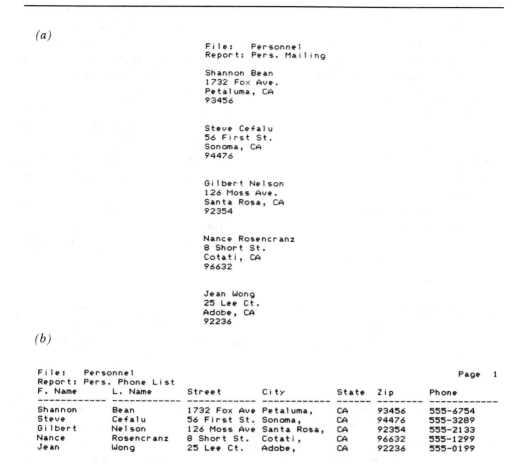

```
File:    Personnel
Report: Pers. Mailing

Shannon Bean
1732 Fox Ave.
Petaluma, CA
93456


Steve Cefalu
56 First St.
Sonoma, CA
94476


Gilbert Nelson
126 Moss Ave.
Santa Rosa, CA
92354


Nance Rosencranz
8 Short St.
Cotati, CA
96632


Jean Wong
25 Lee Ct.
Adobe, CA
92236
```

(b)

| File: Personnel
Report: Pers. Phone List | | | | | | Page 1 |
F. Name	L. Name	Street	City	State	Zip	Phone
Shannon	Bean	1732 Fox Ave	Petaluma,	CA	93456	555-6754
Steve	Cefalu	56 First St.	Sonoma,	CA	94476	555-3289
Gilbert	Nelson	126 Moss Ave	Santa Rosa,	CA	92354	555-2133
Nance	Rosencranz	8 Short St.	Cotati,	CA	96632	555-1299
Jean	Wong	25 Lee Ct.	Adobe,	CA	92236	555-0199

Figure 4-2.   a) Printed label-style report and b) table-style report

4.02 Tip: You can create up to eight customized report formats for your data base information.

When you create a report format for a data base file, you have to give it a name. It is best to choose a name that indicates the file that it was created for and the purpose of the particular report.

The report format used to print the label-style report in Figure 4-2 was called Pers. Mailing (the Pers. stands for Personnel). The table-style report (b) shown in the same figure was created with a format named Pers. Phone List. This tells you that both of these files were created from the Personnel data base and that one is used for mailings while the other is used as a phone list. A report format can be renamed at any time by issuing the OPEN APPLE-N command.

You can create and name up to eight report formats that will be linked to your data base file until you make changes in it or erase it completely (see option 5 on the screen shown in Figure 4-1, accessed by pressing OPEN APPLE-P). Any of the report formats that you create can be retrieved by choosing option 1, "Get a report format," from the Report menu screen (Figure 4-1) and picking the format you want from the options listed.

All report formats that you create for a data base file will be saved with it when you save the file. The next time you use that file and want to print a report using one of the formats you have already created, just press OPEN APPLE-P and choose "Get a report format."

4.03 Tip: *Start with "Duplicate an existing format" (option 4) in the Report menu if you want to create a new report format that contains many of the same characteristics as an existing format.*

Often you will want to print a report that varies slightly from previous reports that you have printed. You realize that you need to change only a few things on a report format that you have used before. But you may be reluctant to make these changes on a report format that you know you will use in the future and do not want to keep reshaping.

AppleWorks had this situation in mind when it created option 4, "Duplicate an existing format," on the Report menu screen. With this feature you are automatically provided with a clone of the format that you want to change slightly. You can change it without affecting the original format and save yourself the time it takes to re-create all the features in the old format that you want in the new one.

Be sure to give the new format a name of its own. You will have an additional report format that will be saved with the data base file and can be used at any time.

4.04 Trap: *You will permanently erase all report formats if you insert or delete a category from the data base while in Change Name/Category.*

At times you may need to make category changes to a data base file after you have already set it up. Do this by pressing OPEN APPLE-N and deleting or inserting new category headings on the Change Name/Category screen, an example of which follows:

```
File: Personnel           CHANGE NAME/CATEGORY     Escape: Review/Add/Change



Category names
==============================================================================
F. Name                          I
L. Name                          I Options:
Street                           I
City                             I Change category name
State                            I Up arrow   Go to filename
Zip                              I Down arrow Go to next category
Phone                            I 3-I          Insert new category
                                 I 3-D          Delete this category
                                 I
                                 I
```

These changes will cause you no problems unless you have already created one or more report formats that you want to keep intact for further use. In this case, the Delete or Insert command will erase all existing report formats, and you will have to re-create them when you are ready to print the report. Issuing either of these commands also sets any custom record layouts you have created (OPEN APPLE-L) back to standard.

If you must insert a new category, you have little choice. But if you want to delete a category from the report that you are printing, you can accomplish this from the Report Format screen without doing permanent damage to anything. The deleted category can even be reinserted into the report format at any time with the Insert command (OPEN APPLE-I).

Although this Trap can cause you some frustration, it will not catch you by surprise. If you should happen to try deleting or inserting a category from the Change Name/Category screen, you will be warned of the consequences. The following screen will appear, notifying you of the results of your actions.

```
File: Personnel              CHANGE NAME/CATEGORY      Escape: Review/Add/Change


Category names
==============================================================================
F. Name                                        |
L. Name                                        |
Street                                         | If you add or delete category
City                                           | names at this point...
State                                          |
Zip                                            | Report formats for this file
Phone                                          | will be erased.
                                               |
                                               | Custom record layouts, made
                                               | using ⌐-L, will be set back
                                               | to standard.
                                               |
                                               |
                                               |
                                               |  --
```

Of course, you are free to ignore the warning, go through with the command, and pay the consequences.

Label-Style Reports

4.05 Tip: *The setup and operation features in a label-style report format are similar to those in the single-record layout.*

Figure 4-3 shows the Report Format screen that you get when you press OPEN APPLE-P and choose "Create a new labels format" (see Figure 4-1) for the Personnel data base file. As you can see, category names are listed much as they are in a single-record layout. In fact, these report format categories can be repositioned for a printed report using the same techniques employed when you make changes in a single-record layout from Change Record Layout (OPEN APPLE-L).

You can use the OPEN APPLE key in combination with the arrow keys to reposition categories any way you want. The following illustration shows the result of that, moving the last name category (L. Name) so that it is next to the first name category (F. Name), juxtaposing the City and State categories, and then bringing the other categories up to fill the gaps.

```
File: Personnel              REPORT FORMAT            Escape: Report Menu
Report: Pers. Mailing
Selection: All records



===========================================================================
F. Name       L. Name
Street
City          State
Zip


Phone
-----------------------Each record will print  7 lines----------------------
```

The phone category remains where it was because phone numbers are not included on mailing labels. If you delete the phone category from the report format with OPEN APPLE-D, you will see the following screen:

```
File: Personnel              REPORT FORMAT            Escape: Report Menu
Report: Pers. Mailing
Selection: All records



===========================================================================
F. Name       L. Name
Street
City          State
Zip



-----------------------Each record will print  7 lines----------------------
```

Now you are ready to print the report. Press OPEN APPLE-P while in the Report Format screen and give the necessary responses to the few prompts that follow until the report finally prints.

Figure 4-4 shows a printout of the results. The first and last names seem disconnected, as do the entries for city and state. There should also be a comma after the city but before the state. To make sure that a comma is printed after each city, return to Review/Add/Change and add a comma after each city entry. This is most easily accomplished from the multiple-record layout of the data base file.

The procedure for juxtaposing categories so that they do not have too many spaces between them is explained in the following Trap.

```
File: Personnel            REPORT FORMAT           Escape: Report Menu
Report: Pers. Mailing
Selection: All records



================================================================================
F. Name
L. Name
Street
City
State
Zip
Phone
-----------------------Each record will print  7 lines-----------------------
```

Figure 4-3. Label-style Report Format screen

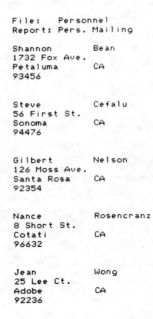

Figure 4-4. Unsatisfactory printed report

✋ **4.06 Trap:** *You will get unwanted spaces when you print a label-style report if you do not left justify categories that you place next to each other in the Report Format.*

The previous Tip showed that a label-style report can be set up so that two categories can be placed next to each other and printed on the same line. (Look at the F. Name and L. Name and City and State categories illustrated in that Tip. However, the report that was printed from this format turned out to be less than satisfactory because of excess space between the first and last name and the city and state (see Figure 4-4).

Fortunately, AppleWorks has a built-in feature that you can use when you are setting up a report format to prevent this problem. This feature left justifies the category that occupies the rightmost position on a line shared by two categories. Left justification assures that only one space will be left between the justified category and its left-hand partner.

To add this aesthetic improvement to your label-style report, place the cursor on the first character of the right-hand category in question. In the following example, the right-hand categories are L. Name and State. Issue the Left Justify command by pressing OPEN APPLE-J.

A left arrow mark appears to the left of each justified category.

```
File: Personnel              REPORT FORMAT              Escape: Report Menu
Report: Pers. Mailing
Selection: All records



================================================================================
F. Name        <L. Name
Street
City           <State
Zip


-----------------------Each record will print  6 lines----------------------
```

Now when you print the report, you will get the more acceptable result shown in Figure 4-5.

💡 **4.07 Tip:** *The Insert and Delete commands work in tandem to provide flexibility in printing label-style reports.*

When you are creating a label-style report from the Report Format screen (accessed with OPEN APPLE-P), you can delete categories that you don't want

---

```
File:   Personnel
Report: Pers. Mailing

Shannon Bean
1732 Fox Ave.
Petaluma, CA
93456


Steve Cefalu
56 First St.
Sonoma, CA
94476


Gilbert Nelson
126 Moss Ave.
Santa Rosa, CA
92354


Nance Rosencranz
8 Short St.
Cotati, CA
96632


Jean Wong
25 Lee Ct.
Adobe, CA
92236
```

Figure 4-5. Acceptable printed report

printed in the current report (OPEN APPLE-D) and reinsert them (OPEN APPLE-I) later, when you print a report that should include them.

In the report format used as an example in the previous two Tips, OPEN APPLE-D was used to delete the phone category from the report format for printed mailing labels. In the future, you may want to include that category in printed reports.

To accomplish this, position the cursor in the Report Format screen on the spot where you want to reinstall the phone category. From there you press OPEN APPLE-I, and you are presented with the following screen:

```
File: Personnel              INSERT A CATEGORY        Escape: Report Format
Report: Pers. Mailing
Selection: All records


===========================================================================
1.  Phone
2.  A spacing line above cursor position
3.  A spacing line below cursor position
```

There is the banished category waiting to be accepted back into the flock. You do this with the RETURN key and are placed back in the Report Format screen, where you can see that the phone category has reappeared.

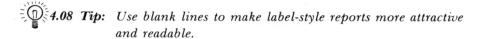 **4.08** ***Tip:*** *Use blank lines to make label-style reports more attractive and readable.*

When you are printing mailing labels, you rarely need to insert extra line spaces between lines of the address, but you may run across other instances when you can make label-style reports more attractive and readable by inserting blank lines before and after each category entry. You can also set off a particular category by inserting spaces around it.

To do this, simply place the cursor on the category adjacent to the position where you want the blank line to go, and issue the Insert command (OPEN APPLE-I). This brings you to the Insert a Category screen illustrated in the previous Tip.

As you can see, you are given the option of inserting a spacing line above or below the cursor position. By highlighting your choice and pressing RETURN, you will be brought back to the Report Format screen, where the new spacing line will be displayed. You can create spacing lines around each category if you wish, but you will have to issue the Insert command for each line that you add.

It is important to make sure that you have at least one blank line at the end of a label-style report format. If you look at the following illustration, you will notice a four-line address label for the Pers. Mailing report.

```
File: Personnel              REPORT FORMAT              Escape: Report Menu
Report: Pers. Mailing
Selection: All records


===================================================================================
F. Name      <L. Name
Street
City         <State
Zip


----------------------Each record will print  6 lines----------------------
```

The message centered on the dotted line below the label tells you that each record will print on six lines. That leaves two blank lines between records. This results in a highly readable label-style report like the one in Figure 4-5.

On the other hand, if you use the Delete command (OPEN APPLE-D) to eliminate the two spacing lines that were below each record and then print the report, you end up with the unsatisfactory results shown in Figure 4-6.

```
File:    Personnel
Report:  Pers. Mailing

Shannon Bean
1732 Fox Ave.
Petaluma, CA
93456
Steve Cefalu
56 First St.
Sonoma, CA
94476
Gilbert Nelson
126 Moss Ave.
Santa Rosa, CA
92354
Nance Rosencranz
8 Short St.
Cotati, CA
96632
Jean Wong
25 Lee Ct.
Adobe, CA
92236
```

Figure 4-6. Printed report without spacing between records

If you want to increase the number of blank lines below the format you have created for your report categories, you can use either the down arrow or the RETURN key. You can create a maximum of 15 lines for each printed record in a label-style report. You will be reminded of this by a persistent beep if you try to exceed this limit.

4.09 Tip: *Use OPEN APPLE-Z from the Report Format screen to zoom in to view the actual records as they will be printed in a report.*

The previous Tips have used a personnel data base for examples, such as the report format for a label-style report (see the illustration in Tip 4.08). This screen shows the relative positions that category entries will occupy when the report is printed, but it displays the category headings, not the entries themselves.

You can see the actual records that will be printed by using the Zoom command (OPEN APPLE-Z). If you issue this command from the Report Format screen, you are brought to the following display:

```
File: Personnel                REPORT FORMAT              Escape: Report Menu
Report: Pers. Mailing
Selection: All records


================================================================================
Shannon        <Bean
1732 Fox Ave.
Petaluma,       <CA
93456


----------------------Each record will print  6 lines----------------------
```

The data in the first record of the data base is displayed as it will be printed. (The < marks indicate that the entry to the right will be left justified, so it will print one space to the right of the entry on the left that shares its line.)

To view the other records in the data base from this screen, you can use AppleWorks' ruler (OPEN APPLE-1 through -9), or you can use OPEN APPLE-right arrow to go to the next record and OPEN APPLE-left arrow to go to the previous record. It is a good idea to check your records in this way before you print them. Any mistakes that you detect can be fixed before printing.

Once you have completed your check, press OPEN APPLE-Z again, and you will be returned to the report format displaying category headings. From there OPEN APPLE-P will enable you to print a hard copy.

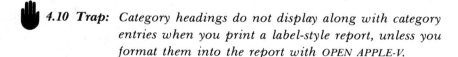 **4.10 Trap:** *Category headings do not display along with category entries when you print a label-style report, unless you format them into the report with OPEN APPLE-V.*

The label-style report in Figure 4-5 contains the entry data for each record in the data base displayed just as you specified it in the report format. As you can see in this figure, the category headings are not printed with the records.

You can format a report so that it will print the category headings that you specify along with each record. Suppose, for instance, that you want the headings Street, City, State, and Zip to be included in the printed report.

Begin from the Report Format screen. Position the cursor on the first letter of the category heading Street and press OPEN APPLE-V. Repeat this procedure as you move to the first letter of each of the other category headings you want to print. The screen on the next page shows the results.

AppleWorks Tips and Traps

```
File: Personnel                REPORT FORMAT              Escape: Report Menu
Report: Pers. Mailing
Selection: All records



================================================================================
F. Name       <L. Name
Street: 1732 Fox Ave.
City: Petaluma, <State: CA
Zip: 93456


-----------------------Each record will print  6 lines-----------------------
```

Each time you give the command, the screen adds the record entry next to the category heading. Note that there is no change on the F. Name and L. Name headings, since these were left as they were.

To see what the actual records will look like when they are formatted in this way, use the Zoom command (OPEN APPLE-Z). From the zoomed-in screen, you can see how each record will look when it is printed.

```
File: Personnel                REPORT FORMAT              Escape: Report Menu
Report: Pers. Mailing
Selection: All records



================================================================================
Shannon       <Bean
Street: 1732 Fox Ave.
City: Petaluma, <State: CA
Zip: 93456


-----------------------Each record will print  6 lines-----------------------
```

OPEN APPLE-right arrow takes you to the next record, OPEN APPLE-left arrow takes you to the previous record, and the ruler feature (OPEN APPLE-1 through -9) sends you to relative positions within the records.

Everything seems okay, so zoom back to the original Report Format screen and initiate the printing procedure (OPEN APPLE-P). Figure 4-7 shows the printed report including the category headings that you specified.

Table-Style Reports

4.11 Tip: *When you format a table-style report, you can add up to three calculated categories that use numerical data from other categories to perform mathematical calculations.*

```
File:   Personnel
Report: Pers. Mailing

Shannon Bean
Street: 1732 Fox Ave.
City: Petaluma, State: CA
Zip: 93456


Steve Cefalu
Street: 56 First St.
City: Sonoma, State: CA
Zip: 94476


Gilbert Nelson
Street: 126 Moss Ave.
City: Santa Rosa, State: CA
Zip: 92354


Nance Rosencranz
Street: 8 Short St.
City: Cotati, State: CA
Zip: 96632


Jean Wong
Street: 25 Lee Ct.
City: Adobe, State: CA
Zip: 92236
```

Figure 4-7. Printed report with OPEN APPLE-V formatting

Look at the Report Format screen in the following illustration:

```
File: Food List              REPORT FORMAT                Escape: Report Menu
Report: July Order
Selection: All records



===============================================================================
--> or <--  Move cursor                    ⌂-J  Right justify this category
  >  ⌂  <   Switch category positions       ⌂-K  Define a calculated category
--> ⌂ <--   Change column width            ⌂-N  Change report name and/or title
⌂-A  Arrange (sort) on this category       ⌂-O  Printer options
⌂-D  Delete this category                  ⌂-P  Print the report
⌂-G  Add/remove group totals               ⌂-R  Change record selection rules
⌂-I  Insert a prev. deleted category       ⌂-T  Add/remove category totals
-------------------------------------------------------------------------------


Food Type    Food Name    Price      Unit        Quantity      Order Date   L
-A---------- -B---------- -C--------- -D--------- -E----------- -F---------- e
Fruit        Orange       .49        lb.         50            Jun  7       n
veg.         cabbage      .19        lb.         25            Jun 15       7
bev.         Ap. juice    2.00       gal.        10            May 85       8


-------------------------------------------------------------------------------
Use options shown above to change report format              25K Avail.
```

Sample records from a food co-op's Food List data base are displayed at the bottom of the screen much as they might be on a Change Record Layout screen.

The help that is shown above the sample records lists all the commands that can be used to format a table-style report. Some of these features are familiar from having used them to change the layout of a multiple-record display. Others will be discussed in later Tips and Traps in this section.

One choice is @-K, "Define a calculated category." A calculated category is a new category added specifically for the current report you are formatting. It does not appear in the data base from Review/Add/Change and only exists in other report formats if you specifically define it.

In this case you want to create a category that will calculate the cost of each food item listed based on quantity ordered and price per unit. You want this category to be placed just after the quantity column, so use the right arrow key to move the cursor into position at column F, Order Date.

When you press OPEN APPLE-K from this position, the Order Date category is pushed to the right (to column G), and a new category entitled Calculated takes its place and fills up with 9s, which is AppleWorks' way of letting you know that this column will automatically be right justified. Notice the 9s in the following illustration:

```
Food Type    Food Name    Price        Unit         Quantity     Calculated    O
-A---------- -B---------- -C---------- -D---------- -E---------- -F---------- -
Fruit        Orange       .49          lb.          50           9999999999 J
veg.         cabbage      .19          lb.          25           9999999999 J
bev.         Ap. juice    2.00         gal.         10           9999999999 M

------------------------------------------------------------------ More --->
Type a name for the calculated category:  Calculated            25K Avail.
```

The prompt at the bottom of the screen invites you to accept Calculated as the category's name or delete it (CONTROL-Y) and type another name in its place.

You want the calculated category to be called Cost, so you supply this in place of Calculated. Next, you are prompted to type in the actual formula that the calculated column will perform. Using the alphabetical headings supplied under each category name as formula references, type **C*E** and press RETURN.

```
Food Type    Food Name    Price        Unit         Quantity     Cost          O
-A---------- -B---------- -C---------- -D---------- -E---------- -F---------- -
Fruit        Orange       .49          lb.          50           9999999999 J
veg.         cabbage      .19          lb.          25           9999999999 J
bev.         Ap. juice    2.00         gal.         10           9999999999 M

------------------------------------------------------------------ More --->
Type calculation rules (Example: A+B+C/5.75):  C*E
```

You have let AppleWorks know that you want your calculated column, which you have named Cost, to display the results of multiplying entries in the Price category with those in the Quantity category for each record in the data base.

The next two prompts let you choose the number of decimal places that you want displayed in the calculated category and then the number of blank spaces between this category and its neighbor to the right. Choose two decimal places, and accept the suggestion of three blank spaces. The Report Format screen now shows the 9s in Cost category set off by two decimal places, as shown in the following illustration:

```
Food Type     Food Name    Price        Unit         Quantity     Cost          O
-A----------  -B---------- -C---------- -D---------- -E---------- -F--------    -
Fruit         Orange       .49          lb.          50           9999999.99    J
veg.          cabbage      .19          lb.          25           9999999.99    J
bev.          Ap. juice    2.00         gal.         10           9999999.99    M

----------------------------------------------------------------- More --->
Use options shown above to change report format                  25K Avail.
```

By now you are probably tired of looking at those meaningless 9s and would like to see the actual results of the calculation that you defined without printing the whole report. You can do this by printing the report to the screen. The steps are essentially the same as for any other printing, except that after pressing OPEN APPLE-P you choose item number 4, "The screen," from the Print the Report menu shown in Figure 4-8.

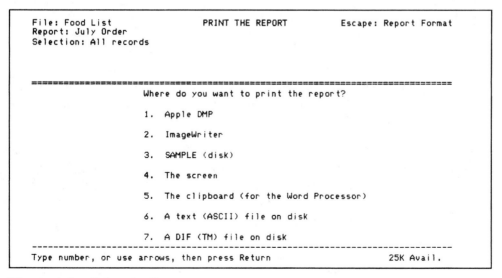

```
File: Food List              PRINT THE REPORT          Escape: Report Format
Report: July Order
Selection: All records


================================================================================
                   Where do you want to print the report?

            1.  Apple DMP

            2.  ImageWriter

            3.  SAMPLE (disk)

            4.  The screen

            5.  The clipboard (for the Word Processor)

            6.  A text (ASCII) file on disk

            7.  A DIF (TM) file on disk
----------------------------------------------------------------------------
Type number, or use arrows, then press Return                  25K Avail.
```

Figure 4-8. Print the Report menu

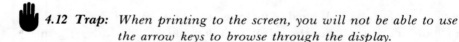

```
File:   Food List                                           Page  1
Report: July Order
Food Type     Food Name    Price      Unit         Quantity         Cost  0
----------    ----------   ---------  ----------   ----------   ---------  -
Fruit         Orange       .49        lb.          50               24.50  J
veg.          cabbage      .19        lb.          25                4.75  J
bev.          Ap. juice    2.00       gal.         10               20.00  M
cheese        Edam         2.79       lb.          12               33.48  J
veg.          mushrooms    1.19       lb.          18               21.42  J
```

Figure 4-9. Screen print of a formatted report

As you can see in Figure 4-9, the screen print shows the desired formula results displayed in the Cost category, which confirms that the specified calculations were carried out and will be included in the printed report.

✋ **4.12 Trap:** *When printing to the screen, you will not be able to use the arrow keys to browse through the display.*

The previous Tip had you printing the date base report to the screen as a preliminary step to printing hard copy. Although this procedure offers an important preprinting check, it has a significant limitation in that it does not give you access to off-screen categories.

Looking at the screen print shown in Figure 4-9, you can see that only the first letters of the entries in the Order Date category are visible. It would be nice to be able to use the right arrow to move over to see the rest of that category. However, you will find that the cursor, flashing at the bottom of the screen, does not respond to any direction that you give it.

Your view is obviously limited to the left-hand extreme of the report. Neither can it extend downward below the bottom of the screen, which limits your view of off-screen records in a large data base.

✋ **4.13 Trap:** *If you have a data base that has more than 26 categories, the report format stops labeling them alphabetically, and you are left without a category reference with which to create a formula.*

In addition to the category name you assign to each category you create in your data base, AppleWorks provides a lettered heading for each column in any table-style report format that you define. These letters are intended to be used to reference categories that you want included in any formula you define for calculated categories in a report.

All works well as long as you are dealing with a data base that has 26 categories or less. But remember that AppleWorks allows a maximum of 30 categories in each data base file. This poses a potential problem if one of the categories you want included in a calculated formula has no letter heading that can be used as a formula reference.

There are two possibilities for a solution to this problem. One is to delete any categories that you feel are not necessary for this specific report, thereby pulling categories that fall beyond column 26 back into the lettered positions. The other is to use the OPEN APPLE along with the left or right arrow keys to move categories that are not part of formulas past column 26 and move categories that are part of formulas under a letter heading.

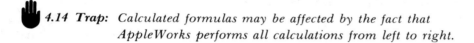 **4.14 Trap:** *Calculated formulas may be affected by the fact that AppleWorks performs all calculations from left to right.*

If you are creating a report format that includes only one calculated category, you do not have to worry about this Trap. But you can include as many as three calculated categories in one report. Calculated categories can also use the results of other calculated categories in their formulas.

If you plan to set up a report in which this latter condition exists, it is important to place any calculated categories referenced in other calculated categories to the left of the category that includes them in further calculations. This placement is crucial because AppleWorks performs its calculations in a left-to-right order. This means that there will be no formula results for another formula to manipulate further if the placement hierarchy is not observed. In this case, the result of the calculation would be zero.

If none of the calculated categories in your report refer to other calculated categories, the order of columns will not matter.

4.15 Trap: *If your columns are not wide enough to display the result of a formula you have formatted into a data base report, you will end up with a cell full of meaningless characters.*

When you use OPEN APPLE-K to specify that calculations be performed in a certain category in your report format, you must also be sure that the column that houses such a category is wide enough to display the results of the calculation. Since you do not see the calculation results from the Report Format screen, you may find yourself in this Trap after your report has already been printed.

The problem will be obvious if you look at the printed report and see what looks like a series of blank tic-tac-toe screens in the column where you expected calculation results displayed. Notice the Cost category in the following illustration:

```
File:    Food List                                              Page  1
Report: July Order
Food Type     Food Name     Price        Unit          Quantity       Cost     Order D
------------- ------------- ------------- ------------- ------------- ----     --------
Fruit         Orange        $  .49       lb.           50            ####     Jun  7
veg.          cabbage       $  .19       lb.           25            4.75     Jun 15
bev.          Ap. juice     $2.00        gal.          10            ####     May 85
cheese        Edam          $2.79        lb.           12            ####     Jun 10
veg.          mushrooms     $1.19        lb.           18            ####     Jun 21
```

The only thing to do in this case is to return to the Report Format screen and use the OPEN APPLE and right arrow keys to add the necessary width to the column in question.

It is most auspicious to print a report to screen before you print the final report. You can thus look for such pitfalls and correct them before the results are set in black and white.

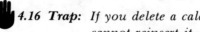 **4.16 Trap:** *If you delete a calculated category in a report format, you cannot reinsert it, as you can the other categories.*

Deleting categories from the Report Format screen is easily accomplished by placing the cursor on the category that you want deleted and giving the Delete command (OPEN APPLE-D). It is also easy to reinsert any category that you have deleted by using the Insert command (OPEN APPLE-I). Any category, that is, except a calculated one.

```
    ----------------------------------------------------------------------------
    Food Type     Food Name     Price        Unit          Quantity       Cost            O
    -A----------  -B----------  -C---------- -D----------- -E----------- -F--------      -
    Fruit         Orange        $  .49       lb.           50            9999999.99      J
    veg.          cabbage       $  .19       lb.           25            9999999.99      J
    bev.          Ap. juice     $2.00        gal.          10            9999999.99      M
                                                                         ==========
    ----------------------------------------------------------------------- More --->
    ----------------------------------------------------------------------------
```

Figure 4-10. Cost category formatted for totals

Data Base Reporting

Calculated categories cannot be recovered when they are deleted from the Report Format screen. If you delete such a category and then wish you had not, the only way to get it back in the report is to create it again from scratch with OPEN APPLE-K.

 4.17 Trap: *Calculated categories do not display dollar signs in their results.*

There is no way in AppleWorks to format a category so that all of its entries will display in currency format. In the following illustration you see dollar signs in the price category only because they were entered with the amounts.

```
File: Food List            REVIEW/ADD/CHANGE            Escape: Main Menu

Selection: All records


Food Type       Food Name      Price   Unit    Quantity  Order Date
========================================================================
Fruit           Orange        $ .49   lb.     50        Jun  7
veg.            cabbage       $ .19   lb.     25        Jun 15
bev.            Ap. juice     $2.00   gal.    10        May 85
cheese          Edam          $2.79   lb.     12        Jun 10 85
veg.            mushrooms     $1.19   lb.     18        Jun 21 85
```

When the calculated category of Cost was added in Figure 4-10, it was defined as Price times Quantity. The data entry person expected the results of this formula to be printed in currency for every record in the report. Figure 4-11 shows the printed results. You can see that the dollar signs were not considered in the calculations. The price is shown in decimals, not currency.

```
File:    Food List                                        Page  1
Report: July Order
Food Type       Food Name    Price        Unit         Quantity        Cost    0
-----------     ----------   ----------   ----------   ----------   ----------  -
Fruit           Orange       $ .49        lb.          50              24.50    J
veg.            cabbage      $ .19        lb.          25               4.75    J
bev.            Ap. juice    $2.00        gal.         10              20.00    M
cheese          Edam         $2.79        lb.          12              33.48    J
veg.            mushrooms    $1.19        lb.          18              21.42    J
                                                                      104.15*
```

Figure 4-11. Total displayed is Cost category minus dollar sign

4.18 Tip: *You can format a data base report so that category totals will be displayed for any category that you specify.*

In Figure 4-10, OPEN APPLE-T was used to format the Cost category, to add all the entries in that category and to display the results at the bottom of the column when the report was printed.

As soon as the Totals command is issued, you are prompted to choose the number of decimal places that you want for a totals display and the number of blank spaces after this category when the report is printed. In this case, you would choose two decimal places and accept the suggestion of three blank spaces.

Once these choices are locked in with the RETURN key, you will notice that the category that you formatted for the totals display has filled up with 9s, indicating that it will be right justified, set off by two decimal places as was specified, and underlined with two rows of dashes, which is a sign that totals will be displayed for this category.

If you print to the screen to check the result of this format, you will see (in Figure 4-11) the total of 104.15 at the bottom of the Cost category. The asterisk sets it off as the category total.

If you want to undo the totals on a certain category, move to that category and press OPEN APPLE-T again. The totals format will immediately toggle off.

4.19 Tip: *When you use the Arrange command in the Report Format screen, it also affects the arrangement of records in Review/ Add/Change.*

The Arrange command (OPEN APPLE-A) can be used on any Report Format categories that you want sorted according to the options shown here:

```
File: Food List              ARRANGE (SORT)        Escape: Review/Add/Change

Selection: All records



================================================================================

              This file will be arranged on
              this category: Food Type

              Arrangement order:

                   1.  From A to Z
                   2.  From Z to A
                   3.  From 0 to 9
                   4.  From 9 to 0
```

When you issue this command from the Report Format screen, you will find that when you return to Review/Add/Change, the specified sort was carried out on all data base records.

 4.20 Trap: *When you format a data base report with OPEN APPLE-G, you may get strange results if you do not use the Arrange command first.*

Another example of the small food co-op's data base is shown in Figure 4-12. If you look at the Food Type category in this figure, you will see that the food types bev. and veg. have more than one listing.

You can bunch like food types so that their records will be printed in a group with several spaces setting them off from the other records, also grouped by food type. (AppleWorks calls this printing group totals.)

Move the cursor to the food type category from the Report Format screen and press OPEN APPLE-G. (This command works like a toggle switch. To remove group totals on a category that has been formatted with OPEN APPLE-G, press this key combination again.) The following screen shows the results so far:

```
File: Food List                  GROUP TOTALS          Escape: Report Format
Report: Group Report
Selection: All records


Group totals on: Food Type
===============================================================================
--> or <--   Move cursor              @-J   Right justify this category
 >  @  <     Switch category positions @-K   Define a calculated category
--> @ <--    Change column width       @-N   Change report name and/or title
@-A  Arrange (sort) on this category   @-O   Printer options
@-D  Delete this category              @-P   Print the report
@-G  Add/remove group totals           @-R   Change record selection rules
@-I  Insert a prev. deleted category   @-T   Add/remove category totals
-------------------------------------------------------------------------------

Food Type    Food Name    Price       Unit        Quantity     Order Date   L
-A---------- -B---------- -C--------- -D--------- -E---------- -F---------- e
cheese       Edam         2.79        1b.         12           Jun 10 85    n
veg.         mushrooms    1.19        1b.         18           Jun 21 85    7
Fruit        Oranges      .49         1b.         50           Jun  7       8
                                                   ⁑
-------------------------------------------------------------------------------

Print group totals only?  No  Yes
```

In the previous illustration, notice the message on the left, just above the double row of dashes, confirming that group totals have been formatted to print for the Food Type category. The prompt at the bottom of the screen asks you if you want to print group totals only. If you answer Yes to this, the only categories in the

```
 ┌─────────────────────────────────────────────────────────────────────────┐
 │  File: Food List              REVIEW/ADD/CHANGE           Escape: Main Menu│
 │                                                                           │
 │  Selection: All records                                                   │
 │                                                                           │
 │                                                                           │
 │  Food Type        Food Name        Price   Unit    Quantity Order Date    │
 │  ═══════════════════════════════════════════════════════════════════════ │
 │  cheese           Edam             2.79    1b.     12       Jun 10 85      │
 │  veg.             mushrooms        1.19    1b.     18       Jun 21 85      │
 │  Fruit            Oranges          .49     1b.     50       Jun  7         │
 │  veg.             cabbage          .19     1b.     25       Jun 15         │
 │  bev.             Ap. juice        2.00    gal.    10       May 85         │
 │  bev.             Rasp.-Ap.juice   2.00    gal.    6        May 85         │
 │  bev.             Ap.-Straw. juice 2.00    gal.    12       May 85         │
 │  bev.             Grpfrt. juice    2.00    gal.    8        May 85         │
 └─────────────────────────────────────────────────────────────────────────┘
```

Figure 4-12. Food List data base — no group totals

printed report that will contain any information will be the ones that you have formatted to display group totals. In this case, it would mean a printout of the Food Type category only. The rest of the columns would be blank. Because you want the report to contain the information from each category, choose No.

Next, you are asked if you want to go to a new page after each group. If you are printing a large data base report with many records in each group, it might be nice to have the records within each group printed on separate pages. In this case, you would choose Yes and go to a new page after each group total. Since this is not necessary in this example, choose No, assuring that the records will be grouped but printed on the same page.

Before making a hard copy print of the report, conduct a test by printing to the screen. When you look at the results shown in Figure 4-13, you will be glad that you took this precaution. Although the group of records with bev. entries in Food Type have been grouped as you would have expected, the two veg. records have been treated as if they do not belong together.

Why has this happened? Looking back at the original arrangement of records in Figure 4-12, you will notice that the bev. entries are positioned next to each other, whereas the veg. entries are separated. To avoid falling into this Trap, make sure that the like values in the controlling category are arranged in adjacent rows.

You can remedy the situation by escaping back to the report format and rearranging the records according to the Food Type category. With the cursor on Food Type, press OPEN APPLE-A, and choose to sort the records from *A* to *Z*, knowing that this will group both the bev. and veg. entries together. While you are there, widen the Food Name category so that the juice entries in the final report will not

```
File:   Food List                                             Page   1
Report: Group Report
Food Type      Food Name    Price      Unit         Quantity     Order Date
-----------    ----------   --------   ----------   ----------   -----------
cheese         Edam         2.79       lb.          12           Jun 10 85


veg.           mushrooms    1.19       lb.          18           Jun 21 85


Fruit          Oranges       .49       lb.          50           Jun  7


veg.           cabbage       .19       lb.          25           Jun 15


bev.           Ap. juice    2.00       gal.         10           May 85
bev.           Rasp.-Ap.ju. 2.00       gal.          6           May 85
bev.           Ap.-Straw. j 2.00       gal.         12           May 85
```

Figure 4-13.   Group totals for Food Type — not correct

be truncated as they were in the test (See Figure 4-13). A second print-to-screen test verifies your success (see Figure 4-14). The categories bev. and veg. are grouped together, and each juice entry is displayed in full.

```
File:   Food List                                             Page   1
Report: Group Report
Food Type      Food Name         Price      Unit        Quantity     Order Dat
-----------    ---------------   --------   ---------   ----------   ---------
bev.           Ap. juice         2.00       gal.        10           May 85
bev.           Rasp.-Ap.juice    2.00       gal.         6           May 85
bev.           Ap.-Straw. juice  2.00       gal.        12           May 85
bev.           Grpfrt. juice     2.00       gal.         8           May 85


cheese         Edam              2.79       lb.         12           Jun 10 85


Fruit          Oranges            .49       lb.         50           Jun  7


veg.           mushrooms         1.19       lb.         18           Jun 21 85
veg.           cabbage            .19       lb.         25           Jun 15



Press Space Bar to continue                                12K Avail.
```

Figure 4-14.   Successful group totals (Food Type)

In this example, the Group Totals command was issued on a category that contained alphabetical entries. This command follows the same pattern when it is used on categories that contain numeric values. Duplicate entries that are adjacent to each other will be displayed in groups when the report is printed.

4.21 Tip: *If you press OPEN APPLE-T for every category you would like subtotaled, you can create a report that displays sub-totals for each set of records you have grouped with OPEN APPLE-G.*

The previous Trap discussed how to use the Group Totals command (OPEN APPLE-G) to group like entries within a category for a printed report. You can maximize the benefits of this feature by using it in conjunction with the OPEN APPLE-T command. These two functions can produce a report that lists subtotals for each set of records it has grouped.

In Figure 4-10, the Cost category was formatted to add all the entries within that category and display their total when the report was printed (Figure 4-11). Then the Group Totals command was used on Food Type to group like entries within this category.

To make the report more useful to the food co-op that created this data base, you want to meld these two features. Format the Cost category with OPEN APPLE-T and the Food Type category with OPEN APPLE-G. The result in Figure 4-15 shows subtotals for each set of records grouped by food type and a grand total at the bottom of the category. Now the food co-op coordinator knows the check amount needed for each food supplier.

Although only one category at a time can be formatted for group totals, the OPEN APPLE-T format can be applied to any number of categories in the same report format, giving you a report that displays subtotals in every category where you issued this command.

4.22 Tip: *You can format a data base report so that both alphabetical and numeric categories are right justified.*

Previous Tips have shown that creating a calculated category within a table-style report or formatting categories to display totals or group totals automatically right justifies the entries in the categories where these formats have been applied.

```
File:    Food List                                                   Page  1
Report: Group Report
Food Type       Food Name         Price        Unit          Quantity       Cost
------------    ----------------  ------------  ------------  ------------  -------
bev.            Ap. juice         2.00          gal.          10             20.00
bev.            Rasp.-Ap.juice    2.00          gal.          6              12.00
bev.            Ap.-Straw. juice  2.00          gal.          12             24.00
bev.            Grpfrt. juice     2.00          gal.          8              16.00
                                                                             72.00

cheese          Edam              2.79          lb.           12             33.48
                                                                             33.48

Fruit           Oranges           .49           lb.           50             24.50
                                                                             24.50

veg.            mushrooms         1.19          lb.           18             21.42
veg.            cabbage           .19           lb.           25              4.75
                                                                             26.17

                                                                            156.15*
```

Figure 4-15. Printed report displaying subtotals for Cost category

AppleWorks always lets you know that the Right Justification feature is in effect by filling the justified categories with 9s. You can apply this format to any category by moving to the appropriate column and issuing the OPEN APPLE-J command. Alphabetical as well as numeric categories can be affected by this command.

In each case, the sample entries within that category on the Report Format screen will fill up with 9s. When the report is printed, entries in the categories that have been right justified will be positioned at the far right extreme of the column where they reside. Of course, the original entry, not the 9s, will show up in the printed report.

Other Report Format Features

 4.23 Trap: *Record selection rules created in Review/Add/Change are adopted as part of the report format unless different record selection rules have been created there.*

If you specify record selection rules in Review/Add/Change, they will be applied to all report formats that you create for that data base, whether you create the report formats before or after you specify the record selection rules. This applies to both label and table-style report formats. The only time these selection rules are not transferred to a report format is when other selection rules have already been specified for that format. The imported selection rules can always be overridden by assigning record selection rules to any particular report format.

When you print a report from a report format that record selection rules have been assigned to, only the records that match the selection rules will be printed.

When you save a file with associated report formats that contain record selection rules, the record selection rules will be saved along with the format as the file is saved.

4.24 Trap: *If you delete a category that you have made certain changes on in the Report Format screen, those changes will be gone when you reinsert the category into your records.*

One of the greatest characteristics of the Report Format screen is its ability to reinsert categories (OPEN APPLE-I) that have been deleted (OPEN APPLE-D). However, in certain cases, you may be in for a surprise when you reinsert deleted categories.

If the categories in question had any of the following operations performed on them before they were deleted, they will no longer apply once they are returned to the format screen:

- Width adjustments (OPEN APPLE with right or left arrow)
- Right justification (OPEN APPLE-J)
- Formatting for totals (OPEN APPLE-T).

5

The Spreadsheet

5.01 Tip: *Use the Find command (OPEN APPLE-F) to access different areas of your spreadsheet quickly.*

The Find command can be useful in several ways. If you want to move the cursor to a specific cell, you select the Coordinates option of the Find command and enter the column and row coordinates of the cell you want to move to. This option requires keeping track of specific worksheet locations, however.

The other Find option is Text, which searches cell contents to match text characters that you specify. Up to 25 characters can be specified. By naming areas in the worksheet and using the Text option, you can access these areas from anywhere in the worksheet.

5.02 Tip: *Use OPEN APPLE-1 through -9 to move through the spreadsheet quickly.*

OPEN APPLE-1 positions the cursor at the beginning of the spreadsheet (cell A1). OPEN APPLE-9 moves the cursor to the end of the active worksheet area. Using OPEN APPLE-2 through -9 will move the cursor in proportional steps from beginning to end. See the following Trap.

✋ **5.03 Trap:** *You cannot always use OPEN APPLE-1 through -9 with a worksheet that has been altered by insertions or deletions.*

Once you insert or delete a row or a column, these commands may not always work as intended. The cursor will move to random locations throughout the active worksheet area. You can still use the OPEN APPLE-arrow commands and the Find command to move the cursor quickly to specific locations. See the previous Tip.

Entering and Editing Information

💡 **5.04 Tip:** *For maximum efficiency, use the arrow keys instead of RETURN to enter information into cells and move to the next cell.*

When you enter information in a cell, you have to let the program know that you have completed the entry. You can either press RETURN or use one of the arrow keys. When you use an arrow key, the data is entered into the current cell, and the cursor moves to the next cell, all in one step. Following this procedure is particularly efficient when you are entering a lot of data in adjacent cells, such as a column of numbers.

✋ **5.05 Trap:** *If you are not careful, lengthy label entries may overwrite the contents of the adjacent cell to the right.*

If your label entry contains more characters than can fit into the current cell, AppleWorks will enter the additional characters in the adjacent cell(s) to the right, if that cell is not protected or does not contain a numeric entry. Label entries are blanked and overwritten, causing loss of information.

Once a label extends into an adjacent cell, AppleWorks treats it as two separate cell entries. If you subsequently change the column width or reformat, each label segment will be affected differently. Editing can then be a cumbersome task — you are forced to edit each segment as a separate entry.

The spreadsheet that follows shows how AppleWorks handles labels.

```
File: SPREADSHEET              REVIEW/ADD/CHANGE            Escape: Main Menu
=========A==========B==========C==========D==========E==========F=====
  1| LAURIE'S   TOY  SHOP
  2|
  3|     Item     # in Stock  Reorder Code
  4|
  5|Puzzles             10        9327
  6|Cabbage Patc        12        3621            Example 1
  7|Bicycles             8        7773
  8|Books               85        2615
  9|Stuffed Toys       128        2745
 10|===============================================.
 11|
 12|     Item     Stock on Hand
 13|
 14|Puzzles             10        9327
 15|Cabbage Patc        12        3621            Example 2
 16|Bicycles             8        7773
 17|Books               85        2615
 18|Stuffed Toys       128        2745
----------------------------------------------------------------------
A6: (Label) Cabbage Patch Dolls

Type entry or use ? commands                          ?-? for Help
```

Examples 1 and 2 are identical except for the label entries in B3 and B12. Changing the label in B12 overwrites C12 and loses the original entry. The label entered in A6 (and A15) is truncated because it cannot overwrite the value in B6 (and B15). The cell indicator (bottom left corner) displays the actual entry.

The following illustration shows the effect of enlarging the columns:

```
File: SPREADSHEET              REVIEW/ADD/CHANGE            Escape: Main Menu
=============A===================B===================C==========
  1|     LAURIE'S        TOY   SHOP
  2|
  3|        Item         # in Stock          Reorder Code
  4|
  5|Puzzles                           10               9327
  6|Cabbage Patch Dolls               12               3621
  7|Bicycles                           8               7773
  8|Books                             85               2615
  9|Stuffed Toys                     128               2745
 10|========================================================
 11|
 12|        Item         Stock on Han         d
 13|
 14|Puzzles                           10               9327
 15|Cabbage Patch Dolls               12               3621
 16|Bicycles                           8               7773
 17|Books                             85               2615
 18|Stuffed Toys                     128               2745
----------------------------------------------------------------------
A6: (Label) Cabbage Patch Dolls

Type entry or use ? commands                          ?-? for Help
```

Cell A6 is now wide enough to display the entire entry. However, the entry in B12 is adversely affected by enlarging the column width.

Plan a worksheet design before you make any cell entries. If necessary, widen the columns to accommodate labels. It takes less time to do some advance planning than to edit and re-enter fragmented labels. If you work from left to right when entering labels, you can avoid overwriting existing labels.

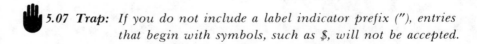

5.06 Tip: *AppleWorks makes assumptions about whether an entry is a label or a value, based on the first character that you enter.*

AppleWorks interprets each spreadsheet entry by keying on the first character. There are basically two categories of entries: labels and values. The following chart outlines how AppleWorks distinguishes them:

LABELS

Leading character   A-Z

                         "   [any character(s) that
                                   follows will be taken
                                   as a label]

VALUES

Leading character   0-9

                         +   [denotes formula]
                         −   [denotes formula]
                         @   [denotes function]

See the following two Traps.

5.07 Trap: *If you do not include a label indicator prefix ("), entries that begin with symbols, such as $, will not be accepted.*

If the first character of a label is not a letter of the alphabet, a double quotation mark (") must precede it. In fact, AppleWorks will not accept an entry that begins with a symbol other than +, −, and @; you will hear a beep and have to re-enter the data. If a symbol follows alphabetic characters, AppleWorks will allow the entry.

To enter dollar figures, do not include the dollar symbol ($). Enter the value and then select the Dollars format.

 5.08 Trap: *You cannot enter a number as a label unless you include a label indicator prefix (").*

Sometimes you may want to enter numbers as labels. Data is often reported by year, and labels might look like those shown in row 5 of the following spreadsheet:

```
File: SALES                    REVIEW/ADD/CHANGE              Escape: Main Menu
========A========B========C========D========E========F========G========H====
   1|           PERFECT INDUSTRIES - PROJECTED SALES
   2|
   3|
   4|    Sales
   5|    Staff    Div.    1986    1987    1988    1989    1990
   6| -------  -------  -------  -------  -------  -------  -------
   7|Laurie         1   $3,000  $3,150  $3,308  $3,473  $3,647
   8|Deeni          1   $2,500  $2,625  $2,756  $2,894  $3,039
   9|Arlene         2   $2,400  $2,520  $2,646  $2,778  $2,917
  10|Nancy          3   $2,350  $2,468  $2,591  $2,720  $2,856
  11|Linda          3   $2,285  $2,399  $2,519  $2,645  $2,777
  12|Sue            4   $2,100  $2,205  $2,315  $2,431  $2,553
  13|Pat            2   $2,400  $2,520  $2,646  $2,778  $2,917
  14|Judy           4   $2,050  $2,152  $2,260  $2,373  $2,492
  15|                   -------  -------  -------  -------  -------
  16|           TOTAL:  $19,085 $20,039 $21,041 $22,093 $23,198
  17|
  18|
-------------------------------------------------------------------------
C5: (Label, Layout-C) 1986

Type entry or use a commands                              a-? for Help
```

The entries in cells C5 through G5 were entered as labels by using the label indicator prefix ("). The cell indicator shows that the entry is a label, and the center layout is assigned. Using this convention, you can assign label formats, if desired, but if this number had been entered without the double quotation marks, AppleWorks will treat it as a value and not allow you to justify the entry.

5.09 Tip: *If you use the spreadsheet Edit command (OPEN APPLE-U) instead of the Blank command (OPEN APPLE-B), assigned format options will not be affected.*

Once you blank a cell, both the contents and the formatting are wiped out. But when you edit a cell, you can maintain the current format settings.

In AppleWorks' Spreadsheet environment, you can use OPEN APPLE-U to delete all the characters in a label entry. However, AppleWorks will not let you delete a value entry with the Edit command. When you press RETURN, you will hear a beep, and your original entry will be restored. To delete an entry, you have to use the Blank command and then reformat the cell. You could also use the following trick.

Copy a blank but formatted cell to the cell you want deleted. The format of the copied cell is carried forward to the destination cell. You can thus copy a blank as easily as a label or a value.

5.10 Tip: *You can edit cells that have been "fixed" by the Titles command.*

Even though fixed rows and columns remain stationary when you scroll to the right and down, you can access and modify cell entries. Notice the duplicate columns in the following worksheet:

```
File: SALES                    REVIEW/ADD/CHANGE    Escape: Restore former entry
========A========A========B=======C=======D========E========F========G=======
 1|                             SALES   PROJECTIONS
 2|
 3|
 4|  Sales    Sales            Current   Proj.    Proj.    Proj.    Proj.    P
 5|  Staff    Staff    Div.    Qtr.      Qtr.1    Qtr.2    Qtr.3    Qtr.4   Yr.
 6|  -------  -------  -------  -------   -------  -------  -------  ------- --
 7|Laura J.  Laurie             2 $45,000 $50,850  $57,460  $64,930  $73,371 $24
 8|Doris N.  Doris N.           2 $42,000 $47,460  $53,630  $60,602  $68,480 $23
 9|Edward G.Edward G.           1 $43,000 $49,450  $56,868  $65,398  $75,207 $24
10|Sandra D.Sandra D.           4 $30,000 $32,400  $34,992  $37,791  $40,815 $14
11|Steven R.Steven R.           3 $21,000 $23,520  $26,342  $29,503  $33,044 $11
12|                             -------   -------  -------  -------  ------- --
13|                   TOTAL:    $181,000 $203,680 $229,292 $258,225 $290,917 $98
14|
15|
16|
17|
18|
-------------------------------------------------------------------------------
A7: (Label) Laura J.
Label: Laurie
Complete the label                                              51K Avail.
```

If you scroll to the far left, the cursor will enter duplicate column A. If you change the name in cell A7 from Laura to Laurie, you are in fact changing the entry in both copies of column A. If you remove the fixed title option, cell A7 still reflects the modified entry.

 5.11 Trap: *You cannot use OPEN APPLE-U to edit repeated labels.*

AppleWorks does not allow you to use the OPEN APPLE-U (Edit) command to modify a cell containing a repeated label. The only way to change this type of entry is to highlight the cell and re-enter the label.

 5.12 Tip: *You can quickly replace cell contents by selecting and retyping.*

The fastest way to replace the contents of a cell is to select the cell and then type the new entry. The old entry will then be replaced by the new one. For short entries, this procedure is faster than using the Edit command, but for lengthy or complex entries, using the Edit command could save unnecessary retyping.

Formatting Cells

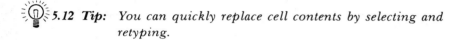 **5.13 Trap:** *Formatting affects the display of a value, not the value itself, which sometimes results in totals that do not "add to the penny."*

AppleWorks stores values as entered, and all calculations are performed on stored values. By assigning different format attributes, you alter only the display of a value.

The distinction between stored and displayed values often explains why the total of a column of formatted numbers does not "add to the penny."

Another related issue is the precision of a number — the total number of digits to the right of the decimal point. The next spreadsheet example demonstrates how to test for equal precision.

```
File: SPREADSHEET                 REVIEW/ADD/CHANGE              Escape: Main Menu
===============A====================B====================C===========
  1|PRECISION TEST:
  2|
  3|
  4|    DISPLAYED ENTRY          ACTUAL  ENTRY
  5|
  6|          123.1234568        123.123456789
  7|          123.1234568        123.123456789123
  8|
  9|                  0          @IF(A6=A7,1,0)    Logical Test
 10|
 11|-------------------------------------------------------------
 12|
 13|          123.1             123.1
 14|          123.1             123.1
 15|
 16|                  1         @IF(A13=A14,1,0)   Logical Test
 17|
 18|

  -------------------------------------------------------------
A1: (Label) PRECISION TEST:

Type entry or use @ commands                        @-? for Help
```

Consider the example in the top half of the spreadsheet. The values in A6 and A7 appear to be identical. However, cells B6 and B7 show the numbers as entered, and as you can see, they are not the same. The @IF function in A9 performs a logical test to determine if the two entries are mathematically precise. The zero result indicates that the test failed—the numbers are not equal.

The reason for this discrepancy is that although AppleWorks can store a number that has up to 25 decimal places, it displays up to only 8 decimal places. The number in A6 actually has 9 decimal places (as shown in B6), while the number in A7 has 12 decimal places (B7).

The example in the bottom half of the spreadsheet shows the results of a positive logical test, indicating that the values entered in A13 and A14 are exactly equal.

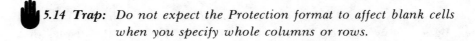

5.14 Trap: *Do not expect the Protection format to affect blank cells when you specify whole columns or rows.*

Blank cells are not affected by assigning the Protection format with the Columns or Rows option. If you want to protect blank cells, use the Entry or Block method of specifying those cells.

5.15 Trap: *If your label headings and values are misaligned, the only solution is to re-align the labels, since values cannot be aligned to the left.*

The default setting for the Label format is left justified. The default setting for the Value format is appropriate, which means that values are displayed as entered. Although labels can also be centered or right justified, values are always aligned to the left.

The only way to re-align a value is to define it as a label by adding a label prefix and then assign a format attribute. But when you do this, AppleWorks no longer considers the entry a value and will not perform calculations on it.

5.16 Tip: *Using the Block option to highlight cells that you want formatted affords the greatest flexibility.*

In AppleWorks, formatting cells is referred to as changing the layout. The command for formatting cells is OPEN APPLE-L. After executing the command, you are asked to select one of four options: Entry, Rows, Columns, or Block. Some special rules apply to how you can use these options. Only the Entry and Block options can be used to format cells prior to making entries. You cannot preset an entire row (127 cells) or column (999 cells), because doing so would use up valuable Desktop memory.

Using the Rows or Columns option, you can format all entries in the highlighted rows or columns. Of course, subsequent entries will not be formatted until you repeat the OPEN APPLE-L command. The Entry option applies to one cell at a time. The Block option affords the most selectivity. With it you can highlight any combination of partial rows and columns. In other words, you can select any rectangular block of cells for a particular format attribute. You can even select a single cell with the Block option. Because the Block option is so flexible, it is the best one to use to change the layout of entries.

5.17 Tip: *Use the Protection format to prevent inadvertently making changes to important cell entries, such as formulas.*

You can protect worksheet cells from inadvertent entries or deletions. This Protection feature helps you keep labels and formulas from being inadvertently altered when other people use the spreadsheet. This can be an important option when you are creating a worksheet into which others will regularly enter data, or when you have an application that includes complex formulas. Once a cell is protected, changes cannot be made unless the protection is revoked.

You can selectively protect single cells or blocks of cells by assigning the Protection format attribute using the Block option. But activating protection is a two-step process. You can use the OPEN APPLE-L (Layout) command to assign the protection attribute to individual cells. However, protection is not in effect unless the standard value setting for Protection is set to On, the default value whenever AppleWorks is started. By using the OPEN APPLE-V command, you can change the global Protection setting to Off.

By switching the worksheet protection to Off, you can access cells that have been assigned the Protection format. This is an important option when you are developing a spreadsheet application and need to make changes as you go. You can then turn protection back on when you have completed your changes.

✋ *5.18 Trap: Selecting the appropriate protection option can be confusing.*

It is easy to get confused when you are using the Protection format because of the way AppleWorks refers to the available options. It is natural to assume that whatever option you choose will not be allowed; that is, the specified cell(s) will be protected against that type of entry. In fact, the opposite is the case. For example, if you choose "Values Only," AppleWorks will let you enter values in the specified cell(s). It is the Nothing option that prohibits entries of any kind from being entered into specified cells. To cancel the Protection setting for individual cells, select the Anything command.

✋ *5.19 Trap: If you blank a cell entry, all formats (including Protection) are removed.*

When you blank a cell (OPEN APPLE-B), AppleWorks automatically resets the format attribute to the standard setting. However, if you attempt to blank a protected cell, AppleWorks displays the following warning:

```
You are about to clear
or remove protected cells.
```

If you respond in the affirmative, protection will be eliminated, and subsequent entries in that cell will not be protected unless you re-assign the protection attribute.

5.20 Tip: *You can make changes in the physical appearance of a spreadsheet by changing the standard values or changing the layout of individual cells.*

The key to planning the physical design of a spreadsheet is to set your standard values. These settings are in effect at all times and govern how data is displayed when it is entered. When you start up AppleWorks, the following default standard values are in effect:

- All labels are left justified.

- All numbers will be displayed as typed (if columns are wide enough).

- All columns are nine characters wide.

- All calculations are performed automatically.

- Calculations are performed from the top down in columns and then across rows.

Using the OPEN APPLE-V (Values) command, you can change the standard values of a spreadsheet. If you know in advance that you want all the labels centered, for example, you can change the standard label format from left justified to centered.

5.21 Tip: *When you copy an individual cell or range of cells, the assigned formats are included.*

When you execute a copy, the format of the copied cells is carried forward to the destination cells, replacing any previous format assignment.

Manipulating the Spreadsheet

 5.22 Trap: *Before you execute a move or a copy, the cursor must be in the proper starting location.*

After you invoke the Move (OPEN APPLE-M) or Copy (OPEN APPLE-C) command, AppleWorks asks you to highlight the cells that are to be moved or copied. You must have the cursor in the appropriate starting cell, because AppleWorks will not let you move the cursor except to highlight the cells that you want included. If you need to cancel a command, press the ESC key.

✋ **5.23 Trap:** *When using the Move command, you are limited to moving whole rows or columns.*

The Move command enables you to easily move a row or column of information to another location within your worksheet. You are, however, restricted to whole rows or columns. This means that you cannot highlight single cells or blocks of cells. Because of this limitation, it is important to examine the contents of rows or columns before you use the Move command. If you do not heed this warning, you may end up moving information that you did not want moved. It may be that the information was in a part of the row or column not visible on the screen at the time of the move.

To move a single cell or block of cells, use the Copy command (and indicate No Change for formulas) to duplicate the entries to a new location and then use OPEN APPLE-B (Blank) to erase the original entries.

✋ **5.24 Trap:** *You cannot use the Copy command on more than one row or column at a time.*

AppleWorks prevents you from selecting multiple rows or columns to be copied. You can highlight cells in one direction only, which forces you to work with only one row or column at a time. Copying to the Clipboard can be a solution if the layout of the worksheet allows for whole rows or columns to be copied. The smallest area that can be selected is an entire row or column. In fact, you can select up to 250 rows or 125 columns to be placed on the Clipboard. Keep these limitations in mind when you are planning a spreadsheet application. If you anticipate the need to copy worksheet segments regularly, arrange the entries so that you can use the Copy command effectively.

💡 **5.25 Tip:** *You can save time when using the Copy command if you copy from as few cells as possible to as many cells as possible.*

The Spreadsheet

Creating the worksheet in Figure 5-1 was expedited by using the Copy command in the most efficient way. By carefully planning the development of a worksheet, you can minimize manual entries by applying generic formulas to multiple cells. The @SUM function entered in B13 can also be used to get totals for columns C through G. Using the Copy command, you can enter the appropriate formulas with a minimum of effort. Similarly, the @SUM function entered in cell G7 can be copied to cells G8 through G11.

The dashed-line pattern in row 6 of Figure 5-1 was created by entering dashes in cell A6 and then copying the repeated pattern to B6 through G6 and B12 through G12. All this was accomplished in only two steps.

5.26 Tip: *When you use the Move command, AppleWorks maintains relative referencing and adjusts all formulas accordingly.*

After you move a row or a column of information to another location in a worksheet, AppleWorks closes up the vacant space and re-assigns column letters and row numbers accordingly. All formulas are adjusted so that cell references remain valid. It makes the Move command virtually trouble-free.

```
File: SALES                  REVIEW/ADD/CHANGE              Escape: Main Menu
========A========B========C========D========E========F========G========H====
 1|              SALES  PROJECTIONS
 2|
 3|
 4|   Sales   Current   Proj.    Proj.    Proj.    Proj.    Proj.
 5|   Staff    Qtr.     Qtr.1    Qtr.2    Qtr.3    Qtr.4   Yr.Total
 6| -------   -------   -------  -------  -------  -------  -------
 7|Laura J.  $45,000   $47,250  $49,612  $52,093  $54,698 $203,653
 8|Doris N.  $42,000   $44,100  $46,305  $48,620  $51,051 $190,077
 9|Edward G. $43,000   $45,150  $47,408  $49,778  $52,267 $194,602
10|Sandra D. $30,000   $31,500  $33,075  $34,729  $36,465 $135,769
11|Steven R. $21,000   $22,050  $23,152  $24,310  $25,526  $95,038
12|          -------   -------  -------  -------  -------  -------
13|         $181,000  $190,050 $199,552 $209,530 $220,007 $819,139
14|
15|
16|
17|
18|
-------------------------------------------------------------------------
B13: (Value, Layout-D0) @SUM(B7...B11)

Type entry or use @ commands                            @-? for Help
```

Figure 5-1. Sample worksheet

Like the Move command, the Insert command (OPEN APPLE-I) maintains accurate cell referencing. On the other hand, the Delete command (OPEN APPLE-D) can be problematical if you delete a row or a column containing a cell referenced by a formula.

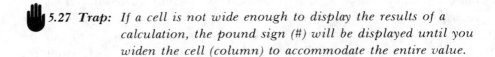 **5.27 Trap:** *If a cell is not wide enough to display the results of a calculation, the pound sign (#) will be displayed until you widen the cell (column) to accommodate the entire value.*

The default column width setting is nine characters. If you enter a value in a cell not wide enough to display the entire value, the cell will fill with pound signs (#). The same display takes place for formula results exceeding the current column width setting. The following spreadsheet is identical to the one in Figure 5-1, except for the values in column B:

```
File: SALES                      REVIEW/ADD/CHANGE              Escape: Main Menu
========A========B========C========D========E========F========G=======•H====
  1|              SALES  PROJECTIONS
  2|
  3|
  4|   Sales  Current   Proj.    Proj.    Proj.    Proj.    Proj.
  5|   Staff    Qtr.    Qtr.1    Qtr.2    Qtr.3    Qtr.4   Yr.Total
  6|  -------  -------  -------  -------  -------  -------  -------
  7|Laura J. $56,000  $58,800  $61,740  $64,827  $68,068 $253,435
  8|Doris N. $47,000  $49,350  $51,818  $54,408  $57,129 $212,705
  9|Edward G. $57,000  $59,850  $62,842  $65,985  $69,284 $257,961
 10|Sandra D. $35,000  $36,750  $38,588  $40,517  $42,543 $158,397
 11|Steven R. $30,000  $31,500  $33,075  $34,729  $36,465 $135,769
 12|          -------  -------  -------  -------  -------  -------
 13|         $225,000 $236,250 $248,062 $260,466 $273,489 ##########
 14|
 15|
 16|
 17|
 18|
-------------------------------------------------------------------------------
G13: (Value, Layout-DO) ƏSUM(G7...G11)

Type entry or use Ə commands                              Ə-? for Help
```

The projected figures are now larger, and the formula results in G13 cannot be displayed because the column is too narrow. But you can widen the cell. Keep in mind, however, that adjusting the column width of any one cell in a worksheet will affect all others unless you use the OPEN APPLE-L command to change the width of a single column.

✋ **5.28 Trap:** *Under certain circumstances, AppleWorks will not let you insert columns or rows.*

If you have created a worksheet application that extends to the maximum number of columns (127) or rows (999), you will not be allowed to insert another column or row.

Chances are you will not be affected by this restriction, since memory limitations usually prevent you from using the maximum number of columns or rows (unless you have a memory expansion card installed in your system).

Insertions cannot be made if the cursor is located after existing information.

✋ **5.29 Trap:** *Be careful about where you place the cursor before using the Insert Rows/Columns command. AppleWorks inserts rows or columns relative to the cursor location.*

Inserted columns will appear to the left of the cursor and inserted rows above the cursor. With this in mind, place the cursor one column to the right or one row below where you want the insertion, and then issue the OPEN APPLE-I command. Be sure to position the cursor before executing the command.

✋ **5.30 Trap:** *You cannot insert more than nine rows or columns at a time.*

AppleWorks limits you to a total of nine rows or columns each time you execute the Insert command. However, you can repeat the procedure should you need to insert more than nine rows or columns in any one worksheet location.

✋ **5.31 Trap:** *If you delete the first or last cell of a range referenced in a formula, you will get an error.*

Cell B13 in Figure 5-1 contains the function @SUM, and the specified range is B7..B11. Suppose that a member of the sales staff leaves the company, and you

AppleWorks Tips and Traps

delete the entries in row 10 to reflect this change. The entries in row 11 move up to the vacant space left by deleting row 10. Everything below the deleted line moves up, and the formula in B12 adjusts accordingly: @SUM(B7..B10). The spreadsheet should look as follows:

```
File: figure 1                  REVIEW/ADD/CHANGE              Escape: Main Menu
=======A=======B=======C=======D=======E=======F=======G=======H====
  1|           SALES  PROJECTIONS
  2|
  3|
  4|  Sales  Current  Proj.    Proj.    Proj.    Proj.    Proj.
  5|  Staff  Qtr.     Qtr.1    Qtr.2    Qtr.3    Qtr.4    Yr.Total
  6| -------  -------  -------  -------  -------  -------  -------
  7|Laura J. $45,000  $47,250  $49,612  $52,093  $54,698 $203,653
  8|Doris N. $42,000  $44,100  $46,305  $48,620  $51,051 $190,077
  9|Edward G.$43,000  $45,150  $47,408  $49,778  $52,267 $194,602
 10|Steven R.$21,000  $22,050  $23,152  $24,310  $25,526  $95,038
 11|          -------  -------  -------  -------  -------  -------
 12|         $151,000 $158,550 $166,478 $174,801 $183,541 $683,370
 13|
 14|
 15|
 16|
 17|
 18|
---------------------------------------------------------------------
B12: (Value, Layout-D0) @SUM(B7...B10)

Type entry or use @ commands                              @-? for Help
```

However, should you delete a row or column that includes the first or last cell in a specified range, your formula will return an error. Refer to this next example:

```
File: figure 1                  REVIEW/ADD/CHANGE              Escape: Main Menu
=======A=======B=======C=======D=======E=======F=======G=======H====
  1|           SALES  PROJECTIONS
  2|
  3|
  4|  Sales  Current  Proj.    Proj.    Proj.    Proj.    Proj.
  5|  Staff  Qtr.     Qtr.1    Qtr.2    Qtr.3    Qtr.4    Yr.Total
  6| -------  -------  -------  -------  -------  -------  -------
  7|Laura J. $45,000  $47,250  $49,612  $52,093  $54,698 $203,653
  8|Doris N. $42,000  $44,100  $46,305  $48,620  $51,051 $190,077
  9|Edward G.$43,000  $45,150  $47,408  $49,778  $52,267 $194,602
 10|Sandra D.$30,000  $31,500  $33,075  $34,729  $36,465 $135,769
 11|          -------  -------  -------  -------  -------  -------
 12|          ERROR    ERROR    ERROR    ERROR    ERROR    ERROR
 13|
 14|
 15|
 16|
 17|
 18|
---------------------------------------------------------------------
B12: (Value, Layout-D0) @SUM(B7...@ERROR)

Type entry or use @ commands                              @-? for Help
```

Row 11 has been deleted from the original in Figure 5-1, and the @SUM function returns an error. AppleWorks is confused since one of the cell references in the specified range has been eliminated. The cell entry now looks like the following illustration:

@SUM(B7..@ERROR)

The formula will have to be edited or re-entered. You can take steps to prevent this from happening by following the suggestion in Tip 5.48.

 5.32 Trap: *Do not assume that blanking a row or a column is the same as deleting a row or a column.*

When you blank a row or a column, the contents are erased and the format reverts to the standard setting. A blank row remains, and other formulas in the worksheet are unchanged. The following spreadsheet shows the effect of blanking a row:

```
File: figure 1                REVIEW/ADD/CHANGE              Escape: Main Menu
========A========B========C========D========E========F========G========H====
 1 |              SALES  PROJECTIONS
 2 |
 3 |
 4 |  Sales   Current  Proj.    Proj.    Proj.    Proj.    Proj.
 5 |  Staff   Qtr.     Qtr.1    Qtr.2    Qtr.3    Qtr.4    Yr.Total
 6 |  ------- -------  -------  -------  -------  -------  -------
 7 |Laura J.  $45,000  $47,250  $49,612  $52,093  $54,698 $203,653
 8 |Doris N.  $42,000  $44,100  $46,305  $48,620  $51,051 $190,077
 9 |
10 |Sandra D. $30,000  $31,500  $33,075  $34,729  $36,465 $135,769
11 |
12 |          -------  -------  -------  -------  -------  -------
13 |          $117,000 $122,850 $128,992 $135,442 $142,214 $529,499
14 |
15 |
16 |
17 |
18 |
-------------------------------------------------------------------------------
B13: (Value, Layout-D0) @SUM(B7...B11)

Type entry or use @ commands                              @-? for Help
```

Rows 9 and 11 have been blanked. The rows did not move, and the formula in B13, @SUM(B7..B11), remains unchanged. Subsequent entries in these rows will be accounted for in the formula cells; however, the results will not be displayed in currency format.

A deletion causes the entire row or column and its contents to disappear from the worksheet. The remaining gap is closed, with rows renumbered and columns relettered.

5.33 Trap: *Review the contents of an entire row or column prior to deleting it because the Delete command permanently removes all information contained in the affected row(s) and column(s).*

You could lose valuable information if you carry out a row or column delete without viewing the entire row or column first. Since most spreadsheet applications exceed the limits of the viewing window, you must remember to scan the entire length of a row or a column prior to issuing the Delete command. If you save the worksheet before making significant deletions, you can always revert to a previously saved version if the spreadsheet gets messed up.

5.34 Tip: *Use the Titles command (OPEN APPLE-T) to keep row and column headings visible at all times.*

Most spreadsheet applications are larger than one screen wide or deep. When you move the cursor to the lower-right portion of the active worksheet area, column headers in the upper rows and row labels in the left columns disappear. It is difficult to remember what type of information each row or column contains when header labels are not visible.

The Titles command lets you "fix" the titles (keep them from moving off the screen). All columns and rows will scroll, except those that you have fixed with the Titles command. The worksheet in the following illustration has fixed top and left titles and has room for entries to be made in columns H through L while the row and column headings are still visible.

```
File: PERFECT                    REVIEW/ADD/CHANGE              Escape: Main Menu
========A========F========G========H========I========J========K========L====
   1|
   2|
   3|
   4|   Sales
   5|   Staff     1989     1990     1991     1992     1993     1994     1995
   6| -------  -------  -------  -------  -------  -------  -------  -------
   7|Arlene    $2,778   $2,917
   8|Deeni     $2,894   $3,039
   9|Judy      $2,373   $2,492
  10|Laurie    $3,473   $3,647
  11|Linda     $2,645   $2,777
  12|Nancy     $2,720   $2,856
  13|Pat       $2,778   $2,917
  14|Sue       $2,431   $2,553
  15|          -------  -------  -------  -------  -------  -------  -------
  16|          $5,846   $6,138       $0       $0       $0       $0       $0
  17|
  18|
-----------------------------------------------------------------------------
H7

Type entry or use а commands                              а-? for Help
```

Do not be confused if you see a double set of columns or rows when the titles are fixed. This feature makes it possible to edit the titles while the Titles command is in effect.

5.35 Tip: *Use the Windows command (OPEN APPLE-W) to access areas of the spreadsheet that are normally out of view.*

The AppleWorks Windows command lets you juxtapose two sets of information that would normally be out of viewing range. Suppose you have a spreadsheet that contains quarterly sales projection figures for two years. You want to compare the figures for the first quarter of each year. The next illustration shows a split view of the screen, with which you can view columns D (1986) and I (1987) as adjacent columns.

```
File: SALES                      REVIEW/ADD/CHANGE                Escape: Main Menu
========A========B========C========D============I=========J========K====
  1|                        SALES  PROJECTIO   1|
  2|                                            2|
  3|                                            3|
  4|   Sales            Current    1986         4|   1987      1987      1987
  5|   Staff     Div.    Qtr.      Qtr.1        5|   Qtr.1     Qtr.2     Qtr.3
  6| -------   -------  -------   -------       6| -------   -------   -------
  7|Laura J.        2  $45,000   $50,850        7| $40,000   $36,000   $42,500
  8|Doris N.        2  $42,000   $47,460        8| $38,000   $34,200   $37,000
  9|Edward G.       1  $43,000   $49,450        9| $38,500   $34,650   $39,000
 10|Sandra D.       4  $30,000   $32,400       10| $27,000   $24,300   $21,000
 11|Steven R.       3  $21,000   $23,520       11| $24,000   $21,600   $18,500
 12|                   -------   -------       12| -------   -------   -------
 13|        TOTAL:    $181,000  $203,680       13|$167,500  $150,750  $158,000
 14|                                           14|
 15|                                           15|
 16|Division Growth Factor:                    16|
 17|      1         2        3        4         17|
 18|     .15       .13      .12      .08        18|
------------------------------------------------------------------------
I18

Type entry or use 2 commands                              2-? for Help
```

The Windows command enables you to divide the screen either horizontally or vertically. You can easily switch the cursor from one viewing window to another with the Jump command (OPEN APPLE-J). Before invoking the Windows command, remember to position the cursor where you want the screen to be split.

In addition to creating a split image of the worksheet, the Windows command lets you specify whether or not you want the two images to scroll in a synchronized fashion. Unsynchronized scrolling is the default setting.

Synchronizing windows often make it easier to work with two at once, because the rows and columns remain aligned in a meaningful way. To select the synchronization option, you must first specify what kind of window you want AppleWorks to create:

Windows?   Side by side   Top and bottom

When you press OPEN APPLE-W a second time, you will see the following:

Windows?   One   Synchronized

You can either revert back to a single screen view, or you can select synchronized scrolling. Once you have opted for synchronization, your command options are as follows:

Windows?   One   Unsynchronized

Entering Formulas and Functions

5.36 Trap: *Formula entries are restricted to a maximum length of 75 characters.*

Under no circumstances can you exceed this limit. If you try, the formula will be truncated into a meaningless entry. In AppleWorks, an entry can be only as long as the screen is wide. As you enter a formula, it is displayed in the cell indicator, and that line offers a total of 75 spaces.

5.37 Trap: *When you type a formula into a cell, AppleWorks will interpret it as a label unless you begin with one of the following: plus sign (+), minus sign (−), decimal point, digits 0-9, left parenthesis, or the @ sign.*

Without the proper prefix, formula entries become labels because AppleWorks keys on the first character to determine the nature of the entry. The following are examples of legitimate formula entries:

    +A7*.37
    −B2+D2
    60*B7
    (A3*C7)−J37
    @SUM(J1..J40)

If you just enter A7*B7, for instance, AppleWorks will turn it into a label, not a formula.

5.38 Tip: *To help prevent errors, point to specify cell addresses and ranges in formulas.*

Instead of typing cell coordinates, use the cursor to point to individual cells and ranges of cells that are referenced in formulas. After you type a formula indicator

$(+, -)$ or function prefix (@), you can point to cell locations with the cursor; AppleWorks keys in the actual coordinates.

If you are not familiar with this method of entering formulas, refer to the *AppleWorks Reference Manual.* Once you get accustomed to it, you may find that this method of entering formulas is easier and more efficient than typing them in. It is often less error-prone since you are working visually. As you highlight a cell or a range of cells, you can easily determine the accuracy of your selection. You cannot, however, use this method when editing a cell entry.

5.39 Trap: *If the parentheses in a formula are not balanced correctly, AppleWorks will beep and prevent you from entering the formula.*

A balanced formula has the same number of open and closed parentheses. AppleWorks will not let you enter a formula unless it is balanced. If you try to enter an unbalanced formula, AppleWorks will beep, and the formula will remain on the entry line until it is properly balanced.

5.40 Tip: *AppleWorks performs calculations from left to right, regardless of the type of mathematical operation.*

Some spreadsheet programs follow what is called order of precedence for mathematical operations. Simply put, it means that certain operations are performed before others. AppleWorks, however, performs calculations in a left-to-right order, without regard for the type of operation, except when an operation is enclosed in parentheses. This simplifies the formula entry process, and the calculation order can easily be determined by looking at the entry order.

5.41 Trap: *A formula will return an error if you have deleted a row or a column that contains a value referenced in it.*

Deleting rows or columns can wreak havoc on formulas. If you inadvertently delete a cell entry that is referenced in a formula, an error message will be displayed in the cell containing the formula. To eliminate the error, either re-enter the formula or go into edit mode to specify a valid cell reference.

5.42 Tip: *When specifying arguments for an @IF function, you can use a formula, a function, or a cell address.*

For any of the three arguments of an @IF statement, you can specify

- A cell address (B7)

- A formula (A10*.25)

- A function (@LOOKUP(C3,A37..K58).

The following example incorporates all three possibilities:

@IF(C7>30000,@LOOKUP(B7,A17..D17),@LOOKUP(A10,A25..F25)*5)

In words, the formula says: If the value in C7 is greater than 30,000, return the result of looking up the value in B7 and finding the corresponding value in the lookup table located at A17..D17. If the value in C7 is less than or equal to 30,000, look up A10 in A25..F25 and multiply by 5.

5.43 Trap: *When entering formulas, always begin in the cell where you want the formula result to be displayed.*

Before starting a formula entry, be sure that the cursor is highlighting the cell where you want the calculation result to be entered. It is particularly easy to fall prey to this Trap when you use pointers to enter formula references. If you are not careful, you could end up with misleading results.

5.44 Tip: *You can refer to the cell indicator for the coordinates of the highlighted cell, the cell's contents, and format attributes if there are any.*

Visually determining the coordinates of a highlighted cell is not always accurate. Your eyes can deceive you. The cell indicator (located in the bottom left corner) indicates the coordinates of the highlighted cell and describes the cell's content and assigned format attributes. The cell indicator in the next illustration shows the formula behind the value displayed in the highlighted cell.

```
File: SALES                  REVIEW/ADD/CHANGE              Escape: Main Menu
========A========B========C========D========E========F========G========H====
 1|                      SALES  PROJECTIONS
 2|
 3|
 4| Sales           Current  Proj.    Proj.    Proj.    Proj.    Proj.
 5| Staff     Div.   Qtr.    Qtr.1    Qtr.2    Qtr.3    Qtr.4   Yr.Total
 6| -------  -------  -------  -------  -------  -------  -------  -------
 7|Laura J.     2 $45,000 $50,850 $57,460 $64,930 $73,371 $246,612
 8|Doris N.     2 $42,000 $47,460 $53,630 $60,602 $68,480 $230,171
 9|Edward G.    1 $43,000 $49,450 $56,868 $65,398 $75,207 $246,922
10|Sandra D.    4 $30,000 $32,400 $34,992 $37,791 $40,815 $145,998
11|Steven R.    3 $21,000 $23,520 $26,342 $29,503 $33,044 $112,410
12|          -------  -------  -------  -------  -------  -------
13|      TOTAL: $181,000 $203,680 $229,292 $258,225 $290,917 $982,114
14|
15|
16|Division Growth Factor:
17|      1        2        3        4
18|     .15      .13      .12      .08
--------------------------------------------------------------------------
C13: (Value, Layout-D0) @SUM(C7...C11)

Type entry or use @ commands                               @-? for Help
```

"Value" refers to the type of entry. "Layout" identifies how the cell entry is formatted; "D0" refers to the Dollars format with zero decimal places. "@SUM(C7..C11)" is the formula entered in C13.

✋ **5.45 Trap:** *When you construct a lookup table, make sure that the values are unique and in ascending order.*

If you do not, the results may be unpredictable. The LOOKUP function expects to find the values in the search range listed in ascending order. For large tables, you might find it easier to use the Arrange (sort) command on the lookup table.

✋ **5.46 Trap:** *If your lookup table does not include entries for the lowest and highest possible values, you may get unexpected results from lookup formulas.*

Consider the lookup table in the following illustration.

```
File: PERFECT                  REVIEW/ADD/CHANGE              Escape: Main Menu
========A========B========C========D========E========F========G========H====
 1 I             PERFECT INDUSTRIES - PROJECTED SALES
 2 I                                                        Lookup Table:
 3 I   Sales
 4 I   Staff     Div.    1986    1987    1988               Division % Growth
 5 I ------     -------  -------  -------  -------           -------  -------
 6 ILaurie         1    $3,000      NA      NA                  2     .05
 7 IDeeni          3    $2,500  $2,675  $2,782                  3     .07
 8 IArlene         2    $2,400  $2,520  $2,621                  4     .03
 9 IPat            2    $2,400  $2,520  $2,621                  5     .06
10 INancy          6    $2,350  $2,444  $2,542                  6     .04
11 ILinda          3    $2,285  $2,445  $2,543
12 ISue            7    $2,100  $2,184  $2,271
13 IJudy           4    $2,050  $2,112  $2,196
14 I                    -------  -------  -------
15 I      TOTAL:      $19,085      NA      NA
16 I
17 I
18 I
------------------------------------------------------------------------------
D6: (Value, Layout-DO) +C6*@LOOKUP(B6,G6...G10)+C6

Type entry or use @ commands                          @-? for Help
```

Note that the search range goes from 2 to 6 (G6..G10), and the search values range from 1 to 7 (B6..B13). The lookup formula in D6 returns NA because the search value is smaller than the first entry in the search range. The lookup formula in D12 returns a growth factor of 4 percent because the search value (7) is larger than the largest value (6) in the search range; in such a case a lookup formula returns the last value in the search range. These results may or may not be what you want. The solution is to anticipate the lowest and highest possible values and include them in the search range. On the low end, you could enter 0 and avoid the NA result.

✋ **5.47 Trap:** *The @AVG function treats an empty cell and a cell containing a zero differently.*

The @AVG function first sums the specified range and then divides by the number of cells in the range. Consider the two examples in the spreadsheet that follows.

```
File: FUNCTIONS                REVIEW/ADD/CHANGE              Escape: Main Menu
=======A========B=======C=======D=======E=======F=======G=======H===
  1 |EXAMPLE A:                         EXAMPLE B:
  2 |
  3 |
  4 |            467                                  467
  5 |            783                                  783
  6 |            239                                  239
  7 |              0
  8 |            117                                  117
  9 |            202                                  202
 10 |        ---------                            ---------
 11 |        301.3333  @AVG(B4..B9)                  361.6  @AVG(F4..F9)
 12 |
 13 |
 14 |
 15 |
 16 |
 17 |
 18 |
    --------------------------------------------------------------------------
B11: (Value) @AVG(B4...B9)

Type entry or use @ commands                              @-? for Help
```

The range in example A includes a zero entry, and the range in example B includes a blank cell. Since the @AVG function considers zero a valid entry, the total of the range in example A is divided by 6 to determine the average.

In the case of example B, the blank cell is ignored and the divisor becomes 5, thus accounting for the difference in results.

The @MIN function, which returns the minimum of all values in a range, and the MAX function, which returns the maximum of all values in a range, handle blanks and zeroes the same way that @AVG does.

5.48 Tip: *When specifying @SUM ranges, include an extra row or column to allow for insertions and deletions.*

If possible, try to include an extra row or column at the boundaries of the @SUM ranges to allow for later entries to fall within the specified range. Consider the following spreadsheet example:

```
File: PERFECT                    REVIEW/ADD/CHANGE              Escape: Main Menu
=======A========B========C========D========E========F========G========H====
   1|           PERFECT INDUSTRIES - MONTHLY SALES
   2|
   3|
   4|   Sales
   5|   Staff     JAN      FEB      MAR      APR      MAY
   6| -------  -------  -------  -------  -------  -------
   7|Laurie    $3,000   $3,000
   8|Deeni     $2,500   $2,500
   9|Arlene    $2,400   $2,400
  10|Pat       $2,400   $2,400
  11|Nancy     $2,350   $2,350
  12|Linda     $2,285   $2,285
  13|Sue       $2,100   $2,100
  14|Judy      $2,050   $2,050
  15|          -------  -------  -------  -------  -------
  16|         $19,085  $19,085       $0       $0       $0
  17|
  18|
----------------------------------------------------------------------------
C16: (Value, Layout-D0) @SUM(C7...C15)

Type entry or use @ commands                          @-? for Help
```

The @SUM function in cell B16 specifies the range B7..B14, and the @SUM function in cell C16 specifies the range C7..C15, which includes the dashed-line entry in cell C15. Since the results are identical, you might conclude that it does not matter which format you use.

But suppose that a new salesperson joins the staff, which means that a new line will have to be inserted in the worksheet. According to Trap 5.31, you could successfully insert a new line in the middle of the range, but not at the beginning or the end of the range. The illustration on the next page demonstrates how the @SUM functions in cells B16 and C16 are affected when a new row is inserted after row 14.

```
File: PERFECT                 REVIEW/ADD/CHANGE          Escape: Main Menu
========A========B========C========D========E========F========G========H====
 1|         PERFECT INDUSTRIES - MONTHLY SALES
 2|
 3|
 4|  Sales
 5|  Staff    JAN     FEB     MAR     APR     MAY
 6|  -------  -------  -------  -------  -------  -------
 7|Laurie    $3,000   $3,000
 8|Deeni     $2,500   $2,500
 9|Arlene    $2,400   $2,400
10|Pat       $2,400   $2,400
11|Nancy     $2,350   $2,350
12|Linda     $2,285   $2,285
13|Sue       $2,100   $2,100
14|Judy      $2,050   $2,050
15|J.G.      $3,000   $3,000
16|          -------  -------  -------  -------  -------
17|         $19,085  $22,085      $0      $0      $0
18|
----------------------------------------------------------------------------
C17: (Value, Layout-D0) @SUM(C7...C16)

Type entry or use @ commands                              @-? for Help
```

The results in cell C17 demonstrate how AppleWorks automatically adjusts the formula to account for the new row. In contrast, the formula in B17 remains @SUM(B7..B14).

✋ *5.49 Trap:* *If you do not specify either "No change" or "Relative"*
for both coordinates of a range to be copied, you may get
the wrong results from your formula.

When copying a formula, you are asked whether the various components of the formula are relative or constant. As each reference is highlighted in the entry line, you must respond by choosing "No change" or "Relative." Consider the example in the following illustration:

```
File: figure 1                    REVIEW/ADD/CHANGE              Escape: Main Menu
========A========B========C========D========E========F========G========H====
 1|              SALES  PROJECTIONS
 2|
 3|
 4|  Sales   Current   Proj.    Proj.    Proj.    Proj.    Proj.
 5|  Staff    Qtr.     Qtr.1    Qtr.2    Qtr.3    Qtr.4   Yr.Total
 6| -------  -------  -------  -------  -------  -------  -------
 7|Laura J.  $12,000  $12,600  $13,230  $13,892  $14,586  $54,308
 8|Doris N.  $10,000  $10,500  $11,025  $11,576  $12,155  $45,256
 9|Edward G. $12,500  $13,125  $13,781  $14,470  $15,194  $56,570
10|Sandra D.  $8,000   $8,400   $8,820   $9,261   $9,724  $36,205
11|Steven R.  $6,000   $6,300   $6,615   $6,946   $7,293  $27,154
12|          -------  -------  -------  -------  -------  -------
13|          $48,500  $50,925  $53,471  $56,145  $58,952 $219,493
14|          $48,500
15|
16|
17|
18|
--------------------------------------------------------------------------------
B14: (Value, Layout-D0) ƏSUM(B7...B11)

Type entry or use Ə commands                              Ə-? for Help
```

The formula in B13 is copied to B14, specifying "No change" for both references, B7 and B11. Cell B14 is therefore an exact duplicate of B13. In the next illustration, the formula in B14 is copied to the range C14..G14. B7 is given "Relative" status, while B11 is referenced as "No change."

```
File: figure 1                  REVIEW/ADD/CHANGE              Escape: Main Menu
========A========B========C========D========E========F========G========H===
   1|             SALES  PROJECTIONS
   2|
   3|
   4|  Sales   Current   Proj.    Proj.    Proj.    Proj.    Proj.
   5|  Staff   Qtr.      Qtr.1    Qtr.2    Qtr.3    Qtr.4    Yr.Total
   6| -------  -------   -------  -------  -------  -------  -------
   7|Laura J.  $12,000   $12,600  $13,230  $13,892  $14,586  $54,308
   8|Doris N.  $10,000   $10,500  $11,025  $11,576  $12,155  $45,256
   9|Edward G. $12,500   $13,125  $13,781  $14,470  $15,194  $56,570
  10|Sandra D.  $8,000    $8,400   $8,820   $9,261   $9,724  $36,205
  11|Steven R.  $6,000    $6,300   $6,615   $6,946   $7,293  $27,154
  12|          -------   -------  -------  -------  -------  -------
  13|          $48,500   $50,925  $53,471  $56,145  $58,952 $219,493
  14|          $48,500   $99,425 $152,896 $209,041 $267,993 $487,486
  15|
  16|
  17|
  18|
------------------------------------------------------------------------
C14: (Value, Layout-D0) @SUM(C7...B11)

Type entry or use @ commands                              @-? for Help
```

This results in B11 being identified as a constant, and the value does not change. But B7, being relative, changes according to the column (C7, D7, E7, and so on). The results in cells C14..G14 are not accurate.

5.50 Tip: Use the @NA function in cells where there will be a value but one is not yet available.

This function is used to place the notation NA in a cell when you have formulas that reference that cell but you do not yet have data in it. When appropriate, the NA can be replaced with a value, and all dependent formulas will recalculate.

5.51 Tip: You can sort columns alphabetically or numerically, in ascending or descending order.

You can use the worksheet environment as a quick and easy alternative to the AppleWorks data base for creating and sorting short lists. When you execute the

OPEN APPLE-A (Arrange) command, the screen should look similar to the following illustration:

```
File: SALES                       ARRANGE            Escape: Review/Add/Change
========A========B========C========D========E========F========G========H====




              Rows 7 through 14 will be arranged
              based on the contents of column A

              Arrangement order:

                   1.   Labels from A to Z
                   2.   Labels from Z to A
                   3.   Values from 0 to 9
                   4.   Values from 9 to 0



--------------------------------------------------------------------------------

Type number, or use arrows, then press Return              52K Avail.
```

If you select the A to Z arrangement order, you will get an alphabetically ordered list like this one:

```
File: SALES                    REVIEW/ADD/CHANGE           Escape: Main Menu
========A========B========C========D========E========F========G========H====
  1I          PERFECT INDUSTRIES - PROJECTED SALES
  2I
  3I
  4I    Sales
  5I    Staff    Div.    1986    1987    1988    1989    1990
  6I -------    -------  ------- ------- ------- ------- -------
  7IArlene          2   $2,400  $2,520  $2,646  $2,778  $2,917
  8IDeeni           1   $2,500  $2,625  $2,756  $2,894  $3,039
  9IJudy            4   $2,050  $2,152  $2,260  $2,373  $2,492
 10ILaurie          1   $3,000  $3,150  $3,308  $3,473  $3,647
 11ILinda           3   $2,285  $2,399  $2,519  $2,645  $2,777
 12INancy           3   $2,350  $2,468  $2,591  $2,720  $2,856
 13IPat             2   $2,400  $2,520  $2,646  $2,778  $2,917
 14ISue             4   $2,100  $2,205  $2,315  $2,431  $2,553
 15I                    ------- ------- ------- ------- -------
 16I          TOTAL:    $5,050  $5,302  $5,568  $5,846  $6,138
 17I
 18I
--------------------------------------------------------------------------------
A7: (Label) Arlene

Type entry or use ? commands                         ?-? for Help
```

The names have been arranged in ascending alphabetical order.

☀️ **5.52 Tip:** *Use the Zoom command (OPEN APPLE-Z) to view formula entries.*

AppleWorks lets you view both formulas and the resulting values by toggling the Zoom command. This feature lets you view formulas, pointers, and functions. You can also "audit" your spreadsheet by using the Zoom command and then printing either a block of cells or the entire worksheet. This is one of the best ways to detect errors in formulas and provide documentation that shows the formulas that you have used. The following illustration is what your spreadsheet should look like after you invoke the Zoom command:

```
File: figure 1                   REVIEW/ADD/CHANGE              Escape: Main Menu
==============A==============B==============C==============D=======
 1|                      SALES     PROJECTIONS
 2|
 3|
 4|      Sales          Current        Proj.          Proj.
 5|      Staff           Qtr.          Qtr.1          Qtr.2
 6| -------            -------        -------        -------
 7|Laura J.            12000          +B7*.05+B7     +C7*.05+C7
 8|Doris N.            10000          +B8*.05+B8     +C8*.05+C8
 9|Edward G.           12500          +B9*.05+B9     +C9*.05+C9
10|Sandra D.            8000          +B10*.05+B10   +C10*.05+C10
11|Steven R.            6000          +B11*.05+B11   +C11*.05+C11
12|                    -------        -------        -------
13|                    ƏSUM(B7...B11) ƏSUM(C7...C11) ƏSUM(D7...D11)
14|
15|
16|
17|
18|
 ------------------------------------------------------------------
A1

Type entry or use Ə commands                              Ə-? for Help
```

There are two print commands. OPEN APPLE-P is the standard print command and has the following options:

PRINT?   All   Rows   Columns   Block

OPEN APPLE-H prints a hard copy of an AppleWorks screen display. This command can be useful if you need a printout of just a few formula cells.

☀️ **5.53 Tip:** *For accuracy to the penny, you can use the @INT function to round numbers with decimals.*

If you work with dollar values and want accuracy to the penny, you may have to round each entry. Although AppleWorks does not have a rounding function, you can use the @INT function and get accurate results.

Suppose you have the number 10.0498 in cell Al. Use the following formula to round this value:

@INT((A1+.005)*100)/100

The calculation steps are as follows:

10.0498+.005=10.0548
10.0548*100=1005.48

The integer value of 1005.48=1005

1005/100=10.05

If you apply this formula to a group of values, the total will be accurate to the penny.

Recalculating the Spreadsheet

5.54 Tip: *By selecting manual recalculation, you can speed up the entry process.*

Unless you specify otherwise, all calculations will be performed automatically as you enter data. This is called automatic recalculation, and as one of the default options, it is in effect when AppleWorks is started. For small worksheets that have simple formulas, automatic recalculation is appropriate. But if your application takes up considerable space or contains complex formulas, you will find that making entries in this mode is a slow process. By setting recalculation to manual, you can significantly speed up the data entry process. See the following Trap for more information.

5.55 Trap: *The previous Tip could easily become a Trap if you forget to recalculate before evaluating formula results or printing.*

It is easy to forget that you have set a worksheet to manual recalculation, because AppleWorks does not display a message on the screen to remind you to recalculate. Once you have switched from automatic to manual recalculation, it is up to you to remember to recalculate formulas before evaluating calculation results or printing. If you do not recalculate, you will be drawing conclusions that could be misleading.

Consider the following spreadsheet, in which cell B7 was changed from $12,000 to $60,000:

```
File: figure 1                 REVIEW/ADD/CHANGE            Escape: Main Menu
========A========B========C========D========E========F========G========H====
  1|             SALES  PROJECTIONS
  2|
  3|
  4|  Sales   Current   Proj.    Proj.    Proj.    Proj.    Proj.
  5|  Staff    Qtr.     Qtr.1    Qtr.2    Qtr.3    Qtr.4  Yr.Total
  6|  -------  -------  -------  -------  -------  -------  -------
  7|Laura J.  $60,000  $12,600  $13,230  $13,892  $14,586  $54,308
  8|Doris N.  $10,000  $10,500  $11,025  $11,576  $12,155  $45,256
  9|Edward G. $12,500  $13,125  $13,781  $14,470  $15,194  $56,570
 10|Sandra D.  $8,000   $8,400   $8,820   $9,261   $9,724  $36,205
 11|Steven R.  $6,000   $6,300   $6,615   $6,946   $7,293  $27,154
 12|           -------  -------  -------  -------  -------  -------
 13|           $48,500  $50,925  $53,471  $56,145  $58,952 $219,493
 14|
 15|
 16|
 17|
 18|
-------------------------------------------------------------------------
B7: (Value, Layout-DO) 60000

Type entry or use 2 commands                               2-? for Help
```

Prior to making this entry, the worksheet was set to manual recalculation. A quick review of formula results in columns B through G reveals that the modified entry in B7 has not been accounted for. The formulas will not be recalculated until you select the Recalculate option. Notice the lack of on-screen messages reminding you to recalculate. The following illustration shows the same worksheet after it has been manually recalculated:

```
File: figure 1                  REVIEW/ADD/CHANGE              Escape: Main Menu
========A=========B=========C=========D========E========F========G========H====
  1|              SALES  PROJECTIONS
  2|
  3|
  4|  Sales   Current   Proj.    Proj.    Proj.    Proj.    Proj.
  5|  Staff    Qtr.     Qtr.1    Qtr.2    Qtr.3    Qtr.4   Yr.Total
  6| -------   -------  -------  -------  -------  -------  -------
  7|Laura J.  $60,000  $63,000  $66,150  $69,458  $72,930 $271,538
  8|Doris N.  $10,000  $10,500  $11,025  $11,576  $12,155  $45,256
  9|Edward G. $12,500  $13,125  $13,781  $14,470  $15,194  $56,570
 10|Sandra D.  $8,000   $8,400   $8,820   $9,261   $9,724  $36,205
 11|Steven R.  $6,000   $6,300   $6,615   $6,946   $7,293  $27,154
 12|           -------  -------  -------  -------  -------  -------
 13|          $96,500 $101,325 $106,391 $111,711 $117,296 $436,723
 14|
 15|
 16|
 17|
 18|
---------------------------------------------------------------------------
B7: (Value, Layout-D0) 60000

Type entry or use ∂ commands                              ∂-? for Help
```

It is also wise to recalculate before you save a file, unless you have a specific reason not to. If you do not, the next time you retrieve that file, you may find that the formula results are inaccurate.

 5.56 Trap: *If you do not pay attention to the order of recalculation, your formulas may yield inaccurate results.*

The standard order of recalculation for AppleWorks is from top to bottom in columns (column-wise). In other words, AppleWorks spreadsheets calculate down columns, starting with the leftmost column and moving to the right. This is the default setting; it is always in effect unless you change it.

There are, however, spreadsheet applications that require a row-wise recalculation order. Consider the model in the next illustration.

```
File: FUNCTIONS                  REVIEW/ADD/CHANGE              Escape: Main Menu
==========A==============B=============C===========D=============E======
 1|Rate:
 2|          .75
 3|
 4|                                 Earnings
 5|      Month        Beginning     Current        Ending
 6|      Year         Balance       Month          Balance
 7|      ----------   ----------    ----------     ----------
 8|                                                $200
 9|Apr - 1986             $200         $350          $550
10|May - 1986             $550         $962        $1,512
11|Jun - 1986           $1,100       $1,925        $3,025
12|Jul - 1986           $2,200       $3,850        $6,050
13|
14|
15|
16|
17|
18|
-------------------------------------------------------------------
B10: (Value, Layout-D0) +D9

Type entry or use ? commands                            ?-? for Help
```

"Beginning Balance" (column B) is derived from the previous "Ending Balance" (column D). Using the standard order of recalculation, the formulas in column B require a value that has not been calculated yet (column D). In order for this spreadsheet to calculate accurately, the order of recalculation should be changed from down columns to across rows. You can do this by using the OPEN APPLE-V (Standard Values) command and selecting the Recalculation option. When asked whether you want to change the order or frequency, choose "Order" and then "Rows." You have now changed the standard order of recalculation from column-wise to row-wise. If you then recalculate, the formula results are then accurate, as in the following illustration:

```
File: FUNCTIONS                  REVIEW/ADD/CHANGE              Escape: Main Menu
==========A==============B=============C===========D=============E======
 1|Rate:
 2|          .75
 3|
 4|                                 Earnings
 5|      Month        Beginning     Current        Ending
 6|      Year         Balance       Month          Balance
 7|      ----------   ----------    ----------     ----------
 8|                                                $200
 9|Apr - 1986             $200         $350          $550
10|May - 1986             $550         $962        $1,512
11|Jun - 1986           $1,512       $2,647        $4,159
12|Jul - 1986           $4,159       $7,279       $11,438
13|
14|
15|
16|
17|
18|
-------------------------------------------------------------------
B10: (Value, Layout-D0) +D9

Type entry or use ? commands                            ?-? for Help
```

Managing Memory

 5.57 Trap: *Because of memory limitations, you cannot use all 127 columns and 999 rows offered by AppleWorks.*

The AppleWorks worksheet contains 127 columns and 999 rows, for a total of 126,873 cells. But it is unlikely that you could create an application that will fill all available cells due to memory limitations of the Apple IIe and IIc. Most systems are equipped with either 64K or 128K of RAM.

With a 64K system, approximately 1000 cells are accessible. Using an Apple with 128K, you could create a worksheet with about 6000 cells. Even though these figures are significantly less than the maximum of over 126,000 cells, they are adequate for most home and business applications.

Because RAM expansion boards are now available for the Apple IIe and IIc, you can conceivably create a worksheet that utilizes considerably more of the available worksheet area.

5.58 Tip: *Use the OPEN APPLE-? command to check available memory.*

When you are working in Spreadsheet mode, AppleWorks does not display the amount of available memory. But keeping track of memory usage can be very important when you are creating large spreadsheet models. To find out the current available memory, use the Help command (OPEN APPLE-?). Notice the indicator in the bottom right corner of the following illustration:

```
File: figure 1                    HELP              Escape: Review/Add/Change
===========================================================================
                 ⌐-A    Arrange (sort) a column

                 ⌐-B    Blank an entry or entries

                 ⌐-C    Copy entries (includes cut and paste)

                 ⌐-D    Delete rows or columns

                 ⌐-F    Find coordinates or information

                 ⌐-I    Insert rows or columns

                 ⌐-J    Jump to other split view

                 ⌐-K    Calculate all values

                 ⌐-L    Change layout of entries

    ----------------------------------------------------------------------

Use arrows to see remainder of Help                        48K Avail.
```

Printing a Spreadsheet

 5.59 Trap: *If your columns are not wide enough, you will not be able to decipher a printout of your formulas.*

Tip 5.52 suggests using the Zoom command to display worksheet formulas and then printing a hard copy of these entries. If you do not first check that your columns are wide enough to display the entire formula, you will end up with truncated formulas that cannot be deciphered. The following illustration is a good example:

```
File: figure 1                REVIEW/ADD/CHANGE           Escape: Main Menu
=======A=======B=======C=======D=======E=======F=======G=======H===
 1|             SALES  PROJECTIONS
 2|
 3|
 4|  Sales   Current  Proj.    Proj.    Proj.    Proj.    Proj.
 5|  Staff   Qtr.     Qtr.1    Qtr.2    Qtr.3    Qtr.4    Yr.Total
 6| -------  -------  -------  -------  -------  -------  -------
 7|Laura J.  60000    +B7*.05+B+C7*.05+C+D7*.05+D+E7*.05+E∂SUM(C7..
 8|Doris N.  10000    +B8*.05+B+C8*.05+C+D8*.05+D+E8*.05+E∂SUM(C8..
 9|Edward G. 12500    +B9*.05+B+C9*.05+C+D9*.05+D+E9*.05+E∂SUM(C9..
10|Sandra D. 8000     +B10*.05++C10*.05++D10*.05++E10*.05+∂SUM(C10.
11|Steven R. 6000     +B11*.05++C11*.05++D11*.05++E11*.05+∂SUM(C11.
12|          -------  -------  -------  -------  -------  -------
13|          ∂SUM(B7..∂SUM(C7..∂SUM(D7..∂SUM(E7..∂SUM(F7..∂SUM(G7..
14|
15|
16|
17|
18|
-------------------------------------------------------------------------
A7: (Label) Laura J.

Type entry or use ∂ commands                              ∂-? for Help
```

Planning Ahead

 5.60 Tip: *When you are planning a complex worksheet, keep a list of the various components and their spreadsheet coordinates or labels so you can use the Find command for easy access.*

A good approach to planning complex worksheet models is to reserve a small area in the upper-left corner (starting in A1) for a list of the various components and their names or coordinates. By starting in A1, you can use the OPEN APPLE-1 command to access the list quickly, without having to remember its location. To access a particular component, use the Text or Coordinates option of the Find command.

To further document your model, you might include a brief description of the purpose of each section. This extra step can save you hours of frustration with an application that you use infrequently.

6

Data Transfer

If you have ever created a file and found that you needed to use part of it again for another purpose, you will appreciate the ability to transfer the original data rather than having to enter it again and risk the chance of introducing new errors. As more sophisticated programs enter the marketplace, you may find that you want to transfer data from your once-adequate programs to some of these newer, more versatile applications packages.

AppleWorks enables you to transfer data both internally (between separate environments within AppleWorks) and externally (between AppleWorks files and those created by other programs).

The first section of this chapter, "The Clipboard: AppleWorks' Data Transfer Station," covers Tips and Traps that will broaden your expertise in using the Clipboard with the Move and Copy commands to share data between environments of the same type within AppleWorks.

The second section, "Using the Clipboard to Transfer Data From Spreadsheet and Data Base Files to the Word Processor," provides valuable insights about the second type of internal data exchange that is built into AppleWorks — using the Print command to print data to the Clipboard from either the Spreadsheet or the Data Base environment for transfer to the Word Processor.

Finally, the section "Creating and Accepting ASCII and DIF Files" covers techniques for sharing data between AppleWorks and files created with other programs.

The Clipboard: AppleWorks' Data Transfer Station

6.01 Tip: *The Clipboard provides a quick and easy means of transferring data between files within the same AppleWorks environment.*

Anytime you want to move information from one data base file to another, one spreadsheet file to another, or one word processing file to another, you can use the AppleWorks Clipboard as a transfer station. Issue either the Move (OPEN APPLE-M) or Copy (OPEN APPLE-C) command. Use the Move command if you no longer want the information to remain in the source document; otherwise, use the Copy command.

When you issue the Move or Copy command, you will be given the following options for moving or copying: (1) Within document, (2) To Clipboard (cut), or (3) From Clipboard (paste). To initiate a data transfer via the Clipboard, choose "To Clipboard (cut)." A prompt at the bottom of the screen will advise you to "Use cursor moves to highlight block, then press Return." With the press of the RETURN key, the information that you highlighted is sent to the Clipboard.

The next task is to make current the file that you have slated to receive the waiting Clipboard information. If the destination file is already on your Desktop, you need only call up the Desktop Index with OPEN APPLE-Q and choose it from the resulting list. If you have not yet added it to the Desktop, you will need to retrieve it from disk by choosing "Add files to Desktop" from the Main Menu.

When you are viewing the destination file, move the cursor to the exact location where you want the transferred information to be placed. Now issue the appropriate command (OPEN APPLE-M if you want the information to be moved out of the Clipboard or OPEN APPLE-C if you want to leave the information in the Clipboard to be transferred to another file), and choose "From Clipboard (paste)" from the options at the bottom of the screen. Presto—the transfer is complete, and you have been saved a lot of duplicating effort.

6.02 Tip: *You can create a new file with Clipboard data from another AppleWorks file.*

The Clipboard performs its wizardry splendidly when you want to move information from one file into another. Keep in mind that you can also create new files from data sent to the Clipboard. This Tip is especially valuable if you wish to use

```
File: Grade 1                    REVIEW/ADD/CHANGE              Escape: Main Menu
========A========B========C========D========E========F========G========H====
   1|1986 SPENDING ALLOWANCE FOR GRADE 1: $660.00
   2|
   3|NUMBER IN CLASS:          33
   4|
   5|PROJECTED USES:
   6|
   7|CLASS PARTIES: 20%       FIELD TRIPS: 50%          MISC. EQUIP: 30%
   8|
   9| $132.00                    $330.00                    $198.00
```

Figure 6-1. Original information used to create a new file

information from an existing file as the basis for a new file.

Transferring information is only one advantage that Clipboard data transfer has to offer. When you use the Copy or Move command to move information from one file to another via the Clipboard, you will find that you have also imported its formats. Thus, a new word processing file can be created with preassigned printer options from another file, whether or not the file's text is useful. You can take advantage of the same situation when you are creating a spreadsheet file if an already existing file has entries or formulas and functions that could provide a head start in creating a new spreadsheet file.

Look at the simple spreadsheet in Figure 6-1 for an example of how this works. The sample spreadsheet shows a record kept by the school secretary, who is budgeting spending money for Grade 1 during 1986. Spending money is determined by multiplying the number of children in the class by $20, which is then divided among three categories, each category benefiting according to a percentage determined by the teachers each year. Figure 6-2 shows a zoomed-in view of the formulas used to arrive at these numbers.

```
File: Grade 1                    REVIEW/ADD/CHANGE              Escape: Main Menu
========A========B========C========D========E========F========G========H====
   1|1986 SPENDING ALLOWANCE FOR GRADE 1:+C3*20
   2|
   3|NUMBER IN CLASS:  33
   4|
   5|PROJECTED USES:
   6|
   7|CLASS PARTIES: 20%       FIELD TRIPS: 50%          MISC. EQUIP: 30%
   8|
   9|+E1*.2                   +E1*.5                    +E1*.3
```

Figure 6-2. Zoomed-in file showing formulas

As you might expect, each class in the school is allotted spending money based on the same formulas. The school secretary maintains a similar file for grades 1 through 6. Knowing that the formulas she created in the Grade 1 file will apply to all the other files, she realizes that she can save time by sending the original file to the Clipboard with the Copy command (OPEN APPLE-C) and then copying it from the Clipboard after she creates the other grade files.

Once the file has been copied to the destination file(s), a number of changes will need to be made. If you compare the spending allowance file for Grade 2 (Figure 6-3) with the original file for Grade 1 (Figure 6-1), you can see that the numbers in the file have changed. But the secretary made only two changes. She changed the grade number from 1 to 2 and the number of children in the class from 33 to 29. The rest of the changes were automatic because of built-in formulas imported from the original file.

Using this same technique, the secretary created six files in a fraction of the time that it would take to enter the same information in each file separately.

Unfortunately, when spreadsheet information is sent to the Clipboard, all currency formats are lost; therefore each file had to be reformatted to display dollar amounts.

If you have a situation for which this Tip would work well, send the "model information" to the Clipboard and then create the destination file(s) that you want to receive it, or you can create a new file from scratch.

Once your destination file exists, move to the source file to extract the necessary information and send it to the Clipboard. When this is done, you can move back to the destination file, move or copy the incoming data from the Clipboard, and applaud yourself for having successfully pulled off this time-saving coup.

6.03 Trap: *The Clipboard can hold up to 250 lines, whether they come from the AppleWorks Word Processor, Data Base, or Spreadsheet environment.*

```
File: Grade 2                    REVIEW/ADD/CHANGE              Escape: Main Menu
=======A=======B=======C=======D=======E=======F=======G=======H====
 1|1986 SPENDING ALLOWANCE FOR GRADE 2: $580.00
 2|
 3|NUMBER IN CLASS:          29
 4|
 5|PROJECTED USES:
 6|
 7|CLASS PARTIES: 20%        FIELD TRIPS: 50%        MISC. EQUIP: 30%
 8|
 9| $116.00                  $290.00                 $174.00
```

Figure 6-3. Original information imported and changed for a new file

When you copy, move, or print data to the Clipboard, you will not be allowed to exceed AppleWorks' Clipboard limit of 250 word processing lines, 255 data base records (the actual limit is closer to 253), or 250 spreadsheet rows. Because of these limitations, it is wise to count the lines that you want to transfer before you begin the operation.

This task can easily be accomplished from AppleWorks' Word Processor environment, since the current line number is always displayed at the bottom of the word processing screen. If you are beginning a data transfer at the beginning of a word processing file, watch the line counter as you are highlighting lines to be included in the transfer. If you are specifying a section within a file, subtract the number of the line at the beginning of the selection from the number of the line at the end of the selection to determine if the selection is under the 250-line limit. You must determine the line count before you initiate the Move or Copy command, because the line tally displayed at the bottom of the screen is replaced with other information once these commands are made.

You can monitor the number of rows in a spreadsheet just as easily, because row numbers are always shown in the far left margin of the Spreadsheet screen.

This line count is not as readily available in AppleWorks' Data Base environment, however. There is no easy way to determine the number of records in a data base from a multiple-record layout. But if you switch to a single-record layout (OPEN APPLE-Z), you will see a message displayed above the single record that tells you the chronological placement of the current record within the data base. Switching back to multiple-record layout, you can use this information to highlight the appropriate number of records to transfer to the Clipboard.

If the information that you want to transfer via the Clipboard exceeds the 250-line limit, you will have to accomplish the transfer in more than one operation.

✋ *6.04 Trap: The amount of space available on the Clipboard can be limited by the amount of total Desktop space available.*

If your computer has a capacity of 128K of RAM, you will have 55K of Apple-Works Desktop space. If you are limited to a total of 64K of RAM, you will have only 10K of Desktop space. Since the Clipboard is included in this Desktop space, its potential capacity of 250 lines, rows, or records may be diminished if the amount of Desktop space needed for this amount of data is not available. With only 10K of Desktop space, you will probably find that your actual limit is well below 250 lines most of the time.

Whenever you attempt to make a transfer that your available RAM cannot support, you will be warned that you are exceeding the 250-line Clipboard limit. If this happens when you know that you are well below this limit (even considering Trap 6.16), you can always check on available Desktop space by looking at the bottom right corner of the help screen (accessed through OPEN APPLE-?).

If you have files on the Desktop that you do not need to complete the data transfer (other than source and destination files), you can create more Desktop space — and thus more Clipboard space — by removing the extraneous files from the Desktop. Be sure to save any files that have been changed before you take this step.

6.05 Tip: *If you are short on Clipboard RAM, you do not have to have the source and destination files on the Desktop at the same time.*

If you are confronted with the problem of limited Desktop space, which further limits Clipboard capacity (see Trap 6.04), you may be able to solve this problem by clearing the Desktop of everything but the source file and then transferring the selected data to the Clipboard.

Once the data is safely in the Clipboard, you can remove the source file from the Desktop (save it if you have not already) and load the destination file onto the Desktop. Now use the Copy or Move command to transfer the Clipboard information to its final resting place in the destination document.

6.06 Trap: *Unless it is necessary, using Copy from the Clipboard instead of Move wastes Desktop space.*

If you have stored data in the Clipboard for a transfer to more than one file, make sure that you use the Copy command when you add that data to each destination file. It will then remain in the Clipboard so that it can be added to subsequent files.

If you intend to transfer data to only one destination file, use the Move command. The Move command takes the data out of the Clipboard and releases RAM for general Desktop use. This is especially crucial if you are dealing with large files that require a great deal of Desktop space, but it is a good habit to get into in any case.

6.07 Tip: *Use the Clipboard as a way to temporarily delete informa-*
tion from a file.

When you are working in an AppleWorks document, whether in the Word Processor, Spreadsheet, or Data Base environment, you may want to print a portion
of the document but still maintain the document as a whole for future printings
and reference. The Clipboard enables you to handle such a situation elegantly.

Issue the Move command (OPEN APPLE-M), and specify that you want information moved "To Clipboard." Next, highlight the data that you want to temporarily delete, and press RETURN. The highlighted section will disappear from
the document, and you will be free to print the remaining data minus the
unwanted section.

Once the expurgated printing is complete, the original document can be restored by placing the cursor in the appropriate position and reissuing the Move
command, this time specifying "From Clipboard." With very little trouble, you
can make a temporary deletion that gives you flexibility and security.

6.08 Trap: *Do not expect to be able to use the Clipboard as a place*
to store more than one set of information.

Whenever new information is copied, moved, or printed to the Clipboard, the
information that was previously stored there is automatically deleted. This has
nothing to do with available space; it occurs even when the data in question is
only one character.

Be especially attuned to this Trap if you have a tendency to assign data to the
Clipboard for a transfer but put off completing the data exchange until it is more
convenient to switch to the destination file. A situation like this can turn into
disaster if you later assign data to the Clipboard and inadvertently erase the
information that you had been holding there.

6.09 Trap: *When you save a file, the contents of the Clipboard are*
not saved with it.

AppleWorks has no way to save Clipboard information to disk when you save a
file. If you have valuable information in the Clipboard, make sure that you

transfer it to the desired destination before you quit the current AppleWorks work session. Even if you carefully save the file before quitting, you will find that all Clipboard information has disappeared the next time you load the file.

✋ *6.10 Trap:* *You can never actually see the contents of the Clipboard.*

It would be nice to be able to view the contents of the Clipboard to be sure that important data is not lost when you want to assign new data to the Clipboard or quit a work session. Unfortunately, there is no way to view the Clipboard's contents. The only thing that you can do is use the Copy command to do a quick Clipboard check whenever you find it necessary.

Move to the end of the file (use OPEN APPLE-9 to get there quickly), and issue the Copy command (OPEN APPLE-C), specifying "From Clipboard." If you get a message that says "The Clipboard is empty," you will know that you can safely add new data to the Clipboard or quit AppleWorks without losing valuable information. If there is information in the Clipboard, it will be copied to your file. You can assess whether it is worth saving and then delete it with OPEN APPLE-D.

✋ *6.11 Trap:* *If there are more data base categories in a source file than in a destination file, the excess categories will be omitted.*

Moving records from one data base file to another is easy. Just use the Copy or Move command to send a specified selection of data to the Clipboard from the source file, and then issue one of the same commands to relocate the Clipboard data once you have positioned the cursor at the appropriate place in the destination file.

Everything should work fine, unless there are more categories in the records commandeered from the source file than there are accommodations for them in the destination file. In such a case, the transfer will be carried out, but any information that does not fit within the categories available in the destination file will be truncated.

For an example of this, look at the two Book List data bases shown in Figure 6-4. Notice that Book List 1 does not contain the book written by Carmella Manende, nor does it include the "Avail." category shown in Book List 2. Since you want the books in each file to match, you would use the Copy command to

```
File: Book List 1            REVIEW/ADD/CHANGE           Escape: Main Menu

Selection: All records


Author              Title                Publisher        Year
===========================================================================
Burke, Taylor       Never Slow Down      M & B            1977
Collins, Mary       Christopher John     Cross            1972
Cross, Lea          Creative Teaching    Kildare          1983
May, Tim            No Nonsense          Guidelines       1976




File: Book List 2            REVIEW/ADD/CHANGE           Escape: Main Menu

Selection: All records


Publisher      Year      Title              Author           Avail.
===========================================================================
M & B          1977      Never Slow Down    Burke, Taylor    A
Cross          1972      Christopher John   Collins, Mary    A
Kildare        1983      Creative Teaching  Cross, Lea       A
Lightfoot      1974      Thinking Thrift    Manende, Carmella A
Guidelines     1976      No Nonsense        May, Tim         NA
```

Figure 6-4. Similar data bases with different layouts and categories

send the Carmella Manende record to the Clipboard, switch to the Book List 2 file (OPEN APPLE-Q), move to the last record in the file, and copy the Manende record from the Clipboard.

You can see in Figure 6-5 that the new record was added just above the last record in the file. Since the destination file (Book List 1) did not contain the

```
File: Book List 1            REVIEW/ADD/CHANGE           Escape: Main Menu

Selection: All records


Author              Title                Publisher        Year
===========================================================================
Burke, Taylor       Never Slow Down      M & B            1977
Collins, Mary       Christopher John     Cross            1972
Cross, Lea          Creative Teaching    Kildare          1983
Manende, Carmella   Thinking Thrift      Lightfoot        1974
May, Tim            No Nonsense          Guidelines       1976
```

Figure 6-5. The effect of adding a new record with the Copy command

"Avail." category present in the source file (Book List 2), the entry for that category was truncated when the incoming information was placed in the new file.

In this example, there was no real loss because the truncated information was not relevant to the file's purpose. If it is essential that no information be lost in a data base to data base transfer, be sure to set up a category match before you move the information to the new file.

Notice that if you compare the two files in Figure 6-4, their categories are laid out in a different order. This presented no problem when the new record was transferred into Book List 1 (see Figure 6-5). Category placement was adjusted automatically to match the Book List 1 layout. Anytime you perform a record exchange of this type, you can count on the same automatic layout adjustment.

6.12 Tip: *Use OPEN APPLE-F (the Find command) or OPEN APPLE-R (for record selection rules) to select one or more data base records to move to the Clipboard for transfer.*

You can use the Find or Record Selection command to extract specific records from a data base. Once the records have been extracted, the Copy or Move command can send the selected records to the Clipboard for transfer to another file.

6.13 Trap: *You cannot move or copy data base records to or from the Clipboard from a single-record layout.*

The Move and Copy commands are the key to moving data base records to and from the Clipboard for transfer to another data base file. However, if you try to initiate the Move command from a single-record layout, you will get no response from AppleWorks. The Copy command serves only to duplicate the current single record the number of times that you specify.

Since these crucial data movers are ineffective in the single-record layout, the benefits of Clipboard transport are not available in this mode.

6.14 Tip: *When you use the Clipboard to transfer data from one AppleWorks spreadsheet file to another, the formulas and functions will remain intact.*

Although you can transfer spreadsheet information to an AppleWorks word processing document by printing to the Clipboard instead of using the Move or Copy command, all formulas are lost in the process, and only the data itself is transferred. Since data can be moved from one spreadsheet to another via the Clipboard with the Move or Copy command, this debilitating side effect is not a problem. You can easily extract data containing formulas and functions from one spreadsheet and place it into another. Because AppleWorks automatically adjusts for relative referencing, the imported data keeps all the relationships straight that are needed for accurate calculations.

Using the Clipboard to Transfer Data From Spreadsheet and Data Base Files To the Word Processor

6.15 Tip: *You can use the Clipboard to transfer information from a data base or spreadsheet file to a word processing file — but not by using the Move or Copy command.*

In addition to providing a means for transferring information between files of the same environment type, the Clipboard accepts information from a data base or spreadsheet file and passes it to a word processing file. However, the information transferred from these sources must be in a form that the Word Processor can read.

Since the Move and Copy commands maintain the form of the source file, they are ineffective when this type of transfer is required. If you attempt such a move or copy, you will meet with apparent success until you try to paste the information from the Clipboard into the destination word processing document. The following message explains why this will not work:

```
The clipboard does not contain
Word Processor information;
therefore, it can't be used.
```

To perform this operation successfully, you will need to use OPEN APPLE-P to print to the Clipboard. If you print from a data base file, you will first need to create a report format. Its design will determine what gets sent initially to the Clipboard and ultimately to the destination word processing document. Once this is done, OPEN APPLE-P presents you with the choices shown in the menu that follows.

```
File: Sample File              PRINT THE REPORT          Escape: Report Format
Report: Sample Report
Selection: All records

=============================================================================
                    Where do you want to print the report?

                    1.  Apple DMP

                    2.  ImageWriter

                    3.  The screen

                    4.  The clipboard (for the Word Processor)

                    5.  A text (ASCII) file on disk

                    6.  A DIF (TM) file on disk

-----------------------------------------------------------------------------
Type number, or use arrows, then press Return                    42K Avail.
```

Since you want the information to be printed to the Clipboard for the Word Processor, choose option 4. Completion of the first step of the transfer is confirmed by the following message:

```
                    The report is now on the clipboard,
                    and can be moved or copied into Word
                    Processor documents.
```

The same confirmation message signals success when you print from a spreadsheet to the Clipboard, again beginning with OPEN APPLE-P but this time choosing option 3 from the Print menu:

```
File: SS Sample File           PRINT               Escape: Review/Add/Change
=============================================================================
                    The information that you identified
                    is 36 characters wide.

                    The Printer Options values allow
                    80 characters per line.


                    Where do you want to print the report?

                    1.  Apple DMP
                    2.  ImageWriter
                    3.  The clipboard (for the Word Processor)
                    4.  A text (ASCII) file on disk
                    5.  A DIF (TM) file on disk


-----------------------------------------------------------------------------

Type number, or use arrows, then press Return                    42K Avail.
```

To complete the second half of the transfer—from the Clipboard to the word processing document—you must move to the location in the destination document where you want the transferred data to be placed and issue the Copy or Move command. Once you choose "From Clipboard (paste)" from the choices that follow, the new data will be integrated into your word processing document, and the transfer will be complete.

✋ **6.16 Trap:** *Data base and spreadsheet lines that are printed to the Clipboard may exceed the 250-line limit without your realizing it, because they are reformatted to be compatible with the Word Processor.*

If you are using the Clipboard to transfer information from one word processing document to another, you will find that the Clipboard will accept a maximum of 250 word processing lines. When you use OPEN APPLE-P to print to the Clipboard (for the Word Processor) from a data base or spreadsheet, the specified data is translated into a form that is acceptable to the Word Processor.

Depending on how many categories there are in your data base and how many columns are in your spreadsheet, each respective record or row may have to be wrapped around to fit within the Word Processor's margins. This operation could substantially increase the number of lines you thought you were sending to the Clipboard.

You will know that you have fallen into this Trap if you are confronted with the following message when you are attempting to print from a data base or spreadsheet file to the Clipboard:

```
The report exceeds the 250 Word
Processor lines that can be put
on the clipboard.
```

All you can do in a case like this is reissue the Print command, specifying less data for transfer the second time. Repeat the process until your selection is accepted.

✋ **6.17 Trap:** *If the selection that you specify for printing to the Clipboard does not conform to the current printer options, you could lose important data.*

When you are selecting data from your spreadsheet or data base to be printed to the Clipboard for the Word Processor, you can specify rows, columns, or blocks from the spreadsheet or set up a custom report format from a data base. It is natural to assume that all the data that you select this way will be transferred to the Clipboard when you select the Print to Clipboard option.

However, the selections that you specify for printing to the Clipboard are further controlled by the printer options that are in force at the time. The printer option specifications for platen width, characters per inch, and right and left margins create the boundaries for the width of the data printed to the Clipboard, just as they do when you are sending data to the printer.

If you accept the default settings for these specifications, you are allowed a width of 80 characters when selecting data for printing. If the selection that you specify is wider than 80 characters, only the data that falls within the 80-character boundary will be printed. The Tips that follow tell you how to adjust for data that is wider than 80 characters.

6.18 Tip: *Check the width of the selection you have specified for printing to the Clipboard before you actually print.*

The previous Trap explained how important it is to know whether the selection that you have specified for printing to the Clipboard fits within the settings of the printer options. You can determine what these settings are by accessing the Printer Options screen with OPEN APPLE-O. Working in the Spreadsheet environment, you can do this easily from the Review/Add/Change screen. To access the Printer Options screen from the Data Base environment, you must first get to the Report Format screen.

Looking at the Printer Options screen, you can read the current print boundaries (designated by "Char per line") that AppleWorks has calculated. (It is obtained by multiplying the platen width times the characters per inch, making allowances for the right and left margins. If they are set at zero, no allowance is necessary.) The Printer Options screen shows this calculation on the far left, just above "Formatting options." Take a look at the Printer Options screen that follows.

```
File: DB Sample          PRINTER OPTIONS        Escape: Report Format
Report: sample
================================================================

-------Left and right margins--------    ------Top and bottom margins-------
PW: Platen Width        8.0 inches    PL: Paper Length      11.0 inches
LM: Left Margin         0.0 inches    TM: Top Margin         0.0 inches
RM: Right Margin        0.0 inches    BM: Bottom Margin      2.0 inches
CI: Chars per Inch      10            LI: Lines per Inch     6

    Line width          8.0 inches        Printing length    9.0 inches
    Char per line (est) 80                Lines per page     54

        ------------------Formatting options-------------------
    SC: Send Special Codes to printer               No
    PD: Print a Dash when an entry is blank          No
    PH: Print report Header at top of each page      Yes
        Single, Double or Triple Spacing (SS/DS/TS)  SS

-------------------------------------------------------------------
Type a two letter option code                          35K Avail.
```

In this example "Char per line (est)" is 80. Now that you know this controlling number, you can determine whether your selection will fit within it.

The width of a data base report is easy to ascertain from the Report Format screen. As you can see in the following illustration, the report's line length (otherwise known as the width of the report) is printed vertically at the report's right margin.

```
File: Food List          REPORT FORMAT         Escape: Report Menu
Report: Food List
Selection: All records

================================================================
--) or <--  Move cursor              @-J  Right justify this category
  ) @ <     Switch category positions @-K  Define a calculated category
--) @ <--   Change column width       @-N  Change report name and/or title
@-A  Arrange (sort) on this category  @-O  Printer options
@-D  Delete this category             @-P  Print the report
@-G  Add/remove group totals          @-R  Change record selection rules
@-I  Insert a prev. deleted category  @-T  Add/remove category totals
                                                                -----
Food Type    Food Name   Price    Unit        Quantity    Order Date   L
-A----------  -B--------- -C------  -D--------  -E--------- -F---------  e
veg.         cabbage     .19      lb.         25          Jun 15       n
cheese       Edam        2.79     lb.         12          Jun 10 85    7
veg.         mushrooms   1.19     lb.         18          Jun 21 85    8

-------------------------------------------------------------------
Use options shown above to change report format        30K Avail.
```

Because a line length of 78 characters falls within the default width of 80 for both spreadsheet and data base settings, you could print this report to the Clipboard without losing any data.

When you are working in the Spreadsheet environment and want to specify a selection for printing to the Clipboard, you do not have the same built-in line measure available in the data base Report Format screen. However, AppleWorks calculates the width automatically each time you issue the Print command and specify a selection for printing.

As the following Print screen example shows, AppleWorks even offers a comparison between the width of the specified selection and the current width allowed by the printer options.

```
File: SS Sample                    PRINT           Escape: Review/Add/Change
================================================================================


             The information that you identified
             is 108 characters wide.

             The Printer Options values allow
             80 characters per line.


             Where do you want to print the report?

             1.  Apple DMP
             2.  ImageWriter
             3.  The clipboard (for the Word Processor)
             4.  A text (ASCII) file on disk
             5.  A DIF (TM) file on disk




-------------------------------------------------------------------------------

Type number, or use arrows, then press Return                     28K Avail.
```

In this case, you would be warned that the selection you have specified exceeds the width currently allowed. You know from this message that if you printed to the Clipboard under the present conditions, you would lose the data that falls beyond the printer option boundaries. Some adjustments are in order. The next two Tips tell you how to make these adjustments.

6.19 Tip: *You can increase the width of the data you are allowed to print to the Clipboard by adjusting the printer options.*

Traps 6.17 and 6.18 described the crucial role that the printer option settings play in determining the width of data that can be printed to the Clipboard. Since these settings are adjustable, you can use them to expand the boundaries that the printer options impose.

The maximum platen width that you can enter for printer options is 25 inches. A setting of 10 characters per inch would give you a width of 250 characters without making any other adjustments. The maximum entry you can make for characters per inch is 24, and the overall maximum that AppleWorks allows is 255 characters per line.

With this in mind, you can make the necessary adjustments to platen width and characters per inch to meet this limit if the data you are printing requires a maximum width. If your selection still extends beyond these boundaries, the following Tip may come in handy.

6.20 Tip: *You can fit more data within your printer options by adjusting column and category widths.*

As explained in the previous Tip, adjusting certain printer option settings expands the boundaries of data that can be printed to the Clipboard. You can further increase the amount of data that can fit within these boundaries by compressing column widths in Spreadsheet mode and category widths in Data Base mode.

If you have made all the adjustments possible in your printer options in order to stretch the limits to the maximum and you still do not have enough room to send all the data to the Clipboard, examine the layout of the source document and see if any spreadsheet columns or data base categories contain blank spaces that could be eliminated.

If you feel that without the blank spaces the material would be unreadable, that is important to keep in mind. However, once the data has been transported to its destination, spaces can be added.

6.21 Tip: *When printing to the Clipboard, it does not matter if you choose printer options that are incompatible with your printer.*

The discussion of ways to print the maximum amount of data from a data base or spreadsheet to the Clipboard and then to the Word Processor has included the adjustment of printer options so that the platen width is set for up to 25 inches and characters per inch up to 24. You may think that you will never use these maximum settings because your printer cannot handle such extremes.

Do not limit yourself with this unnecessary restriction. Remember that you are not currently using the printer. Printing is being done to the Clipboard, which can handle any extremes that the printer options will allow.

✋ *6.22 Trap: Adjust the Word Processor's printer options to allow for any extra width necessary for incoming spreadsheet or data base information.*

In previous Tips and Traps, you have seen how adjustments to printer options in a source document can enable you to maximize the amount of spreadsheet or data base information that you can print to the Clipboard. Remember, however, that moving the information to the Clipboard is only the first step in transferring data to the Word Processor.

You may wonder how the destination document can accommodate data that has been adjusted to display as many as 24 characters per inch, which would mean 144 characters on a 6-inch-wide line. In fact, an Apple screen cannot display more than 80 characters on one line.

If information imported from the Clipboard exceeds the 80-character screen limit (or a lesser limit that the current printer options allow), any characters that extend beyond will be wrapped around to the next line. This wraparound effect, touted as a valuable attribute in the word processing world, can wreak havoc with the columns and rows that are necessary to the integrity of a spreadsheet or data base layout. However, if your ultimate goal is to print this integrated document as hard copy, you can get these lines to unwrap again by making the proper adjustments to the word processing printer options.

If you increased the width of the data to be transferred before you printed to the Clipboard (see Tip 6.19 for more details), you may have to change the printer options in the destination document to make necessary width allowances for actual printing. (To check the width that has been set, switch to the source document to redetermine it.)

When you set printer options in the source document, your goal was to print to the Clipboard; therefore, you did not need to consider whether your printer could handle the format. However, now you will be held accountable in hard copy for any setting that you apply to the printer options. In short, if you want to print a hard copy, do not assign any settings that your printer cannot carry out.

6.23 *Tip:* *You can edit information that you have transferred into the Word Processor from the Spreadsheet or Data Base once it is part of the word processing document.*

Do not be discouraged if, in spite of all your efforts, the data that you have imported into your word processing document does not align properly. With the flexible formatting options available to you in the Word Processor environment (OPEN APPLE-O), you can make adjustments after the data is transferred. You can change margins, spacing, or characters per inch as needed in the section where the transferred data is, or you can use the Move command to design a layout that is more aesthetic or more suited to your purposes.

6.24 *Trap:* *Specifying a section of a data base file for transfer to the Word Processor can be tricky.*

When you are highlighting information from a spreadsheet to be printed to the Clipboard, you can specify the entire file, certain rows or columns within the file, or a block of the file. Unfortunately, the same flexibility is not available in the Data Base environment.

Since printing from the Data Base requires creating a report format, the selections that you can specify for transfer are limited by the selection rules governing the report format itself. It is easy to omit specific categories from a report format so that only the categories that you specify will be printed. But there is no way to highlight specific rows for printing, as in the Spreadsheet environment.

If you do not want to print all the records in a data base, you can create record selection rules that limit printing to the records that fit those rules. If the records that you want to print are related in a way that is easily defined through these rules, you will have no problem, but if their relationship is obscure, you will have to become more creative to discover a way to shape the rules to encompass them, or create a duplicate file and delete the records that you do not want to print.

6.25 *Tip:* *Printing to the screen can give you a preview of the data base data that you are sending to the Word Processor.*

Printing to the screen is one of the options on the Print the Report screen, which appears when you type OPEN APPLE-P from the data base Report Format screen. To some degree, this option can make it possible for you to get a preview of a data base report that you want to print to the Clipboard for use in a word processing document.

This feature can be especially helpful if the report you are printing is within the 80-character maximum display width of the Apple screen. If such is the case, the screen print that you get will be in a form that you can expect to be maintained when you make a transfer first to the Clipboard and then to the Word Processor.

6.26 Trap: *Categories beyond the screen's 80-character capacity will be truncated when you print to the screen.*

If the data base report that you are printing to the screen for preview exceeds a width of 80 characters, you will not be able to preview anything that falls beyond the 80-character limit. Each line will be chopped off at this point.

If you meet with this unfortunate result, do not worry that your entire report cannot be sent to the Word Processor because of excessive width. Several earlier Tips and Traps in this chapter explain that the key to successful data transfer depends on the relationship between the width of your data selection and the printer option settings that govern line width in the source document. Printing to the screen is a separate procedure that does not affect printing to the Clipboard.

6.27 Trap: *You will not be warned about discrepancies between the width of a data base report and printer options when you are printing data base information to the Clipboard.*

When you are printing spreadsheet data to the Clipboard for transfer to a word processing document, AppleWorks calculates the width of the data that you select and compares it with the width allowed by the printer option settings. Tip 6.18 shows this helpful message displayed on a spreadsheet Print menu.

Unfortunately, you cannot rely on this safeguard when you are printing to the Clipboard from a data base report. You will have to check both the report width and the printer option settings to make sure that the settings are wide enough to accommodate the report. The line length of a data base report is always displayed vertically at the far right margin of the sample records on the Report Format screen.

To find out if the report's line length falls within the width allowed by the printer options, access the Printer Options screen (OPEN APPLE-O) from the Report Format screen. The "Char per line (est)" calculation, displayed to the left above "Formatting Options," will give you the information you need.

6.28 Trap: *When information has been transferred from a spreadsheet to a word processing document, formulas will no longer be in effect.*

When you transfer spreadsheet data from one AppleWorks spreadsheet to another, you use the Copy or Move command to pass the information to and from the Clipboard. With this procedure, formulas and functions are kept intact and are fully operational upon arrival in their new environment.

But neither the Copy nor Move command is effective when you are moving spreadsheet information to the Clipboard for transfer to a word processing document. This type of transfer must be initiated with the Print command (OPEN APPLE-P), a procedure that renders all formulas and functions useless. Keeping this in mind, be sure to perform all necessary calculations before sending information from a spreadsheet to a word processing document. Once in its new home, the spreadsheet data is considered text.

Creating and Accepting ASCII and DIF Files

6.29 Tip: *Sharing information among files saves re-entry time and prevents entry errors.*

AppleWorks' Clipboard helps you integrate data among files within a single AppleWorks environment and from the Spreadsheet and Data Base environments into Word Processor files, minimizing the chance of error and saving steps at the same time.

You can also save time by extracting relevant information from an existing file to create a new file from scratch. A common example of this is a situation that calls for creating a spreadsheet that will make calculations on employees' salaries listed in a Personnel data base. Why build the spreadsheet from scratch, re-entering data that is already in the Personnel data base? This sort of redundancy chews up time and spits out errors. Always be aware of instances when you can transfer data and avoid unnecessary consumption of your most valuable commodity — time.

When you plan to create a data base or spreadsheet file, train yourself to ask the time-saving question, "Is any portion of the data that I need for this file already available somewhere else?" If the answer is yes, the following Tips and Traps should help you identify the sources and rechannel the relevent information into an AppleWorks file.

6.30 Tip: DIF and ASCII files code information in a format that can be understood by otherwise incompatible programs.

ASCII (American Standard Code for Information Interchange) is a binary system of coding information that is used as a standard throughout the computer world. More sophisticated coding systems adopted by different manufacturers are not compatible with each other; thus files created by one manufacturer's program cannot be transferred to another's unless they can be broken down to the compatible level that ASCII provides.

DIF (Data Interchange Format) is an ASCII-coded system that provides additional formatting capabilities that are absent in ASCII. DIF is particularly useful when you are dealing with numeric data, whereas ASCII files are most effective when the information to be transferred is text.

Files saved in one of these forms can share data with otherwise incompatible programs, although a compatible disk format is also necessary if exchanges occur via disk (see Trap 6.43 for further information).

AppleWorks, designed as a program to promote data integration, allows you to save AppleWorks files to disk in ASCII or DIF form (varies with each environment) and load files from disk into AppleWorks if they are in ASCII or DIF form. The circumstances under which this translation is necessary and the process itself are further delineated in the Tips and Traps that follow.

6.31 Trap: You cannot use the Clipboard to transfer information between a data base and a spreadsheet in AppleWorks, or out of the Word Processor into either of these.

AppleWorks' Clipboard facilitates data transfer between data base files, between spreadsheet files, and from either of these sources to word processing files. But it cannot help you get a spreadsheet file and a data base file to share information, nor will it help you send word processing information into either of these environments. To accomplish this exchange, data source files must be saved to disk as an ASCII or DIF file (see the previous Tip) and then loaded into the destination file in this universal form.

6.32 Trap: *Information loaded from disk into AppleWorks cannot be appended to an existing file; it must be used to create a new file.*

When you are working within AppleWorks, the Clipboard allows you to move information between existing files within the same environment and to move data from a spreadsheet or data base file into the word processing environment. With this feature, you can add data base or spreadsheet information to a word processing document or benefit from inter-file data transfer within all three AppleWorks environments.

There is an important distinction between the mix-and-match powers that the Clipboard provides and the data-sharing capabilities that are possible when data is imported from disk into AppleWorks. Files that are imported into Apple-Works via disk cannot be loaded into already existing files (an operation that is easily achieved by the Clipboard), whether they originally came from AppleWorks or other programs. To carry out this sort of importation, start from the Main Menu and choose "Add files to the Desktop" — you cannot add files from within an existing file. The result is the addition of an autonomous file instead of the aggregate that can be created by the Clipboard.

6.33 Tip: *You can use the Clipboard to merge files once an imported file is part of AppleWorks.*

As stated in the previous Trap, you are denied the file-merge powers that the Clipboard provides when you import ASCII or DIF files into AppleWorks. This limitation should not restrict you unnecessarily, however. Once you have created a new AppleWorks file with the imported data, you can use the Clipboard to move information into it from other files (in compatible environments) or out of it into other files.

6.34 Tip: *To send information between AppleWorks' Data Base and*
Spreadsheet environments or from these environments to
other programs, print a DIF file to disk.

As powerful as AppleWorks' Clipboard is for moving information between files, it
cannot move data from a data base file into a spreadsheet file, or vice versa. If you
have data base information that you want to manipulate in an AppleWorks
spreadsheet, print it to disk as a DIF file and then create a new spreadsheet file by
loading the DIF file into the Spreadsheet environment. The same is true for
transporting data from an AppleWorks spreadsheet into an AppleWorks data
base.

You can also print DIF files from either of these environments to disk so that
they can be shared with other data base or spreadsheet programs outside of
AppleWorks. The procedure for printing DIF files is similar to printing to a
printer; it is the same whether you want to use the file within AppleWorks or
share it with an outside program.

From the Data Base environment, you create a report format, press OPEN
APPLE-P, and choose option 6, "A DIF (TM) file on disk," from the Print the
Report menu shown in the following illustration:

```
File: DB Sample              PRINT THE REPORT         Escape: Report Format
Report: Sample
Selection: All records



========================================================================
                    Where do you want to print the report?

                    1.  Apple DMP

                    2.  ImageWriter

                    3.  The screen

                    4.  The clipboard (for the Word Processor)

                    5.  A text (ASCII) file on disk

                    6.  A DIF (TM) file on disk


------------------------------------------------------------------------
Type number, or use arrows, then press Return              42K Avail.
```

From the Spreadsheet environment, OPEN APPLE-P enables you to specify the
portion of the spreadsheet that you want to print (All, Rows, Column, Block) and

then presents you with the standard print destination choices, from which you can choose "A DIF (TM) file on disk."

The next step in both procedures is to enter a pathname for the file you are printing to disk (see Trap 6.42 if you need further explanation of pathnames). When you press RETURN after completing this entry, your file will be printed to disk in DIF format and can be re-read by AppleWorks or used by other programs capable of reading DIF files and operating under ProDOS or DOS 3.3 (see Trap 6.43).

6.35 Trap: *Category headings are not retained when a data base file is transferred as a DIF file.*

Data bases are created in rows and columns with headings naming each category (called field names) occupying the position at the top of each category column. When you create a DIF file and load it into a spreadsheet file, do not be surprised to find these category headings missing. In the process of creating the DIF file, they are deleted.

6.36 Tip: *AppleWorks' Spreadsheet environment will accept data from DIF files created by other programs as well as those created from an AppleWorks data base.*

Creating a DIF file puts information into a form that can be understood by programs operating with ProDOS or DOS 3.3. Since AppleWorks' Spreadsheet environment can read DIF files, it can accept information whose source is a spreadsheet program outside of AppleWorks (external source) or a data base file from an internal or external source if: (1) the information is saved to disk in DIF format, and (2) the program operates with ProDOS or DOS 3.3 (see Trap 6.43).

To load a DIF file into an AppleWorks Spreadsheet environment, place the disk with the file in question in the proper drive and choose "Add files to the Desktop" from the Main Menu. Since you are creating a new spreadsheet file with the imported data, choose "Make a new file for the: Spreadsheet" from the Add Files menu. From the Spreadsheet menu, you can make this new file in three ways, as shown in the following menu:

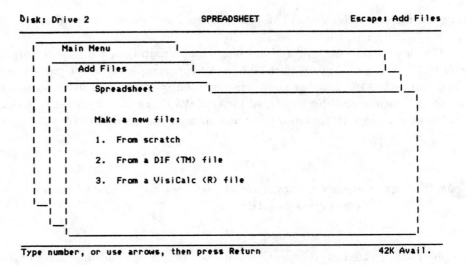

It should be obvious that the proper choice in this case is option 2, "From a DIF (TM) file."

To retrieve this file, AppleWorks has to know the pathname assigned to it (see Trap 6.42 if you need further explanation about pathnames). Once you have provided the pathname and pressed RETURN, you supply a name for the new file (it should be different from the name given to the DIF file because AppleWorks cannot save two files with the same name on the same disk). When this is done, the RETURN key gives the go-ahead signal, and the imported file is loaded into the newly created AppleWorks spreadsheet.

6.37 Trap: *Spreadsheet formulas and functions will not be maintained when you print ASCII or DIF files.*

If you print an ASCII or DIF file from an AppleWorks spreadsheet file, do not expect to find the formulas and functions intact when you load the file to its destination, either inside or outside AppleWorks. If formulas and functions are important to the imported file's function in its new environment, they will have to be added after the transfer is completed.

6.38 Tip: *The order (rows or columns) in which you save spreadsheet information to a DIF file could be very important.*

When you print an AppleWorks spreadsheet file to disk as a DIF file, you have to choose the manner in which to save the data: in column or row order. Since AppleWorks displays incoming DIF files in column order only, choose the Columns option if you are printing a DIF file to be used in AppleWorks. If you choose row order, all the data that was in columns in the original file will be laid out in rows, and all the data that was originally in rows will be displayed in columns when the file is read by AppleWorks. If you are printing DIF files from another program to be used in AppleWorks, pay attention to the same column order mandate.

AppleWorks DIF files destined for transfer to programs outside AppleWorks should be printed in a format that is compatible with the destination program's layout procedures. To allow for the greatest flexibility in transferring DIF files, many programs provide row and column choices for saving and loading files. If you are sharing data with such a program, be sure to maintain a consistent pattern.

If you are sending an AppleWorks DIF file to a program that allows for only one layout pattern, be sure to determine whether that program displays incoming files in rows or columns before printing a DIF file from AppleWorks so that you can choose a compatible format before you print the file.

6.39 Tip: *AppleWorks' Data Base environment accepts DIF or ASCII files created within AppleWorks and DIF, ASCII, and Quick File files created outside AppleWorks.*

As you can see by the Data Base Add Files menu displayed in the following illustration, AppleWorks can import three types of files into its Data Base environment:

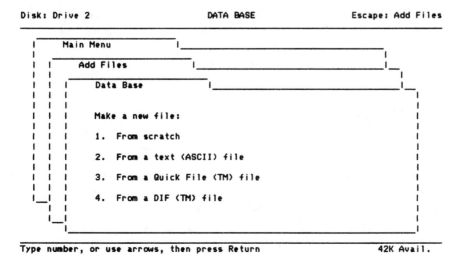

```
Disk: Drive 2                    DATA BASE              Escape: Add Files
_____

I    Main Menu            I_____
I                         _____       I
I  I    Add Files         I_____I__
I  I   _____      I
I  I  I   Data Base       I_____I__
I  I  I                                                         I
I  I  I                                                         I
I  I  I  Make a new file:                                       I
I  I  I                                                         I
I  I  I  1.  From scratch                                       I
I  I  I                                                         I
I  I  I  2.  From a text (ASCII) file                           I
I  I  I                                                         I
I  I  I  3.  From a Quick File (TM) file                        I
I  I  I                                                         I
I__I  I  4.  From a DIF (TM) file                               I
   I  I                                                         I
   I__I                                                         I
      I_____I

_____
Type number, or use arrows, then press Return            42K Avail.
```

Whether these files were originally AppleWorks files that had been saved to disk in ASCII or DIF format, or whether they came from other programs, the procedure for creating new AppleWorks Data Base files with them is the same. Begin by choosing "Add files to the Desktop" from the Main Menu, then "Make a new file from the: Data Base." When the screen in the previous illustration appears, make the appropriate choice and press RETURN. When you are asked for a pathname, type a slash (/), the name of the disk that the incoming file is on, another slash (/), and finally the name of the file. (If you need more information about pathnames, see Trap 6.42.)

The last task you will be asked to perform before the new file is before you is to enter a name for the new file. Be sure to give it a different name from the one assigned to it on the source disk if you expect to save it back to that disk as an AppleWorks file. AppleWorks will not let you keep two files with the same name on a single disk.

✋ **6.40 Trap:** *Avoid using an ASCII file to share data base or spreadsheet information from AppleWorks with other data base programs.*

You can print an ASCII file from an AppleWorks data base or spreadsheet by specifying "A text (ASCII) file on disk" from the menu that begins the print procedure. Such a file could be shared with other data base programs instead of a DIF file. However, because the formatting capabilities of a DIF file are more compatible with data base layout, it is preferable to use DIF files instead of ASCII files when you want to transfer data from an AppleWorks data base or spreadsheet to a data base outside AppleWorks, or from an AppleWorks spreadsheet to an AppleWorks data base. If your destination program can accept only incoming files in ASCII form, you must comply with that restriction and make the necessary format adjustments once the new file is relocated.

🔅 **6.41 Tip:** *AppleWorks' Word Processor can send and receive data to and from other programs by using ASCII files.*

Transferring data via the Clipboard is a convenient AppleWorks feature. You may find this feature most useful in the Word Processor environment, since it can accept data sent to it from files outside its own environment as well as from other word processing files. This flexibility is something that the data base and spreadsheet environments do not have.

The Word Processor can extend its data-sharing facility outside AppleWorks if you print AppleWorks word processing files to disk in ASCII form. By the same token, ASCII files created from other programs (or from AppleWorks' Data Base) can be used to create new AppleWorks word processing files.

To print an ASCII file from an AppleWorks word processing file, begin by typing the Print command (OPEN APPLE-P). Next, select the portion of the word processing document that you would like to have printed. If you choose the first option, "Beginning," the entire file will be printed. "This Page" limits the printed text to the page where the cursor is located. Choosing "Cursor" means that all data from the cursor location to the end of the file will be printed. (To assure that these last two choices are read properly, type OPEN APPLE-K before issuing the Print command.)

Once your selection is specified, the word processing Print menu will appear, along with the query "Where do you want to print the file?" Your choice is option 3, "A text (ASCII) file on disk." Next you will be asked for a pathname. Enter a slash (/), then the exact name of the disk that you are printing to, another slash (/), and the name that you want to assign to the file you are printing. (For more information on pathnames, see the following Trap.) If you have followed all these steps, the file should print to disk, and you will have a record of it in a form that can be shared with many programs outside of AppleWorks.

To load ASCII files from disk into an AppleWorks word processing file, choose "Add files to the Desktop" from the Main Menu. Then choose "Make a new file for the: Word Processor." When the menu in the following illustration appears, the obvious choice is number 2, "From a text (ASCII) file."

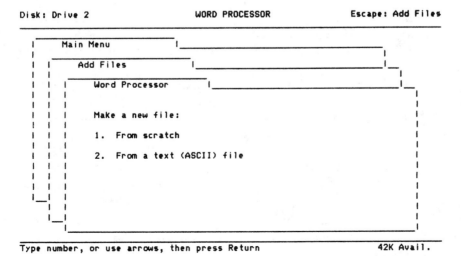

```
Disk: Drive 2              WORD PROCESSOR        Escape: Add Files
_____

 I    Main Menu          I_____
 I   _____                                          I
 I   I   Add Files          I_____I__
 I   I  _____                                       I
 I   I  I  Word Processor      I_____I__
 I   I  I  _____                                    I
 I   I  I                                                                  I
 I   I  I  Make a new file:                                                I
 I   I  I                                                                  I
 I   I  I  1.  From scratch                                                I
 I   I  I                                                                  I
 I   I  I  2.  From a text (ASCII) file                                    I
 I   I  I                                                                  I
 I   I  I                                                                  I
 I   I  I                                                                  I
 I___I  I                                                                  I
     I  I                                                                  I
     I__I                                                                  I
       I_____I

_____
Type number, or use arrows, then press Return            42K Avail.
```

You will be asked for the pathname next. It should be in the following format: a slash (/), the exact name of the disk that the incoming file is on, another slash (/), and the exact name of the file itself. Now press RETURN and the file will be loaded, although it will not appear on the screen until you give it a new name. Once this procedure is completed, you are free to use any AppleWorks features to rearrange the data to meet your needs or to share the data with other AppleWorks files via the Clipboard.

✋ 6.42 Trap: *You will not be able to save or load DIF or ASCII files unless you provide the pathname in the proper format.*

Whenever you want to save or load an ASCII or DIF file, or a VisiCalc or Quick File, AppleWorks will ask you to provide the file's pathname. The pathname it is seeking is the address of the file, from which AppleWorks can determine where to look for the information you have requested it to load and how to address information you have requested it to store.

The first part of the address is the name of the disk (often referred to as the volume) to which you will be printing if you are saving files, or from which you will be reading if you are loading files. It is the name that was assigned to the disk when it was first formatted. (This name must be entered in the same format it was assigned, including spaces and periods — uppercase and lowercase differences are irrelevant.)

The next part of the pathname is the name of the file itself. If you are in the process of saving a file, decide on the name you want assigned to it. It need not be the same name you have previously assigned to it, but you can retain that name if you want to. If you are retrieving a file that is already on disk, you need to provide the name that has been assigned to that file (again, the name must be entered in the same format).

You can find out both the disk and file names by choosing Other Activities from AppleWorks' Main Menu and then specifying option 2, "List all files on the current disk drive." Once you have noted the necessary information, escape back to the Main Menu and renew the process of adding the imported file.

You now know most of what you need to enter the proper pathnames when AppleWorks requests them, with one important exception. The pathname that you provide will not be accepted unless all parts of its address, disk volume name, and file name are preceded by a slash (/). If you follow this convention, you should end up with a pathname such as /Home.Records/Check.Reg. If you keep these few important points in mind, you should have no trouble saving and retrieving ASCII and DIF files to and from disk.

When files have been categorized by subdirectories, pathnames are more complicated. This book does not address this issue in the interest of simplicity and because anyone who has the sophistication necessary to create and work with subdirectories is already well versed in pathname know-how. For more information on subdirectories, see the *ProDOS User's Manual*.

6.43 Trap: *DIF or ASCII files created by a program using DOS 3.3 must be converted to ProDOS before they can be read by AppleWorks.*

AppleWorks is designed to work with ProDOS. However, many other Apple programs that have been around longer operate with DOS 3.3. You can take advantage of the data-sharing advantages that ASCII and DIF files provide for importing or exporting information between AppleWorks (ProDOS) and a DOS 3.3 program if you have the ProDOS User's disk or the System Utilities disk for the Apple IIc.

The ProDOS User's disk is a separate, inexpensive utility program sold by Apple that enables you to convert ProDOS files to DOS, and vice versa. Chapter 7 of the *ProDOS User's Manual* provides an excellent explanation of how to achieve this conversion. If you have an Apple IIc, the System Utilities disk that came with the system can perform ProDOS to DOS 3.3 conversions if you choose "Change a Disk's Format" from the Advanced Operations menu.

6.44 Tip: *You can load Quick Files into an AppleWorks data base and VisiCalc files into an AppleWorks spreadsheet.*

The designers of AppleWorks were aware that many veteran Apple users had already invested quite a bit of time and effort in creating spreadsheet files with the popular VisiCalc program. The same was true for users of Quick File, a favorite Apple data base program. AppleWorks was designed to be able to accept VisiCalc files into its Spreadsheet environment and Quick Files into its Data Base environment.

To carry out either of these file imports, begin from the Main Menu and choose "Add files to the Desktop." From the Add Files menu, choose to make a new file for the spreadsheet if you want to import a VisiCalc file, and for the data base if you are adding a Quick File. The choices that follow should be self-explanatory. If you are asked for a pathname, you must provide it in the form /Disk Name/File Name. (For an explanation of pathnames see Trap 6.42.)

6.45 Tip: Be prepared to make adjustments once you have finished loading imported files.

Files imported from another program or application usually need adjustments once they are in their new environment. Column widths may need to be widened in Spreadsheet mode to display the new data properly. Word processing printer options often need adjustment to accommodate the width of imported spreadsheet or data base information. Meaningful category names will have to replace the headings entitled Category 1, 2 3, and so on that AppleWorks supplies to incoming data base information.

These are only a few of the instances of data reshaping that may be a necessary price you pay for the advantage of inter- and intra-program data exchange. The adjustments are too numerous and specific to go into here. Accept these adjustments as usual; do not assume that the need for adjustments indicates a data transfer error.

6.46 Tip: When saving a DIF or ASCII file, do not worry about the relationship between the material you want printed and the printer options.

When you print data to the Clipboard from an AppleWorks file, any specified information that does not fit within the boundaries set by the source environment's printer options will be truncated in the transfer operation. When you print information from an AppleWorks file to your printer, be sure that the printer can perform the printer options that you assign the file.

When you are printing an ASCII or DIF file to disk, you do not have to think about this. Such specifications are not considered in ASCII or DIF format and thus do not restrict you when you save these files to disk.

6.47 Trap: You may need to divide a large file in two before you can save it to disk as an ASCII or DIF file.

If you are attempting to save a large AppleWorks file to disk in ASCII or DIF format and have followed all the correct steps but keep getting a message stating that the file save is unable to continue, try dividing the file in two and then save it to disk again.

The best way is to load the file, delete a portion of it, and rename the remainder (using OPEN APPLE-N). (Save it to disk as a new file if you want to be able to refer to it in its reduced form in the future.) Then you can create the ASCII or DIF file, which was your original intention.

Next, reload the original file, delete the portion that you have already saved and renamed, and save the rest as a smaller, more acceptable ASCII or DIF file. (Be sure to save it to disk also as an AppleWorks file if you want it in that form for future reference. Remember that if you do not rename it before you do this, it will wipe out the original file, which could cause you some grief if you were not expecting it.)

7

AppleWorks Applications
For Home, School,
And Office

Now that you are familiar with the basic functions of AppleWorks and how to integrate them, it is time to start thinking about creating applications to use in your own work environment. Before you actually create an application, be sure to address the following topics:

- *Common data files and logical organization.* Think in terms of common data files that can be used by several individuals to create different applications. You can thus eliminate duplicate efforts. Organize master files by project for maximum efficiency.

- *Templates.* Create spreadsheet templates for repetitive tasks, such as weekly and monthly reports. Generic templates represent a tremendous time savings.

- *Standard office procedures.* When several people share application files, it is important to establish standard procedures for naming files, documenting applications, tracking updates, and backing up files.

- *Data entry validation.* To ensure accuracy, user input should be validated. This is particularly important when data is entered by users who are unfamiliar with the logic of an application.

These important topics are covered in the first part of this chapter, which focuses on designing effective applications and establishing work group standards that maximize efficiency. These are generic issues that apply to all work environments.

The second part of this chapter demonstrates how to apply these generic concepts to specific work environments: home, office, and school. The following representative applications are included:

- *Integrated Sales Analysis Report.* Demonstrates how to use a master data base and report formats to generate four different monthly reports.

- *Personal Financial Planning.* Includes three components: Checkbook Management, Personal Financial Net Worth Statement, and Loan Summary.

- *The School Office.* Uses a master data base of student information to generate three useful lists: Student Roster, Teacher Roster, and Emergency Contact.

- *Gradebook.* A spreadsheet template that can be used to produce report cards.

- *School Classroom.* Two applications, My Dream Vacation and Cost Comparison Shopping, introduce students to spreadsheet applications. The concept of a data base and the importance of data base report formats are introduced with the Software Catalog and Review application.

Application Design

7.01 Tip: By organizing files by project on your disks, you can work more efficiently.

To optimize the AppleWorks data transfer facility, you should organize data files logically. If you have been using single-function programs, your approach to organizing files has most likely been to save files on a disk until it is full and not be particularly concerned with which files are stored together. Although this approach is economical in terms of the number of disks used, it does not enable you to group files according to subject matter.

AppleWorks Applications

The power of an integrated program like AppleWorks is that you can create different types of data files and then combine them for various applications. If you need to swap disks in and out of the disk drive every time AppleWorks accesses a different data file, you will find the process of data interchange cumbersome and ineffective.

The best approach to organizing AppleWorks files is to plan ahead and think in terms of task-related disks. That means storing all the files needed for a particular task on the same disk. Since integrated applications are developed from different types of data, you will have word processing, spreadsheet, and data base files on one disk.

Say that you are using AppleWorks to create a sales projection model. You could have a task disk called Projection that contains a sales report spreadsheet, a sales projection spreadsheet, a customer data base, and a report format word processing document. With all the data files saved on one disk, you can easily create your application without having to switch disks. Of course, if you are working with large files, they may not all fit on a single disk. For example, a customer data base could be quite large, leaving little room on the disk for other files. It is often best to isolate a data base and not store other files on the same disk so that you do not exceed disk storage limits when you are updating. Or you may want to use the customer data base file for more than one task. This is another instance when it would be appropriate to store a single file on a disk.

If your system includes a hard disk, you will have to develop an organizational scheme just to keep track of files. A standard floppy disk allows for up to 143K bytes of storage, while a hard disk environment offers more than 5 million bytes. Since a floppy disk is limited in size, a physical limitation is automatically imposed that restricts you from saving more files than you could possibly keep track of. However, with considerably more storage space available, you would probably find it impossible to manage files without a well-planned, systematic organizational structure.

Apple's ProDOS operating system offers a hierarchical, or tree-structured, approach to storing files. You can store files in a multilevel arrangement that groups related files in what are called subdirectories. AppleWorks, which is a ProDOS-based program, takes full advantage of this hierarchical filing system. For instructions on how to set up a hard disk and create subdirectories, refer to the AppleWorks and ProDOS manuals. In a hard disk environment, a task disk becomes a task subdirectory.

Whether you are using floppy disks or a hard disk, it is important to plan your AppleWorks applications in advance and to determine how different data files will be used. Planning is time well spent. It can save you hours of frustration when you develop an application that uses data from multiple files.

7.02 Tip: *You can increase productivity in an office environment if all employees assign meaningful file names, accurately respond to the AppleWorks date prompt, and label disks.*

These are three simple yet often overlooked steps that can increase productivity by establishing office standards for handling files and disks.

Meaningful file names make it easier to identify files. If you were handed a file folder labeled PJTD2, you would probably have to open the file to determine its contents. But the contents of a file labeled PROJECT.QTR2 would not have to be examined; the file name alone would be sufficient to identify the contents of the file.

The same principle applies to naming data files. If you had to display the contents of a file on the screen to identify it, you would be spending more time identifying files than using them. File names can be up to 15 characters long. They can contain both letters and numbers, but they must begin with a letter.

File names should not be assigned by chance. People should work together to develop a file-naming convention. Establishing an office standard makes it possible for employees to easily identify a particular file and its contents. This is not unlike a paper filing system. If you did not know where the budget projections file for the current year was, you would be wasting valuable time asking other employees or searching through drawers until you found the right folder. It is more efficient to create an office standard that everyone understands and follows.

You can encode a great deal of meaningful information into file names. You may often be working with an application for which you have a group of related files. Suppose you are creating budget spreadsheets for several departments. Unless you code key descriptive bits of information into the file name, you will soon lose track of the files. A file containing a projected budget for the first quarter of 1986 for the engineering department of a firm might be assigned the following file name:

PROJBUD.ENG.861

The first seven characters identify the file as a projected budget file, the ninth through twelfth characters indicate that it is for the engineering department, and the three numbers identify the year and the quarter.

Whenever you start up AppleWorks, you are asked to enter the current date. AppleWorks stamps your files with this date so that you know when a file was created or last modified. If you bypass the date entry, your files will be stamped incorrectly and you will not have an accurate accounting of file use. Although seemingly trivial, an accurate stamp is important if you need to identify the latest version of a file or one that was updated on a particular day.

You are probably already in the habit of labeling disks. But are your labels effective? Cryptic scribbles are not helpful when you need to locate a particular disk. Labeling disks can be compared to labeling file folders: Labels should be meaningful and descriptive. Again, it is important to establish an office standard that all users adhere to. You want to create labels that help identify the contents of a disk without having to scan it electronically. The following example is of a label affixed to a disk that contains quarterly projected budgets for several departments in a company:

```
PROJECTED BUDGETS
1986        Q1 – Q4
DEPTS: Eng, Adm, Sec
```

The most important detail should be on the first line. Additional information can be abbreviated.

 7.03 Trap: *If you do not establish a routine office procedure for recording changes, users will not be aware of the latest updates to an application.*

A change in office procedure can be documented in a memo or announced at a staff meeting. All employees should be made aware of procedural changes that might affect their work. However, few offices have an established updating procedure.

The best approach is to designate that certain users be responsible for making changes in a particular application and that updates be recorded in a log that is accessible to all users. Only the individuals who are most familiar with a particular application should be making modifications, and all users will be aware of the changes and the dates that the changes were made. The following is a sample log sheet:

Date	File/Disk Name	Change	Initials
4/3/86	PROJBUD.ENG.861 [PROJ.BUD]	Growth assumption: 7% to 8%. Attribute to general upturn in economy and increased advertising budget. (J.M. OK)	LJ
7/13/86	MEMO.STYLE [DOC.STYLE]	Print style changed: from single to double spacing. (D.N. OK)	EG

A log that shows dates, changes, and initials offers a historical perspective of the development and use of an application. When you specify the file name, use the full name, not an abbreviation. Several files can have similar names. For example:

PROJBUD.ENG.861 *(The number 1 refers to first quarter.)*
PROJBUD.ENG.862 *(The number 2 refers to second quarter.)*

When identifying the change, be as specific as possible without being verbose. Express the most important details in as few words as possible. Indicate who instigated the change so that questions can be directed to the appropriate person. It is also important that the person who modified the application initial the log entry in case there are any questions later.

7.04 Tip: *Document all applications internally and externally so that all employees in a work environment can successfully use an application.*

Whether you create an application for yourself or for others, documenting what you have done is essential. You should provide two types of documentation: external and internal. External documentation can be a document file or a print-out that explains the purpose of your model and how to use it. Internal documentation includes notations within the model that enable users to understand how the application functions and make modifications to it. This kind of documenting procedure can be used with all three AppleWorks environments, but it is particularly useful with spreadsheet models.

To demonstrate how to document spreadsheet applications, look at the spreadsheet model in Figure 7-1. The formulas in this spreadsheet appear in Figure 7-2.

External documentation should include the following elements:

- *A brief description of the purpose of the spreadsheet.* Provides users with the fundamental concepts of your design.

- *The date that the application was created or last modified and the name of the person(s) responsible for it.* If something goes wrong, you will know whom to contact.

```
File: SALES                    REVIEW/ADD/CHANGE              Escape: Main Menu
=======A========B========C========D========E========F========G========H===
  1|                          SALES PROJECTIONS
  2|
  3|ASSUMPTIONS:
  4|Base       $700,000
  5|Growth        10.00%
  6|
  7|                    Jan       Feb       Mar       Apr       May       Jun
  8|    Monthly Index:  .05       .06       .04       .08       .07       .08
  9|
 10|
 11|    Total Sales:  $770,000
 12|
 13|                    Jan       Feb       Mar       Apr       May       Jun
 14|
 15|    Sales by Month: $38,500   $46,200   $30,800   $61,600   $53,900   $61,600
 16|
 17|
 18|
-------------------------------------------------------------------------------
D11

Type entry or use ∂ commands                              ∂-? for Help
```

Figure 7-1. Sales projections using monthly sales indexes

```
File: SALES                    REVIEW/ADD/CHANGE              Escape: Main Menu
=======A========B========C========D========E========F========G========H===
  1|                          SALES PROJECTIONS
  2|
  3|ASSUMPTIONS:
  4|Base       700000
  5|Growth     .1
  6|
  7|                    Jan     Feb     Mar     Apr     May     Jun
  8|    Monthly Index: .05      .06     .04     .08     .07     .08
  9|
 10|
 11|    Total Sales:   +B4*(1+B5)
 12|
 13|                    Jan     Feb     Mar     Apr     May     Jun
 14|
 15|    Sales by Month: +C11*C8  +C11*D8  +C11*E8  +C11*F8  +C11*G8  +C11*H8
 16|
 17|
 18|
-------------------------------------------------------------------------------
A1

Type entry or use ∂ commands                              ∂-? for Help
```

Figure 7-2.   Formulas used to create the Sales Projection model

- *The name of the program used to create the application and its version or release number.* Software companies update their products; you will need to know which version was used to create a particular application.

- *A printout of cell formulas.* Having formulas printed out facilitates the debugging process. It is also advisable to include a brief explanation of complex formulas. For example, Figure 7-2 is a printout of the cell formulas for the spreadsheet model shown in Figure 7-1.

- *All file names and disk names involved in an application.* Helps a user locate files easily.

- *Sample data.* It is always a good idea to test a model with sample data. You can determine the accuracy of a model, and a printout of the test run shows expected results. This helps novice users confirm that the model is working correctly.

- *Potential problems.* Cite problems that novices may encounter and offer suggestions for dealing with them.

Figure 7-3 shows external documentation for the Sales Projection model. Internal documentation should include the following elements:

- *Consistent layout.* If your worksheets are organized according to a company standard, users can easily navigate from section to section. The nature of your business will determine the most appropriate layout.

- *Separate assumptions area.* When you are designing a model, it is a good idea to construct the spreadsheet in a way that makes "What if" analysis fast and easy. The spreadsheet design in Figure 7-1 makes it easy for users to change the base amount or growth rate variables.

- *On-line documentation.* Include a brief explanation of the variables and assumptions used in calculations. Figure 7-4 shows sample on-line documentation for the spreadsheet model in Figure 7-1.

- *Manual/Auto recalculation flag.* Since AppleWorks does not indicate that a worksheet has been set to manual recalculation, it is up to you, the creator, to remind users to recalculate the worksheet before analyzing calculation results. One way is to include a recalculation "flag" in the on-line documentation (see Figure 7-4).

7.05 Tip: *In addition to saving files frequently as you work with them, one person in an office environment should be responsible for backing up all disks at the end of the day.*

```
                        SALESPROJ86

Model Documentation:

PURPOSE:   Sales forecast model using monthly sales indexes.

           Variables Defined:

                Base - Previous year's total sales

                Growth - Projected annual growth rate

                Monthly Index - Based on seasonal variations
                                and computed from historical
                                sales data for previous
                                five years.

CREATION DATE:   11/7/85
LAST MODIFIED:   1/13/86

CREATED BY:   R. Seller, Sales Manager (Ext. 123)

CREATED WITH:   Appleworks, Version 1.0

FILE NAME(S):   SALESPROJ86

SAMPLE DATA:   1st Quarter, 1986

File:   SALES
Page   1

                     SALES PROJECTIONS

ASSUMPTIONS:
Base       $700,000
Growth        10.00%

                    Jan       Feb       Mar
        Monthly Index:    .05       .06       .04


    Total Sales:    $770,000

                    Jan       Feb       Mar

  Sales by Month:  $38,500  $46,200  $30,800
```

Figure 7-3.   External documentation for the Sales Projection model

Even if you save your data frequently, various things can go wrong that could result in a loss of data: Power failure, hardware failure, and bad disks are only a few of the possibilities. To prevent disaster, back up all your data disks at the end of the day. If one employee in an office is responsible for following a standard backup procedure, you can be assured that all disks are properly backed up on a

```
File: SALES                    REVIEW/ADD/CHANGE              Escape: Main Menu
========J========K========L========M========N========O========P========Q====
  1|            DOCUMENTATION
  2|
  3|            BASE:  Last year's total sales
  4|
  5|            GROWTH:  Projected annual growth rate
  6|
  7|            MONTHLY INDEX:  Based on last year's totals; each
  8|                            month's sales divided by annual sales
  9|                            (accounts for seasonal sales pattern)
 10|
 11|            ----------------------------------------------------
 12|            ** To find the effect of growth rate on sales,
 13|            change the growth-rate percentage (B5).
 14|            ----------------------------------------------------
 15|
 16|**************    DON'T FORGET TO RECALC SPREADHSEET    *****************
 17|                      ------
 18|
-------------------------------------------------------------------------------
J1

Type entry or use @ commands                              @-? for Help
```

Figure 7-4.   Internal documentation for the Sales Projection model

regular basis. You do not want this important task to be left to chance. By instituting a mandatory backup operation, you can guard against severe data loss. The few minutes it takes to back up a disk could save you hours of frustration.

7.06 Tip: *By using common data files, you can be more effective and efficient in creating applications.*

Think in terms of data management tools, not individual applications. A data management tool is a file or set of files that can be used to create applications that meet different needs. With AppleWorks' data interchange capabilities, you can create an information file that can be transferred and modified to create various applications. Flexible data files can increase productivity by eliminating the need to re-enter data.

The first step in creating an information base is to define your information needs. The following is a list of procedures that can help guide you through the process of analyzing your needs:

- *Determine who will be using the information.*
- *Consult with prospective users to get their input on the types of application(s) they need.*

- *Synthesize user input into two lists: common data needs and specific applications.*

- *Design a master data file.* First, determine which AppleWorks environment is most appropriate for the task at hand. Then decide on the most effective structure for the data, such as categories of data, grouping data types, and presentation of data.

- *Test the model on paper before working on-line.* Is the master data file comprehensive enough to satisfy current and anticipated future data needs? Will you be able to modify your applications easily?

Suppose you are the national sales director for a manufacturing company, and you plan to use AppleWorks to automate office procedures. After consulting with the office staff, you create the following list of specific applications:

- *Sales Analysis.* Reviews product sales and profit patterns.

- *Sales Budget.* Sales projections and sales expense budget.

- *Historical Sales Analysis.* Five-year quarterly sales history.

- *Seasonal Forecast.* A seasonal index, computed from historical sales data, indicates seasonal variations that should be considered when you are forecasting sales.

- *Advertising Analysis.* Tracks advertising campaigns by type, amount spent, sales activity directly related to the campaign, and net profit.

- *Inventory Report.* Tracks inventory levels by amount, cost, and retail value of each product.

- *Salesperson Analysis.* Analyzes the sales performance of each salesperson.

- *Regional Sales Analysis.* Analyzes sales activity by region.

- *Customer List.* Identifies the level of sales activity for each customer.

- *Promotional Letter.* Sent to customers to promote new product lines.

- *Profit/Loss Statement.* Projects the net profit (or loss) of a company.

- *Personnel File.* Contains personal and job-related information about each employee.

- *Salary Budget.* Shows salary history and projections.

The next step is defining common data needs. Once you have done this, the contents of master data files become obvious. The 13 applications listed can be created from the following master data files:

Sales Data
Advertising Data
Inventory Data
Customer Data
Personnel Data
Income and Expense Data

The Sales Data file could contain the necessary information to produce the following reports:

Sales Analysis
Sales Budget
Historical Sales Analysis
Seasonal Forecast
Salesperson Analysis
Regional Sales Analysis
Profit/Loss Statement (income figures)

As you can see, this is an efficient approach to designing and developing applications. The following are some additional benefits:

- *Sharing master data files reduces data entry time.* Employees do not need to maintain individual data files. One person can be responsible for maintaining and distributing all master files.

- *On-line data entry helps standardize input by requiring users to adhere to a structure.*

- *Data can be accessed by in-house employees as well as transmitted to other offices via modem.*

7.07 Tip: *You can create spreadsheet templates for standard applications that you use often.*

If much of your work is repetitive, such as financial statements, budgets, and weekly, monthly, and annual reports, generic spreadsheet templates can save time. Whenever you create an application that can be used more than once, you can turn it into a template by following these steps:

1. Construct the spreadsheet model.

2. Enter sample data and test formulas for accuracy.

3. Erase all data, leaving only labels and formulas. (Be sure that you do not inadvertently erase formulas.)

4. Save the spreadsheet and assign a meaningful file name.

To use a template:

1. Load the spreadsheet template into memory.

2. Enter data into the appropriate cells.

3. When you are finished making entries in the current application and want to save it, assign it a new file name. *Do not* use the template file name. Otherwise, you will replace the template file with the current application file and destroy the generic template.

Suppose you are responsible for quarterly updates of the Sales Projection spreadsheet shown in Figure 7-1. By creating a generic template like the one shown in the following illustration, you would enter data only when you use the template. The labels and formulas are in place and do not have to be re-entered. This procedure represents a tremendous saving of time and helps establish standard reporting formats.

```
File: SALES                    REVIEW/ADD/CHANGE              Escape: Main Menu
========A=======B=======C=======D=======E=======F=======G=======H=======
  1|                          SALES PROJECTIONS
  2|
  3|ASSUMPTIONS:
  4|Base            $0
  5|Growth        0.00%
  6|
  7|                     Jan     Feb     Mar     Apr     May     Jun
  8|    Monthly Index:    0       0       0       0       0       0
  9|
 10|
 11|    Total Sales:    $0
 12|
 13|                     Jan     Feb     Mar     Apr     May     Jun
 14|
 15| Sales by Month:    $0      $0      $0      $0      $0      $0
 16|
 17|
 18|
------------------------------------------------------------------------
A1

Type entry or use 】 commands                              】-? for Help
```

 7.08 Trap: *If you do not assign the Protection format to cells in a generic template that contain labels and formulas, you could inadvertently wipe out these labels and formulas.*

After you develop and test a spreadsheet model, protect all labels and formulas from being inadvertently altered when users interact with the spreadsheet. Several Tips in Chapter 5 discuss some of the important issues related to using the Protection format option. If you do not protect labels and formulas in a template, you are courting disaster. Once you determine that a model is logically sound and that the formulas are accurate, protect the model from being altered. One incorrect entry can destroy an entire spreadsheet. Take the time to protect key cells, and remember that by doing so you may be saving hours of debugging.

7.09 Tip: *By incorporating a few simple formulas in your spreadsheets, you can validate the data entries made by users.*

You can test an application model to determine the accuracy of your formulas, but how do you test user input for accuracy? Although seemingly impossible, it is actually easy to implement. (And you do not have to look over the shoulders of others to do it!) All it takes is a set of simple logical functions located outside the active spreadsheet area. You can validate user input and test the overall validity of the application at the same time.

Now you are going to create an input validation area for the spreadsheet model shown in Figure 7-1. But before you enter validation formulas, you must have a clear understanding of the underlying assumptions. The external documentation in Figure 7-3 indicates the purpose of this application and defines the following variables:

- *Base.* The previous year's total sales figure.

- *Growth.* Projected annual growth rate.

- *Monthly index.* Based on seasonal variations and computed from historical sales data for the previous five years.

After consulting with R. Seller, sales manager and creator of this model, you become aware of four significant logical parameters:

1. A total of the Sales by Month figures must be equal to the Total Sales figure.

2. A total of the monthly indexes must add up to 1.00 (100%).

3. The projected annual growth rate must be between 8 and 12 percent.

4. The base figure must be last year's total sales.

Validating the input for this spreadsheet, then, becomes nothing more than creating a set of logical functions that can mathematically evaluate these four parameters. The built-in @IF function can be used to perform the logical tests. The general form of this function is

@IF*(logical condition, true value, false value)*

The following spreadsheet is a continuation of Figure 7-1 and uses column P as an input validation area, with the appropriate formulas and @IF functions:

```
File: validation              REVIEW/ADD/CHANGE              Escape: Main Menu
========I========J========K========L========M========N========O========P====
  1|                                                            INPUT VALIDATION:
  2|                                                                          0
  3|
  4|                                                                          0
  5|                                                                          0
  6|                                                                          0
  7|      Jul      Aug      Sep      Oct      Nov      Dec
  8|      .09      .09      .11      .11      .11      .11                     1
  9|                                                                          0
 10|
 11|
 12|
 13|      Jul      Aug      Sep      Oct      Nov      Dec
 14|
 15| $69,300  $69,300  $84,700  $84,700  $84,700  $84,700          $770,000
 16|                                                                          0
 17|
 18|
    -------------------------------------------------------------------------
 I4

Type entry or use 2 commands                              2-? for Help
```

To understand the process, examine the formulas that evaluate the first parameter. First, you want to get the total of Monthly Sales figures. The formula looks like this:

@SUM(C15..N15)

You enter it in P15. To test the validity of this result, enter the following @IF function:

@IF(P15<>C11,@ERROR,0)

The conditional test, P15<>C11, checks whether the total of Monthly Sales is less than or greater than (not equal to) Total Sales. If this condition is true, the @ERROR function returns ERROR as a result. If the condition is false, a zero will be returned. By nesting the @ERROR function within the @IF statement, you can flag errors. In the following illustration, inappropriate data has been intentionally entered to demonstrate the usefulness of error flagging. Entries for all four parameters are currently invalid.

```
File: SALES                    REVIEW/ADD/CHANGE            Escape: Main Menu
========I========J========K========L========M========N========O=======P===
 1|                                                            INPUT VALIDATION:
 2|                                                                     ERROR
 3|
 4|                                                                         1
 5|                                                                         0
 6|                                                                     ERROR
 7|      Jul      Aug      Sep      Oct      Nov      Dec
 8|      .09      .09      .11      .09      .11      .11                  .98
 9|                                                                     ERROR
10|
11|
12|
13|      Jul      Aug      Sep      Oct      Nov      Dec
14|
15|  $72,225  $72,225  $88,275  $72,225  $88,275  $88,275           $786,450
16|                                                                     ERROR
17|
18|
    -------------------------------------------------------------------------
I1

Type entry or use @ commands                            @-? for Help
```

While the @IF function flags the error, the accompanying formula serves as a helpful diagnostic tool. The formula in P15 indicates the total sales at $786,450, which is $16,450 more than it should be; $770,000 is correct.

Here are the formulas used in the input validation area. A detailed explanation of the formulas entered in P2..P9 follows:

```
File: validation               REVIEW/ADD/CHANGE            Escape: Main Menu
==============O=====================P========================Q==============
 1|                            INPUT VALIDATION:
 2|                            @IF(B4<>700000,@ERROR,0)
 3|
 4|                            @IF(B5<.08,1,0)
 5|                            @IF(B5>.12,1,0)
 6|                            @IF(P4+P5>0,@ERROR,0)
 7|
 8|                            @SUM(C8...N8)
 9|                            @IF(P8<>1,@ERROR,0)
10|
11|
12|
13|
14|
15|                            @SUM(C15...N15)
16|                            @IF(P15<>C11,@ERROR,0)
17|
18|
    -------------------------------------------------------------------------
P13

Type entry or use @ commands                            @-? for Help
```

- *Cell P2.* @IF(B4<>700000,@ERROR,0) Returns an error if the base figure is a number other than $700,000, last year's total sales.

- *Cell P4.* @IF(B5<.08,1,0) Checks whether the projected annual growth rate is less than 8 percent. If the conditional test is true, 1 is returned; otherwise, 0.

- *Cell P5.* @IF(B5>.12,1,0) Checks whether the projected annual growth rate is more than 12 percent. If the conditional test is true, 1 is returned; otherwise, 0.

- *Cell P6.* @IF(P4+P5>0,@ERROR,0) Adds the results from P4 and P5 to determine if the projected annual growth rate is within the acceptable range, between 8 and 12 percent. If not, an error flag will be displayed.

- *Cell P8.* @SUM(C8..N8) Adds the monthly indexes to check whether they add up to 1.00 (100 percent).

- *Cell P9.* @IF(P8<>1,@ERROR,0) Returns an error if the monthly indexes do not total 100 percent.

In the next sections, you'll examine specific applications that you can create for your office and for your personal financial management at home using some of the Tips and Traps discussed in this book.

Application: Integrated Sales Analysis Report

WORK ENVIRONMENT: Business

DESCRIPTION: This application demonstrates how to use a data base and the report format feature to generate monthly reports.

Suppose you are the sales director for All-Star Products, a company that distributes sporting equipment. You are responsible for tracking and reporting sales activity on a monthly basis by producing four summary reports. Each one has a different format and references different data categories in the master data base.

DEVELOPING AND USING THE APPLICATION:

1. Create a master data base that includes all the data categories needed to produce the summary reports, as shown in the following illustration:

```
File: SALES ANALYSIS          INSERT NEW RECORDS       Escape: Review/Add/Change


Record 8 of 8
=================================================================================
Sales #: -
Customer Name: -
Address: -
City: -
St: -
Zip: -
Phone: -
Contact: -
Rating: -
Product: -
Date Last Order: -
$ Last Order: -
YTD Sales: -

---------------------------------------------------------------------------------
Type entry or use ? commands                                         50K Avail.
```

The data categories are defined as follows:

- *Sales #.* Salesperson number (for in-house reference).
- *Customer Name.* Customer's name.
- *Address.* Customer's street address.
- *City.* Customer's city.
- *St.* Customer's state (two-letter abbreviation).
- *Zip.* Customer's ZIP code number.
- *Phone.* Customer's phone number, including the area code.
- *Contact.* Primary contact person.
- *Rating.* Customer rating code based on sales activity.
- *Product.* Product line purchased by the customer.
- *Date Last Order.* Date of last order.
- *$ Last Order.* Dollar amount of last order.
- *YTD Sales.* Year-to-date sales amount.

2. To simplify the process of producing monthly reports, you can define a library of report formats and reuse them. The following illustration shows a list of the current report formats for this application:

```
File: SALES ANALYSIS          REPORT CATALOG          Escape: Report Menu
Report: MAILING LIST


===============================================================================

              Current report formats:

                  1.  CUSTOMER CONTACT
                  2.  SALES x SALESPERSON
                  3.  SALES x PRODUCT
                  4.  SALES ACTIVITY
                  5.  MAILING LIST




-------------------------------------------------------------------------------
Type number, or use arrows, then press Return              51K Avail.
```

- *Customer Contact.* Includes the mailing address, phone number, and contact person for each customer. With all records selected, you get a master customer list that should look similar to the following example:

```
ALL-STAR PRODUCTS
File:   SALES ANALYSIS
Report: CUSTOMER CONTACT
Customer Name       Address            St   Zip    Phone            Contact
-----------------   -----------------  ---- -----  --------------   --------
Athlete's Foot      10 K St.           MA   33256  (293) 876-0742   Laura
Duffers             4 Fairway Dr.      CA   44444  (521) 812-3218   Arnie
Grand Slam          730 Stadium Way    CA   99376  (321) 234-8777   Tommy
Hang Ten            421 Woody Dr.      CA   93283  (221) 382-3391   Brian
The Goal Post       1 50th Yd.         CA   38476  (765) 772-5514   OJ
The Slam Dunk       543 Center Ct.     CA   42813  (253) 927-1183   Shorty
What a Racket       384 Swing St.      NY   22345  (222) 832-3205   Martina
```

Here is the report format that produces this report:

```
File: SALES ANALYSIS          REPORT FORMAT           Escape: Report Menu
Report: CUSTOMER CONTACT
Selection: All records


===============================================================================
--> or <--  Move cursor                  @-J  Right justify this category
 >  @  <    Switch category positions    @-K  Define a calculated category
--> @ <--   Change column width          @-N  Change report name and/or title
@-A  Arrange (sort) on this category     @-O  Printer options
@-D  Delete this category                @-P  Print the report
@-G  Add/remove group totals             @-R  Change record selection rules
@-I  Insert a prev. deleted category     @-T  Add/remove category totals
-------------------------------------------------------------------------------
ALL-STAR PRODUCTS
Customer Name       Address            St   Zip    Phone            Contact  L
-A--------------    -B------------     -C-- -D---  -E-----------    -F------ e
What a Racket       384 Swing St.      NY   22345  (222) 832-3205   Martina  n
The Slam Dunk       543 Center Ct.     CA   42813  (253) 927-1183   Shorty   7
Grand Slam          730 Stadium Way    CA   99376  (321) 234-8777   Tommy    4

-------------------------------------------------------------------------------
Use options shown above to change report format            51K Avail.
```

Suppose a salesperson leaves the company and you have to hire a new one. You will need to produce a customer contact list for the new employee. Using the Customer Contact report format and specifying that only records with Sales # equal to 3 are to be included, your report will look something like this:

```
ALL-STAR PRODUCTS
File:    SALES ANALYSIS
Report: CUSTOMER CONTACT
Selection: Sales # equals 3
Customer Name      Address             St   Zip     Phone              Contact
-----------------  ------------------  ---- ------- -----------------  --------
Grand Slam         730 Stadium Way     CA   99376   (321) 234-8777     Tommy
Athlete's Foot     10 K St.            MA   33256   (293) 876-0742     Laura
The Goal Post      1 50th Yd.          CA   38476   (765) 772-5514     OJ
```

- *Sales × Salesperson.* Summarizes year-to-date sales activity by salesperson. As sales director, you can use the following report to track the productivity of your sales staff:

```
ALL-STAR PRODUCTS                                              Page  1
File:    SALES ANALYSIS
Report: SALES x SALESPERSON
Sales #  Customer Name      Product   YTD Sales
-------  -----------------  --------  ----------
2        The Slam Dunk      6            1660
2        What a Racket      4            1775
                                         3435

3        Athlete's Foot     8            1853
3        Grand Slam         7            1985
3        The Goal Post      9            1730
                                         5568

4        Hang Ten           7            1450
                                         1450

5        Duffers            8            1520
                                         1520

                                        11973*
```

For each salesperson, a total is indicated, as well as a grand total for the entire sales staff (noted with an asterisk). The following illustration shows a screen view of the report format. Group totals for YTD Sales are reported by Sales #:

```
File: SALES ANALYSIS          REPORT FORMAT              Escape: Report Menu
Report: SALES x SALESPERSON
Selection: All records


Group totals on: Sales #
===========================================================================
--> or <--   Move cursor                  @-J  Right justify this category
   >  @  <    Switch category positions    @-K  Define a calculated category
--> @ <--    Change column width           @-N  Change report name and/or title
@-A  Arrange (sort) on this category       @-O  Printer options
@-D  Delete this category                  @-P  Print the report
@-G  Add/remove group totals               @-R  Change record selection rules
@-I  Insert a prev. deleted category       @-T  Add/remove category totals
---------------------------------------------------------------------------
ALL-STAR PRODUCTS
Sales #  Customer Name     Product  YTD Sales      L
-A------ -B--------------- -C------ -D--------     e
2        What a Racket      4        9999999999    n
2        The Slam Dunk      6        9999999999    4
3        Grand Slam         7        9999999999    9
                                    ============
---------------------------------------------------------------------------
Use options shown above to change report format              51K Avail.
```

- *Sales* × *Product*. Summarizes year-to-date sales activity by product.
  Numbers are used to refer to different product lines, as shown in the following illustration:

```
ALL-STAR PRODUCTS                                          Page   1
File:   SALES ANALYSIS
Report: SALES x PRODUCT
Customer Name    Product   YTD Sales
---------------- --------- ----------
What a Racket     4          1775
                             1775

The Slam Dunk     6          1660
                             1660

Grand Slam        7          1985
Hang Ten          7          1450
                             3435

Athlete's Foot    8          1853
Duffers           8          1520
                             3373

The Goal Post     9          1730
                             1730

                            11973*
```

AppleWorks Tips and Traps

The report format for this report is shown in the next illustration. Group totals for YTD Sales are reported by Product.

```
File: SALES ANALYSIS              REPORT FORMAT            Escape: Report Menu
Report: SALES x PRODUCT
Selection: All records


Group totals on: Product
===============================================================================
--> or <--  Move cursor                    @-J  Right justify this category
  >  @  <   Switch category positions       @-K  Define a calculated category
--> @ <--   Change column width             @-N  Change report name and/or title
@-A  Arrange (sort) on this category        @-O  Printer options
@-D  Delete this category                   @-P  Print the report
@-G  Add/remove group totals                @-R  Change record selection rules
@-I  Insert a prev. deleted category        @-T  Add/remove category totals
-------------------------------------------------------------------------------
ALL-STAR PRODUCTS
Customer Name     Product  YTD Sale   L
-A--------------  -B------  -C------   e
What a Racket     4        99999999   n
The Slam Dunk     6        99999999   3
Grand Slam        7        99999999   7
                                ========
-------------------------------------------------------------------------------
Use options shown above to change report format                    51K Avail.
```

Figure 7-5 demonstrates how the Sales × Product report can be incorporated into a memo with data transfer methods. When printing the data base report, you select the Clipboard option and then use the Copy from Clipboard command to transfer the report to the word processing document.

• *Sales Activity.* The following report summarizes sales activity with year-to-date sales figures and the date and the amount of the last order:

```
ALL-STAR PRODUCTS
File:   SALES ANALYSIS                                          Page   1
Report: SALES ACTIVITY
Customer Name    Rating   Date Last Order  $ Last Order  YTD Sales
---------------  -------  ---------------  ------------  ----------
Grand Slam       AA       Oct 10 85        $437          1985
Athlete's Foot   A        Dec  6 85        $640          1853
What a Racket    B        Nov  7 85        $254          1775
The Goal Post    B        Jan 20 86        $730          1730
The Slam Dunk    B        Nov 21 85        $258          1660
Duffers          C        Dec 18 85        $392          1520
Hang Ten         C        Jan  3 86        $216          1450
                                                         11973*
```

As sales director, you have to track the level of sales activity for your customers and be aware of those who have not placed orders during the last few months. The report format should look like the following example:

```
File: SALES ANALYSIS           REPORT FORMAT           Escape: Report Menu
Report: SALES ACTIVITY
Selection: All records


==========================================================================
--> or <--  Move cursor            @-J  Right justify this category
  >  @  <   Switch category positions  @-K  Define a calculated category
--> @ <--  Change column width      @-N  Change report name and/or title
@-A  Arrange (sort) on this category  @-O  Printer options
@-D  Delete this category           @-P  Print the report
@-G  Add/remove group totals        @-R  Change record selection rules
@-I  Insert a prev. deleted category  @-T  Add/remove category totals
--------------------------------------------------------------------------
ALL-STAR PRODUCTS
Customer Name   Rating  Date Last Order  $ Last Order  YTD Sales    L
-A------------  -B-----  -C----------  -D----------  -E--------   e
Grand Slam       AA      Oct 10 85        $437         9999999999   n
Athlete's Foot   A       Dec  6 85        $640         9999999999   6
What a Racket    B       Nov  7 85        $254         9999999999   6
                                                      ==========
--------------------------------------------------------------------------
Use options shown above to change report format              50K Avail.
```

• *Mailing Labels.* It is hard to imagine a business that does not use mailing labels. With the Labels option, you can easily prepare a report format that will produce mailing labels from your master data base file. Figure 7-6 displays the format of the mailing labels, and the following illustration shows the Labels option of the report format used to produce them:

```
File: SALES ANALYSIS           REPORT FORMAT           Escape: Report Menu
Report: MAILING LIST
Selection: All records


ALL-STAR PRODUCTS
==========================================================================

Customer Name
Address
City      St  Zip


-----------------------Each record will print  6 lines--------------------




--------------------------------------------------------------------------
Use options shown on Help Screen                          @-? for Help
```

```
MEMO

TO:     Joe Jock, President
FROM:   R. Seller, National Sales Director
RE:     Direct Mail Campaign
DATE:   Jan 31, 1986


Here is the PRODUCT ANALYSIS REPORT for January, 1986:

All-STAR PRODUCTS

Report: SALES x PRODUCT

Customer Name      Product   YTD Sales
----------------   --------  ----------

What a Racket      4            1775
                                1775

The Slam Dunk      6            1660
                                1660

Grand Slam         7            1985
Hang Ten           7            1450
                                3435

Athlete's Foot     8            1853
Duffers            8            1520
                                3373

The Goal Post      9            1730
                                1730

                             11973*


Based on the figures above, I recommend that we feature
product lines 4, 6, and 9 in our next direct mail campaign.
```

Figure 7-5. Incorporating the report in a memo

Application: Personal Financial Planning

WORK ENVIRONMENT: Home

DESCRIPTION: This application demonstrates how to use spreadsheets to manage personal finances. You will learn how to create a checkbook management system that not only reconciles your deposit and payment entries, but also sum-

---

```
File:   SALES ANALYSIS
Report: MAILING LIST
ALL-STAR PRODUCTS


Grand Slam
730 Stadium Way
Chavez RavineCA   99376


Athlete's Foot
10 K St.
Marathon      MA   33256


What a Racket
384 Swing St.
Forest Hills NY   22345


The Goal Post
1 50th Yd.
Colliseum     CA   38476


The Slam Dunk
543 Center Ct.
Laker City    CA   42813


Duffers
4 Fairway Dr.
Teeoff        CA   44444


Hang Ten
421 Woody Dr.
Surf City     CA   93283
```

Figure 7-6.   Mailing label format

marizes expenses according to tax categories that correspond to the 1040 tax form. Many people justify the purchase of a microcomputer with the intention of creating an electronic version of their checkbook register. Some follow through in developing this application, but few individuals are disciplined enough to enter all their checkbook transactions on a regular basis. However, if a check register includes a tax deduction summary, the application takes on a new dimension. You can save time by eliminating the frustrating and typically lengthy procedure of summarizing tax-related information at the end of the year.

On another spreadsheet, you summarize current assets and liabilities, indicating your total net worth as of a specified date. The information in this report can help you plan major purchases and set financial goals.

The third spreadsheet analyzes a loan in terms of the monthly payment and total interest paid over the life of the loan. With this application, you can determine the monthly payments on a new loan or the total interest paid out during the life of a loan.

DEVELOPING AND USING THE APPLICATION:

1. *Checkbook Management.* This spreadsheet has three components: Check Register, Tax Categories, and Tax Summary. The following illustration shows the Check Register:

```
File: CHECK MNGMT              REVIEW/ADD/CHANGE            Escape: Main Menu
=====A===B============C============D=====E=====F==========G=====H==
 1|                    CHECKBOOK    MANAGEMENT
 2|=========================================================================
 3|CHECK REGISTER
 4|=========================================================================
 5| Check
 6|Number  Description              Amount   Deposit    Balance   Code
 7|------  ------------------------ -------- ---------- --------- ----
 8|        <Balanced Forwarded>                         $2,100.58
 9| 1001   High Rate Lender         $1,250.00           $850.58    0
10| 1002   Reach Out Phone Co.      $87.22              $763.36    3
11| 1003   Fly By Night Airline     $685.00             $78.36     5
12| 1004   Subscription:Apple-A-Peel $25.00  $1,500.00  $1,553.36  2
13| 1005   Dues:Apple Peelers Inc.  $45.00              $1,508.36  2
14|
15|
16|                        TOTAL    $2,092.22 $1,500.00
17|
18|
-------------------------------------------------------------------------
A1

Type entry or use a commands                          a-? for Help
```

The spreadsheet columns are defined as follows:

- *Column A.* Check number.
- *Column B.* Blank.
- *Column C.* Description of payee.
- *Column D.* Amount of check.
- *Column E.* Blank.
- *Column F.* Amount of deposit.
- *Column G.* Formula to calculate balance.
- *Column H.* Code that corresponds to tax categories.

For every payment, you must indicate the amount paid and the appropriate tax code. The formulas in Column G automatically calculate the running balance. The tax code references the tax categories found in the second component of the following spreadsheet:

```
File: CHECK MNGMT              REVIEW/ADD/CHANGE              Escape: Main Menu
============J==========K==========L==========M==========N=========O====
  1|
  2|                          TAX CATEGORIES
  3|
  4|     Car          Dues &      Business     Business     Business
  5|   Expenses      Subscrp     Telephone    Entertain.     Travel
  6|     (1)           (2)          (3)          (4)          (5)
  7|
  8|
  9|    $0.00         $0.00        $0.00        $0.00        $0.00
 10|    $0.00         $0.00       $87.22        $0.00        $0.00
 11|    $0.00         $0.00        $0.00        $0.00      $685.00
 12|    $0.00        $25.00        $0.00        $0.00        $0.00
 13|    $0.00        $45.00        $0.00        $0.00        $0.00
 14|
 15|
 16|
 17|
 18|
     ----------------------------------------------------------------
J1

Type entry or use ∂ commands                           ∂-? for Help
```

Applying logic in the form of IF statements, you can have each payment analyzed in terms of specified tax categories. Using the Zoom command to display formulas, you get the following:

```
File: CHECK MNGMT              REVIEW/ADD/CHANGE              Escape: Main Menu
============J=================K=================L=================M========
  1|
  2|                          TAX CATEGORIES
  3|
  4|        Car            Dues &          Business         Business
  5|      Expenses        Subscrp         Telephone        Entertain.
  6|        (1)             (2)             (3)              (4)
  7|
  8|
  9|∂IF(H9=1,+D9,0)   ∂IF(H9=2,+D9,0)   ∂IF(H9=3,+D9,0)   ∂IF(H9=4,+D9,0)
 10|∂IF(H10=1,+D10,0) ∂IF(H10=2,+D10,0) ∂IF(H10=3,+D10,0) ∂IF(H10=4,+D10,0)
 11|∂IF(H11=1,+D11,0) ∂IF(H11=2,+D11,0) ∂IF(H11=3,+D11,0) ∂IF(H11=4,+D11,0)
 12|∂IF(H12=1,+D12,0) ∂IF(H12=2,+D12,0) ∂IF(H12=3,+D12,0) ∂IF(H12=4,+D12,0)
 13|∂IF(H13=1,+D13,0) ∂IF(H13=2,+D13,0) ∂IF(H13=3,+D13,0) ∂IF(H13=4,+D13,0)
 14|∂IF(H14=1,+D14,0) ∂IF(H14=2,+D14,0) ∂IF(H14=3,+D14,0) ∂IF(H14=4,+D14,0)
 15|
 16|
 17|
 18|
     ----------------------------------------------------------------
J2

Type entry or use ∂ commands                           ∂-? for Help
```

The third component, a Tax Summary, looks like this:

```
File: CHECK MNGMT              REVIEW/ADD/CHANGE          -Escape: Main Menu
=======A=====B===============C=================D=======E======F========G===
19|
20|
21|==========================================================================
22|TAX SUMMARY
23|==========================================================================
24|        Business Telephone          $87.22
25|        Dues & Subscriptions        $70.00
26|        Business Travel            $685.00
27|        Car Expenses                 $0.00
28|        Business Entertainment       $0.00
29|
30|==========================================================================
31|
32|
33|
34|
35|
36|
--------------------------------------------------------------------------
A19

Type entry or use @ commands                              @-? for Help
```

The following formulas were used to get these results:

```
File: CHECK MNGMT              REVIEW/ADD/CHANGE           Escape: Main Menu
=======A=====B===============C=================D=======E======F========G===
19|
20|
21|==========================================================================
22|TAX SUMMARY
23|==========================================================================
24|        Business Telephone       @SUM(K8...K100)
25|        Dues & Subscriptions     @SUM(J8...J100)
26|        Business Travel          @SUM(M8...M100)
27|        Car Expenses             @SUM(I8...I100)
28|        Business Entertainment   @SUM(L8...L100)
29|
30|==========================================================================
31|
32|
33|
34|
35|
36|
--------------------------------------------------------------------------
A19

Type entry or use @ commands                              @-? for Help
```

This component serves as a year-end summary of tax-related information.

To enter additional payments or deposits, you need to insert a new row and then copy all appropriate formulas from the previous row. The following illustration shows how the spreadsheet accounts for the new entry made on row 14 (check number 1006):

```
File: CHECK MNGMT            REVIEW/ADD/CHANGE          Escape: Main Menu
======A===B=============C===============D======F==========G======H==
  1 |                    CHECKBOOK   MANAGEMENT
  2 |=================================================================
  3 |CHECK REGISTER
  4 |=================================================================
  5 | Check
  6 |Number  Description              Amount    Deposit    Balance  Code
  7 |------  -----------------------  ---------  ----------  ---------  ----
  8 |        <Balanced Forwarded>                            $2,100.58
  9 | 1001   High Rate Lender         $1,250.00               $850.58   0
 10 | 1002   Reach Out Phone Co.         $87.22               $763.36   3
 11 | 1003   Fly By Night Airline       $685.00                $78.36   5
 12 | 1004   Subscription:Apple-A-Peel   $25.00  $1,500.00  $1,553.36   2
 13 | 1005   Dues:Apple Peelers Inc.     $45.00             $1,508.36   2
 14 | 1006   Off Shore Drilling Gas Co   $15.90             $1,492.46   1
 15 |
 16 |                         TOTAL  $2,108.12  $1,500.00
 17 |
 18 |
-----------------------------------------------------------------------
A1

Type entry or use ə commands                          ə-? for Help
```

The Tax Categories section evaluates the new entry, and the results are shown in the following illustration:

```
File: CHECK MNGMT            REVIEW/ADD/CHANGE          Escape: Main Menu
==========J============K===========L===========M=========N=========0====
  1 |
  2 |                        TAX CATEGORIES
  3 |
  4 |     Car         Dues &     Business    Business    Business
  5 |  Expenses      Subscrp    Telephone   Entertain.    Travel
  6 |    (1)           (2)         (3)         (4)         (5)
  7 |
  8 |
  9 |   $0.00         $0.00       $0.00       $0.00       $0.00
 10 |   $0.00         $0.00      $87.22       $0.00       $0.00
 11 |   $0.00         $0.00       $0.00       $0.00     $685.00
 12 |   $0.00        $25.00       $0.00       $0.00       $0.00
 13 |   $0.00        $45.00       $0.00       $0.00       $0.00
 14 |  $15.90         $0.00       $0.00       $0.00       $0.00
 15 |
 16 |
 17 |
 18 |
-----------------------------------------------------------------------
J1

Type entry or use ə commands                          ə-? for Help
```

The Tax Summary reflects the payment entered on row 14:

```
File: CHECK MNGMT                 REVIEW/ADD/CHANGE              Escape: Main Menu
=======A=====B=============C==================D=======E======F========G===
 19|
 20|
 21|==========================================================================
 22|TAX SUMMARY
 23|==========================================================================
 24|            Business Telephone              $87.22
 25|            Dues & Subscriptions            $70.00
 26|            Business Travel                $685.00
 27|            Car Expenses                    $15.90
 28|            Business Entertainment           $0.00
 29|
 30|==========================================================================
 31|
 32|
 33|
 34|
 35|
 36|
-----------------------------------------------------------------------------
A19

Type entry or use 2 commands                               2-? for Help
```

2. *Personal Financial Net Worth Statement.* This application involves listing all assets and liabilities and then creating a formula to calculate net worth. Figure 7-7 shows a sample Net Worth Statement. The categories can be modified to suit your needs.

3. *Loan Summary.* This application is divided into two parts: Loan Summary at the top and the amortization table below it (see Figure 7-8). The Loan Summary includes the principal amount borrowed, the annual interest rate charged, the term of the loan (expressed in months), and the monthly payment, computed with this formula (in English):

(Principal Amount*(Interest Rate/12))/(1−(1/(1+Interest Rate/12))^(Loan Term))

Suppose you want to borrow $12,000 to buy a new car. The Loan Summary in Figure 7-8 determines the monthly payment and summarizes the loan activity

AppleWorks Applications

```
File:   Net Worth                                            Page  1

        PERSONAL   FINANCIAL
        NET WORTH  STATEMENT          AS OF:  APRIL,1986
========================================================================

        ASSETS                        LIABILITIES
        ======                        ===========
Fluid Assets:                     Current Bills Due:
    Cash on Hand        $700           Charge Accounts        $500
    Checking Accounts $1,200           Credit Card Accts.   $2,400
    Savings Accounts $15,000           Medical/Dental         $150
                                       Homeowner's Insur.     $500
         Sub-Total   $16,900           Auto Insurance         $250
                                       Life Insurance         $250
Long-Term Assets:                      Medical Insurance      $800
    Life Insurance   $50,000           Other                    $0
    Certif. of Deposit $2,000
    Retirement Fund   $2,000                 Sub-Total      $4,850

         Sub-Total   $54,000      Taxes:
                                       Real Estate            $650
Current Market Value of Securities:    Self Employment        $500
    Stocks                 $0          Other                    $0
    Options                $0
    Bonds                  $0                Sub-Total      $1,150
    Mutual Funds           $0
                                  Loans:
         Sub-Total          $0          Home Mortgage      $55,000
                                        Mortgage Other RE.       $0
Current Market Value                    Auto                $2,200
of Durable Assets:                      Home Improvement         $0
    Home or Condo   $120,000            Education           $1,200
    Other Real Estate     $0            Life Insurance           $0
    Furn./Appiances   $3,000            Other                    $0
    Automobiles '     $4,000
    Recreational Veh.      $0                 Sub-Total     $58,400
    Clothing          $1,500
    Furs,Jewelry        $800
    Other                  $0

         Sub-Total  $129,300

Other Assets:
    Money Owed You         $0
    Tax Refunds Due      $650
    Other                  $0

         Sub-Total       $650

TOTAL CURRENT ASSETS  $200,850    TOTAL CURRENT LIABILITY    $64,400


   .........NET WORTH AS OF THIS DATE:   $136,450 ..............
   ....................................................................
```

Figure 7-7.   Sample net worth statement

```
File:   LOAN SUMMARY                                                    Page   1

                               LOAN SUMMARY
================================================================================

Loan Amount.......     $12,000              Loan Type......
Interest Rate.....      13.50%
Loan Term.........          36              AUTOMOBILE
Monthly Payment...     $407.22


================================================================================

                        Interest         Principal        Balance
                        ---------        ----------       --------
                                                          $12,000.00
1986       Month  1      $135.00          $272.22       $11,727.78
           Month  2      $131.94          $275.29       $11,452.49
           Month  3      $128.84          $278.38       $11,174.11
           Month  4      $125.71          $281.51       $10,892.59
           Month  5      $122.54          $284.68       $10,607.91
           Month  6      $119.34          $287.88       $10,320.03
           MOnth  7      $116.10          $291.12       $10,028.90
           Month  8      $112.83          $294.40        $9,734.51
           Month  9      $109.51          $297.71        $9,436.80
           Month 10      $106.16          $301.06        $9,135.74
           Month 11      $102.78          $304.45        $8,831.29
           Month 12       $99.35          $307.87        $8,523.42
1987       Month  1       $95.89          $311.33        $8,212.08
           Month  2       $92.39          $314.84        $7,897.25
           Month  3       $88.84          $318.38        $7,578.87
           Month  4       $85.26          $321.96        $7,256.90
           Month  5       $81.64          $325.58        $6,931.32
           Month  6       $77.98          $329.25        $6,602.08
           Month  7       $74.27          $332.95        $6,269.13
           Month  8       $70.53          $336.70        $5,932.43
           Month  9       $66.74          $340.48        $5,591.95
           Month 10       $62.91          $344.31        $5,247.63
           Month 11       $59.04          $348.19        $4,899.44
           Month 12       $55.12          $352.10        $4,547.34
1988       Month  1       $51.16          $356.07        $4,191.27
           Month  2       $47.15          $360.07        $3,831.20
           Month  3       $43.10          $364.12        $3,467.08
           Month  4       $39.00          $368.22        $3,098.86
           Month  5       $34.86          $372.36        $2,726.50
           Month  6       $30.67          $376.55        $2,349.95
           Month  7       $26.44          $380.79        $1,969.16
           Month  8       $22.15          $385.07        $1,584.09
           Month  9       $17.82          $389.40        $1,194.69
           Month 10       $13.44          $393.78          $800.91
           Month 11        $9.01          $398.21          $402.69
           Month 12        $4.53          $402.69             $.00
                        ----------       -----------
Totals                 $2,660.04        $12,000.00
```

Figure 7-8.   Loan statement

from 1986 to 1988. The @SUM function is used to determine the total principal and interest paid. The following illustration displays the formulas used in this spreadsheet:

```
File: LOAN SUMMARY              REVIEW/ADD/CHANGE           Escape: Main Menu
=====A========B=========C=========D==========E=========F======
   1|                          LOAN SUMMARY
   2|================================================================
   3|
   4|Loan Amount.....  12000                      Loan Type......
   5|Interest Rate...  .135
   6|Loan Term.......  36
   7|Monthly Payment.  (C4*(C5/12))/(1-(1/(1+(C5/12))^C6))
   8|
   9|================================================================
  10|
  11|               Interest     Principal       Balance
  12|               --------     ---------       -------
  13|                                            +C4
  14|1986   Month 1  (C5/12)*E13  (C7-C14)       +E13-D14
  15|       Month 2  (C5/12)*E14  (C7-C15)       +E14-D15
  16|       Month 3  (C5/12)*E15  (C7-C16)       +E15-D16
  17|       Month 4  (C5/12)*E16  (C7-C17)       +E16-D17
  18|       Month 5  (C5/12)*E17  (C7-C18)       +E17-D18
      -------------------------------------------------------------
A1

Type entry or use @ commands                          @-? for Help
```

In the next section you'll find some useful models for educational applications, both for the school office and for classroom use. Involving students in projects of interest to them is a quick way to teach AppleWorks, too.

Application: The School Office

WORK ENVIRONMENT: School Administration

DESCRIPTION: This application demonstrates how to use a master data base of student information to generate three typical applications in a school work environment: Student Roster, Teacher Roster, and Emergency Contact. The process of updating the information is simplified by creating report formats.

DEVELOPING AND USING
THE APPLICATION:

1. The structure of the master data base is shown in the following illustration:

```
File: SCHOOL ADMIN          INSERT NEW RECORDS      Escape: Review/Add/Change


Record 11 of 11
=====================================================================================
Last Name: -                         Birth Date: -
First Name: -                        Age: -
Grade: -
Teacher: -
Address: -
City: -
St: -
Zip: -
Phone: -
Mother: -
Work Ph 1: -
Father: -
Work Ph 2: -
Emerg (Mr/Ms): -
Emerg Ph: -
-------------------------------------------------------------------------
Type entry or use @ commands                                    47K Avail.
```

2. The next illustration shows a list of the current report formats for this application:

Current report formats:

1. STUDENT ROSTER
2. TEACHER ROSTER
3. EMERGENCY

- *Student Roster.* An alphabetized list of all students, birth date and age, current grade level, and assigned teacher. The report looks like this:

```
File:   SCHOOL ADMIN
Report: STUDENT ROSTER
Last Name           First Name  Grade Teacher          Birth Date Age
----------------    ----------  ----- ---------------- ---------- ---
Ahab                Andy        2     Mr. Queequeg     Apr  3 78  7
Applestein          Johnny      3     Ms. Ippi         Jun  5 77  8
Defarge             Missy       6     Mr. Rothschild   Nov  7 74  11
Finn                Hank        3     Ms. Ippi         Jun 21 76  9
Hatcher             Becky       3     Ms. Ippi         Jul 13 77  8
Holmes              Sherrie     1     Mr. Watson       Oct 31 78  7
Potter              Muffy       3     Ms. Ippi         Jul  4 77  8
Sawyer              Tommy       3     Ms. Ippi         Feb 14 75  10
Silver              John        5     Ms. Douglas      Aug  4 75  10
Silverfield         David       4     Ms. Dickens      Mar 13 76  9
```

AppleWorks Applications

The report format that produces this report is shown in the following illustration:

```
File: SCHOOL ADMIN           REPORT FORMAT           Escape: Report Menu
Report: STUDENT ROSTER
Selection: All records



===========================================================================
--> or <--   Move cursor                  a-J  Right justify this category
   >  a  <    Switch category positions   a-K  Define a calculated category
--> a  <--    Change column width         a-N  Change report name and/or title
a-A  Arrange (sort) on this category      a-O  Printer options
a-D  Delete this category                 a-P  Print the report
a-G  Add/remove group totals              a-R  Change record selection rules
a-I  Insert a prev. deleted category      a-T  Add/remove category totals
---------------------------------------------------------------------------

Last Name       First Name Grade Teacher       Birth Date Age L
-A------------- -B-------- -C--- -D------------ -E-------- -F- e
Ahab            Andy       2     Mr. Queequeg   Apr  3 78  7   n
Applestein      Johnny     3     Ms. Ippi       Jun  5 77  8   6
Defarge         Missy      6     Mr. Rothschild Nov  7 74  11  5

---------------------------------------------------------------------------
Use options shown above to change report format              51K Avail.
```

- *Teacher Roster.* A list of student's names arranged by grade level and teacher. The report looks like this:

```
File:   SCHOOL ADMIN                                        Page  1
Report: TEACHER ROSTER
Grade Teacher           Last Name        First Name
----- ---------------   -------------    -------------
1     Mr. Watson        Holmes           Sherrie
2     Mr. Queequeg      Ahab             Andy
3     Ms. Ippi          Applestein       Johnny
3     Ms. Ippi          Finn             Hank
3     Ms. Ippi          Hatcher          Becky
3     Ms. Ippi          Potter           Muffy
3     Ms. Ippi          Sawyer           Tommy
4     Ms. Dickens       Silverfield      David
5     Ms. Douglas       Silver           John
6     Mr. Rothschild    Defarge          Missy
```

The report format for this report is shown in the next illustration:

```
File: SCHOOL ADMIN           REPORT FORMAT          Escape: Report Menu
Report: TEACHER ROSTER
Selection: All records


========================================================================
--> or <--   Move cursor                 ∂-J  Right justify this category
   >  ∂  <    Switch category positions   ∂-K  Define a calculated category
--> ∂ <--    Change column width          ∂-N  Change report name and/or title
∂-A  Arrange (sort) on this category      ∂-O  Printer options
∂-D  Delete this category                 ∂-P  Print the report
∂-G  Add/remove group totals              ∂-R  Change record selection rules
∂-I  Insert a prev. deleted category      ∂-T  Add/remove category totals
------------------------------------------------------------------------


Grade Teacher          Last Name         First Name    L
-A---  -B------------   -C-------------   -D----------  e
1      Mr. Watson       Holmes            Sherrie       n
2      Mr. Queequeg     Ahab              Andy          5
3      Ms. Ippi         Applestein        Johnny        3
------------------------------------------------------------------------

Use options shown above to change report format            51K Avail.
```

By using the OPEN APPLE-R command, you can change the record selection rules and generate individual rosters for each teacher at the beginning of a new school year or update them as needed.

• *Emergency Contact.* A list of parents' work numbers and the name and phone number of the person to contact if a parent cannot be reached during an emergency. The report looks like this:

```
File:   SCHOOL ADMIN                                            Page  1
Report: EMERGENCY
Last Name      First   Phone     Mother  Work Ph   Father   Work Ph   Emerg      Emerg Ph
---------      -----   -----     ------  -------   ------   -------   -----      --------
Holmes         Sherri  555-1927  Barbara 555-9115  Robert   555-9999  Danielle   555-3002
Ahab           Andy    555-1234  Allison 555-3263  Captain  555-7321  Dottie     555-2341
Applestein     Johnny  555-0713  Doris   555-1107  Ed       555-0605  Laura      555-0403
Finn           Hank    555-3847  Deeni   555-9932  Howie    555-2222  Marc Rya   555-8921
Hatcher        Becky   555-0299  Ginny   555-5847  John     555-0092  Polly      555-2222
Potter         Muffy   555-9372  Mae     555-4482  Ray      555-0101  Brett      555-7774
Sawyer         Tommy   555-9876  Linda   555-9122  Larry    555-3215  Joe        555-2227
Silverfield    David   555-8827  Sue     555-4432  John     555-9003  Melissa    555-5556
Silver         John    555-0048  Nancy   555-4587  Rick     555-1919  Kathy      555-0999
Defarge        Missy   555-8823  Arlene  555-1112  Jerry    555-3928  Randy      555-5948
```

The report format is shown in the following illustration:

```
File: SCHOOL ADMIN            REPORT FORMAT            Escape: Report Menu
Report: EMERGENCY
Selection: All records


============================================================================
--> or <--   Move cursor                 @-J  Right justify this category
 >  @   <     Switch category positions   @-K  Define a calculated category
--> @  <--    Change column width          @-N  Change report name and/or title
@-A  Arrange (sort) on this category       @-O  Printer options
@-D  Delete this category                  @-P  Print the report
@-G  Add/remove group totals               @-R  Change record selection rules
@-I  Insert a prev. deleted category       @-T  Add/remove category totals
----------------------------------------------------------------------------

Last Name      First  Phone    Mother  Work Ph Father  Work Ph  Emerg     Emerg P
-A---------    -B----  -C------  -D-----  -E------  -F-----  -G------  -H------  -I-----
Holmes         Sherri  555-1927  Barbara  555-9115  Robert   555-9999  Danielle  555-300
Ahab           Andy    555-1234  Allison  555-3263  Captain  555-7321  Dottie    555-234
Applestein     Johnny  555-0713  Doris    555-1107  Ed       555-0605  Laura     555-040

----------------------------------------------------------------------- More --->
Use options shown above to change report format                51K Avail.
```

Application: Gradebook

WORK ENVIRONMENT: School Administration

DESCRIPTION: This application demonstrates how to create a spreadsheet template that can be used by teachers to produce report cards.

Suppose you are a junior high school teacher and for each student in your class you have a series of scores that need to be summarized into a grade. This application is designed to save time by organizing the task into three components: calculating a summary percent from a series of test scores, determining the letter grade by referencing a grading scale, and automatically calculating the overall grade point average.

DEVELOPING AND USING THE APPLICATION:

1. Create a Report Card template that contains all labels and formulas and looks like the template that follows.

```
File: GRADEBOOK                    REVIEW/ADD/CHANGE              Escape: Main Menu
========A==========B==========C========D========E========F========G====
  1|                              REPORT CARD
  2|
  3|STUDENT: _____                        GRADE:_____
  4|
  5|                                  QUARTER: _____   YEAR:_____
  6|
  7|SUBJECTS:              Percent              Grade              Teacher
  8|
  9|      Algebra 1
 10|      English
 11|      Biology
 12|      U.S. History
 13|      Spanish 2
 14|      P.E.
 15|                        ---------          ---------
 16|      Overall G.P.A:    ERROR
 17|
 18|COMMENTS:
-----------------------------------------------------------------------
C16: (Value, Layout-P0) ƏAVG(C9...C14)

Type entry or use Ə commands                            Ə-? for Help
```

As you fill in the information about the student, the underscoring disappears. The list of subjects can be changed as needed. The formula in C16 returns an error because the specified range, C9..C14, is blank before you enter data.

2. Create a Grading Scale like the one shown in the following illustration to convert percent scores into letter grades:

```
File: GRADEBOOK                    REVIEW/ADD/CHANGE              Escape: Main Menu
========H========I========J========K======L========M========N========O====
  1|              GRADING SCALE:    | |   WORK AREA: SCORES
  2|                                | |
  3|              .92       A        | |
  4|              .83       B        | |
  5|              .74       C        | |
  6|              .63       D        | |
  7|          Below         F        | |
  8|                                | |
  9|                                | |
 10|                                | |
 11|                                | |
 12|                                | |
 13|                                | |
 14|                                | |
 15|                                | |
 16|                                | |
 17|                                | |
 18|                                | |
-----------------------------------------------------------------------
O1

Type entry or use Ə commands                            Ə-? for Help
```

3. By creating a work area like the one shown in the previous illustration, you have a designated place to list student test scores. You can then use the @AVG function to calculate the average percent. The Work Area can be accessed easily if you plan where to put it. In this application, the user can quickly get to the Work Area by pressing the OPEN APPLE-left arrow combination twice.

The next two illustrations show a sample Report Card after the grades have been entered:

```
File: GRADEBOOK                REVIEW/ADD/CHANGE            Escape: Main Menu
========A=============B=========C========D========E=======F========G====
  1 I                          REPORT CARD
  2 I
  3 I STUDENT: Albert Einstein                        GRADE:        8
  4 I
  5 I                          QUARTER: Spring      YEAR:        1986
  6 I
  7 I SUBJECTS:                Percent          Grade          Teacher
  8 I
  9 I      Algebra 1            .99               A
 10 I      English              .86               B
 11 I      Biology              .94               A
 12 I      U.S. History         .88               B
 13 I      Spanish 2            .76               C
 14 I      P.E.                 .71               D
 15 I                        ---------        ---------
 16 I         Overall G.P.A:    86%               B
 17 I
 18 I COMMENTS:
---------------------------------------------------------------------
C16: (Value, Layout-P0) @AVG(C9...C14)

Type entry or use @ commands                        @-? for Help
```

```
File: GRADEBOOK                REVIEW/ADD/CHANGE            Escape: Main Menu
=====H========I========J========K======L=======M========N========O====
  1 I          GRADING SCALE:       I I    WORK AREA: SCORES
  2 I                               I I
  3 I      .92         A            I I         .78
  4 I      .83         B            I I         .84
  5 I      .74         C            I I         .93
  6 I      .63         D            I I         .89
  7 I      Below       F            I I         .95
  8 I                               I I         .88
  9 I                               I I         .79
 10 I                               I I         .96
 11 I                               I I       ---------
 12 I                               I I         .88
 13 I                               I I
 14 I                               I I
 15 I                               I I
 16 I                               I I
 17 I                               I I
 18 I                               I I
---------------------------------------------------------------------
M12: (Value, Layout-F2) @AVG(M3...M10)

Type entry or use @ commands                        @-? for Help
```

When you save the Report Card, be sure to assign it a new name. If you do not, you will lose your template. If you name the files by students' names, you can easily retrieve each student's report card.

Application: My Dream Vacation

WORK ENVIRONMENT: School Classroom

DESCRIPTION: This classroom application introduces students to the concept of a spreadsheet. Students are asked to plan a seven-day dream vacation and then contact travel agencies to get a cost breakdown, including hotels, transportation, and meals. Students may also be assigned a budget to work with, and if they exceed the limit, will have to adjust their plans accordingly.

DEVELOPING AND USING THE APPLICATION:

    1. The following illustration shows the spreadsheet layout for this application:

```
File: DREAM VACATION          REVIEW/ADD/CHANGE              Escape: Main Menu
====A=B=====C======D======E=======F==G==H====I====J==K==L==M===N====O=====P=
  1|STUDENT NAME      _____          GRADE      _____
  2|
  3|
  4|                          MY DREAM VACATION
  5|
  6|DAY   LOCATION      HOTEL NAME     COST TRANSPORT  COST  FOOD $ DAY TOTAL
  7|=== ============= =============== ====== ========= ====== ====== =========
  8|  1 London        Palace Place     $85 Air         $650   $10     $745
  9|  2 London        Palace Place     $85              $25     $110
 10|  3 Paris         Le Maison       $105 Air         $120   $30     $255
 11|  4 Paris         Right Bank      $120              $25     $145
 12|  5 Paris         Tres Bon         $90              $20     $110
 13|  6 Paris         Tres Bon         $90              $25     $115
 14|  7 California                          Air         $650   $10     $660
 15|                                                         ---------
 16|                                             TOTAL:       $2,140
 17|                                                          $2,000
 18|                                    COST < or > :          $140 ERR
---------------------------------------------------------------------------
P18: (Value) @IF(O17<O16,@ERROR,0)

Type entry or use @ commands                          @-? for Help
```

The student supplies the following information:

- *Column C.* Location name.
- *Column E.* Hotel name.
- *Column G.* Per-night rate for hotel.
- *Column I.* Mode of transportation.
- *Column K.* Transportation cost.
- *Column M.* Total food costs for the day.

The application template includes all labels. The following are necessary formulas:

- Column O contains @SUM functions to determine the total amount spent each day.
- Cell O16 uses @SUM to get a seven-day total.
- If students are asked to consider a budget limit, that amount is entered in cell O17.
- The formula in O18 uses the formula +O16−O17 to determine whether the student has exceeded the budget. If the formula returns a negative number, it will be displayed in parentheses.
- Cell P18 contains an optional formula that introduces the advanced student to logical formulas: @IF(O17<O16,@ERROR,0). If the student exceeds the budgeted limit, an error flag is displayed.

Application: Cost Comparison Shopping

WORK ENVIRONMENT: School Classroom

DESCRIPTION: This classroom application introduces students to the concept of using a spreadsheet for cost analysis. The students agree on a list of items to price at three stores. The spreadsheet results offer a comparative analysis.

DEVELOPING AND USING THE APPLICATION:

1. Enter all labels and formulas to create a spreadsheet template like the one shown in the following illustration:

```
File: COST COMPARISON        REVIEW/ADD/CHANGE          Escape: Main Menu
=======A==============B==============C==========D===========E======F===G===H==
  1 ISTUDENT _____          GRADE       _____
  2 I
  3 I                        COST COMPARISON SHOPPING
  4 I
  5 I
  6 I       ITEM(s)                 STORE #1   STORE #2   STORE #3   1   2   3
  7 I       ---------------------   ---------  ---------  ---------
  8 I       Springsteen Tape          $5.80      $7.20      $6.50    1   0   0
  9 I       ET&T Telephone           $48.00     $43.00     $62.50    0   1   0
 10 I       3 Ring Binder             $3.95      $2.50      $2.79    0   1   0
 11 I                               =========  =========  =========
 12 I                      TOTALS    $57.75     $52.70     $71.79    1   2   0
 13 I
 14 I
 15 I
 16 I
 17 I
 18 I
-------------------------------------------------------------------------------
F8: (Value) ЭIF(C8=ЭMIN(C8...E8),1,0)

Type entry or use Э commands                              Э-? for Help
```

The formulas are defined as follows:

- Cells C12, D12, and E12 use @SUM to determine store totals.

- The formulas contained in the range F8..H12 use the @IF function to determine which store offers the lowest price on a particular item. For example, the formula in cell F8, @IF(C8=@MIN(C8..E8),1,0), reads in English like this:

> If the value in C8 is equal to the minimum value in the range C8 through E8, then display the number 1; otherwise display 0.

This logical statement serves to flag the lowest price for each item listed. If this concept is too advanced, blank out the range F8..H12. Students enter the following data: in column B the list of items, and in columns C, D, and E the prices.

Application: Software Catalog and Review

WORK ENVIRONMENT: School Classroom

DESCRIPTION: This application demonstrates how to use a data base to catalog and review a library of software disks. Just as books are cataloged in a library, software disks should be organized to facilitate users in making selections. The following are some of the advantages of implementing this application:

- Each software program is evaluated by the students. Student reviews lend credibility to the process of evaluating software because they are the primary users.

- Teachers can use software evaluations to help them decide which programs should be incorporated in their lesson plans.

- Parents can use software evaluations to help them make appropriate software purchases for their children.

- A master list of all software programs can be used for inventory purposes.

- Labels can be generated that make it easy to identify program type and content, and appropriate grade level.

DEVELOPING AND USING THE APPLICATION:

1. The data base structure of this application is shown in the following illustration:

```
File: CATALOG              REVIEW/ADD/CHANGE            Escape: Main Menu

Selection: All records


Record 11 of 11
=======================================================================
PROGRAM NAME: -
COMPANY: -
DESCRIPTION: -
COST: -
LO-GR.: -
HI-GR.: -
TYPE: -
SUBJECT: -
EQUIP.REQUIRED: -
EASY(1)-HARD(5): -




------------------------------------------------------------------------
Type entry or use a commands                         a-? for Help
```

The data categories are defined as follows:

- *Program Name.* The name of the software program.

- *Company.* The name of the software manufacturer.

- *Description.* A short description of the program.

- *Cost.* The retail cost of the program.

- *LO-GR.* The lowest appropriate grade level.

- *HI-GR.* The highest appropriate grade level.

- *Type.* Define the program by type, such as drill or game.

- *Subject.* If appropriate, indicate the specific subject area.

- *Equip. Required.* Specify the required equipment when the standard configuration is not adequate (for example, some programs require a color monitor).

- *Easy(1)-Hard(5).* Students rate the program on a scale of 1 to 5 in terms of ease of use.

2. The following illustration shows a list of the current report formats for this application:

```
Current report formats:
    1.   SOFTWARE REVIEW (1)
    2.   SOFTWARE REVIEW (2)
    3.   SOFTWARE LIST
    4.   SOFTWARE LABELS
```

- *Software Review (1).* Lists the program name, the company name, a description of the program, and the retail cost. The following example is what the report looks like when it is printed:

```
File:   CATALOG                                                     Page  1
Report: SOFTWARE REVIEW (1)
PROGRAM NAME              COMPANY                 DESCRIPTION           COST
----------------------   ---------------------   --------------------  -----
Crossword Fun            2-Across Company        Create crossword puzzles  50.00
Easy Writer              Pen and Pencil Co.      Word processing           45.00
Touch Typing             Keyboard Kompany        practice touch typing     15.00
Alphabet Soup            Little People Products  alphabet recognition      25.00
Story Maker              Starbright Software     create sentences          25.00
Pinball Madness          Tilt Co.                create pinball games      27.00
Max the Math Wizard      Add It Up Software      solve math puzzles        30.00
Word Mixup               Thinking About It       unscramble words          25.00
Glorp I                  Adventure + Inc.        text adventure game       30.00
Monster Math: Multiply   Educare Inc.            multiplication facts      35.00
```

- *Software Review (2).* Lists the program name, the appropriate grade level range, the type of program, the subject area, the required equipment, and a rating of how easy it is to use. The report looks like this:

```
File:   CATALOG                                                     Page  1
Report: SOFTWARE REVIEW (2)
PROGRAM NAME             LO-GR. HI-GR. TYPE      SUBJECT       EQUIP.REQUIRED EASY
---------------------    ------ ------ --------  ------------- -------------- ----
Crossword Fun            3      12     Utility   English       printer        4
Easy Writer              2      12     Utility   English       printer        3
Touch Typing             3      12     drill     non-specific  none           2
Alphabet Soup            Pre    1      drill     Reading       color monitor  1
Story Maker              1      3      creative  English       none           4
Pinball Madness          6      12     creative  non-specific  joystick       5
Max the Math Wizard      3      6      drill     math          none           2
Word Mixup               3      8      drill     English       none           1
Glorp I                  3      12     game      non-specific  none           2
Monster Math: Multip     3      6      drill     math          color monitor  2
```

Both reports were printed with all records selected. The next two illustrations show the report formats that produced Software Review (1) and (2):

```
File: CATALOG                    REPORT FORMAT              Escape: Report Menu
Report: SOFTWARE REVIEW (1)
Selection: All records



=================================================================================
--> or <--  Move cursor                       ɔ-J  Right justify this category
  >  ɔ  <    Switch category positions         ɔ-K  Define a calculated category
--> ɔ <--    Change column width               ɔ-N  Change report name and/or title
ɔ-A  Arrange (sort) on this category          ɔ-O  Printer options
ɔ-D  Delete this category                      ɔ-P  Print the report
ɔ-G  Add/remove group totals                   ɔ-R  Change record selection rules
ɔ-I  Insert a prev. deleted category           ɔ-T  Add/remove category totals
---------------------------------------------------------------------------------

PROGRAM NAME           COMPANY                  DESCRIPTION              COST
-A------------------   -B--------------------   -C----------------------  -D---
Crossword Fun          2-Across Company         Create crossword puzzles 50.00
Easy Writer            Pen and Pencil Co.       Word processing          45.00
Touch Typing           Keyboard Kompany         practice touch typing    15.00

--------------------------------------------------------------------- More --->
Use options shown above to change report format                    51K Avail.
```

```
File: CATALOG                    REPORT FORMAT              Escape: Report Menu
Report: SOFTWARE REVIEW (2)
Selection: All records



=================================================================================
--> or <--  Move cursor                       ɔ-J  Right justify this category
  >  ɔ  <    Switch category positions         ɔ-K  Define a calculated category
--> ɔ <--    Change column width               ɔ-N  Change report name and/or title
ɔ-A  Arrange (sort) on this category          ɔ-O  Printer options
ɔ-D  Delete this category                      ɔ-P  Print the report
ɔ-G  Add/remove group totals                   ɔ-R  Change record selection rules
ɔ-I  Insert a prev. deleted category           ɔ-T  Add/remove category totals
---------------------------------------------------------------------------------

PROGRAM NAME        LO-GR. HI-GR. TYPE      SUBJECT        EQUIP.REQUIRED EASY
-A------------------ -B----- -C---- -D-------  -E----------   -F------------ -G--
Crossword Fun          3      12    Utility   English        printer         4
Easy Writer            2      12    Utility   English        printer         3
Touch Typing           3      12    drill     non-specific   none            2

--------------------------------------------------------------------- More --->
Use options shown above to change report format                    51K Avail.
```

You might want to be more selective in your reporting process. Suppose you are an English teacher and you are planning your next study unit for grades 3 through 8. You would like to know if the school's software library contains programs related to your topic. Just run Software Review (1) and (2) again, this time selecting only the records that satisfy the following selection criteria:

- SUBJECT contains English.

- LO-GR is greater than 2.

- The EQUIP.REQUIRED column does not contain a color monitor.

The reports will look like the following illustrations:

```
File:    CATALOG
Report: SOFTWARE REVIEW (1)
Selection: SUBJECT contains ENGLISH
    and       LO-GR. is greater than 2
    and       EQUIP.REQUIRED does not contain COLOR MONITOR
PROGRAM NAME           COMPANY                  DESCRIPTION                COST
--------------------   --------------------     -------------------------  -----
Crossword Fun          2-Across Company         Create crossword puzzles   50.00
Word Mixup             Thinking About It        unscramble words           25.00
```

```
File:    CATALOG                                                     Page   1
Report: SOFTWARE REVIEW (2)
Selection: SUBJECT contains ENGLISH
    and       LO-GR. is greater than 2
    and       EQUIP.REQUIRED does not contain COLOR MONITOR
PROGRAM NAME           LO-GR. HI-GR. TYPE      SUBJECT         EQUIP.REQUIRED EASY
--------------------   ------ ------ --------- --------------  -------------- ----
Crossword Fun            3      12   Utility   English         printer         4
Word Mixup               3       8   drill     English         none            1
```

- *Software List.* A report that prints out a master software list that looks like this:

```
File:    CATALOG                                                     Page   1
Report: SOFTWARE LIST
PROGRAM NAME           LO-GR HI-GR TYPE       SUBJECT         EQUIP.REQUIRED EASY
--------------------   ----- ----- ---------- --------------  -------------- ----
Crossword Fun            3     12  Utility    English         printer         4
Easy Writer              2     12  Utility    English         printer         3
Touch Typing             3     12  drill      non-specific    none            2
Alphabet Soup          Pre     1   drill      Reading         color monitor   1
Story Maker              1      3  creative   English         none            4
Pinball Madness          6     12  creative   non-specific    joystick        5
Max the Math Wizard      3      6  drill      math            none            2
Word Mixup               3      8  drill      English         none            1
Glorp I                  3     12  game       non-specific    none            2
Monster Math: Multiply   3      6  drill      math            color monitor   2
```

This can be used as a quick reference or for inventory purposes. The report format used is shown in the following illustration:

```
File: CATALOG                    REPORT FORMAT              Escape: Report Menu
Report: SOFTWARE LIST
Selection: All records


===============================================================================
--> or <--  Move cursor                  @-J  Right justify this category
 >  @   <    Switch category positions   @-K  Define a calculated category
--> @ <--   Change column width          @-N  Change report name and/or title
@-A  Arrange (sort) on this category     @-O  Printer options
@-D  Delete this category                @-P  Print the report
@-G  Add/remove group totals             @-R  Change record selection rules
@-I  Insert a prev. deleted category     @-T  Add/remove category totals
-------------------------------------------------------------------------------


PROGRAM NAME            LO-GR HI-GR TYPE       SUBJECT        EQUIP.REQUIRED EASY
-A--------------------- -B--- -C--- -D-------- -E----------- -F----------- -G--
Crossword Fun             3    12   Utility    English        printer         4
Easy Writer               2    12   Utility    English        printer         3
Touch Typing              3    12   drill      non-specific   none            2

----------------------------------------------------------------- More --->
Use options shown above to change report format              51K Avail.
```

• *Software Labels.* You can generate descriptive labels such as those shown in the following illustration and affix them to the floppy disk itself or to a storage box.

```
File:    CATALOG
Report: SOFTWARE LABELS

Crossword Fun
3       12
Utility
English


Easy Writer
2       12
Utility
English


Touch Typing
3       12
drill
non-specific
```

The Labels option of the report format is used to generate the following type of report.

```
File: CATALOG                REPORT FORMAT              Escape: Report Menu
Report: SOFTWARE LABELS
Selection: All records



===============================================================================
PROGRAM NAME
LO-GR.  HI-GR.
TYPE
SUBJECT

----------------------Each record will print  6 lines----------------------




--------------------------------------------------------------------------
Use options shown on Help Screen                         ?-? for Help
```

The applications presented in this chapter make use of various Tips and Traps found throughout this book. You'll find as you use the programs that other applications will suggest themselves, and that they can be a good starting point for designing your own models.

Trademarks

DIF™	Software Arts Products Corp.
VisiCalc®	VisiCorp.
ProDOS®	Apple Computer, Inc.
QuickFile®	Apple Computer, Inc.
Apple®	Apple Computer, Inc.
ImageWriter™	Apple Computer, Inc.
Silentype®	Apple Computer, Inc.
IIc™	Apple Computer, Inc.
Scribe®	Licensed to Apple Computer, Inc.
MX series™	Epson America, Inc.
MX/Graftrax™	Epson America, Inc.
RX series™	Epson America, Inc.
FX series™	Epson America, Inc.
Sprint 5™	Qume Corp.
Sprint 11™	Qume Corp.

Index